the Noodle Shop Cookbook

the Noodle Shop Cookbook

JACKI PASSMORE

MACMILLAN • USA

A Prentice Hall Macmillan Company

15 Columbus Circle
New York, NY 10023

Library of Congress Cataloging-in-Publication Data

Passmore, Jacki.
The noodle shop cookbook/Jacki Passmore

p.   cm.
Includes index.
ISBN 0-02-594705-2
1. Cookery (Pasta)   2. Noodles.   3. Cookery, Southeast Asia.   4. Cookery—Asia, Southeastern.
I. Title
TX809.M17P35   1994
641.8'22'095—dc20   94–1218
CIP

Book design by Chris Welch

Manufactured in the United States of America
10   9   8   7   6   5   4   3   2   1

To Isobel, my daughter, friend, chief taster, and valued critic

contents

acknowledgments

Iowe much to my agent, Judith Weber, for her vision in anticipating the marketability of a book on noodles, for encouraging me to pursue the project, and for taking it to Macmillan for publication. It is an author's greatest joy to know his or her manuscript has been placed in the right hands.

Writing *The Noodle Shop Cookbook* proved to be enormously satisfying. I usually write on Asian cuisines in the widest scope, so it was an interesting challenge to concentrate on only one subject ingredient—to explore the enormous potential of noodles as a food of today, a food that is delicious and nourishing, easy to cook, economical, and inspiring to experiment with in the kitchen. But selecting the recipes, from the over three hundred and fifty possibilities that my files and research uncovered, was only part of the challenge. For the often tedious task of testing, typing, and editing that followed, I had the support of a dedicated team. Without the enthusiasm and reliability of my assistant, Megan Nelson, my time in the kitchen testing and tasting would have been far less enjoyable. Thank you, Megan; your help was invaluable. For Amanda Salmon, who took time from her cooking studies to assist with the recipe testing, I have a special thank you. And a special thank you also to Ann Bradley, who saw to neglected office responsibilities while I had my apron on and chopsticks in hand.

Most especially, I praise my editor, Justin Schwartz. Justin's enthusiasm for the book was inspirational. I admired his close attention to detail in the editing of the manuscript, and I'm delighted with the originality of the artwork and cover design.

introduction

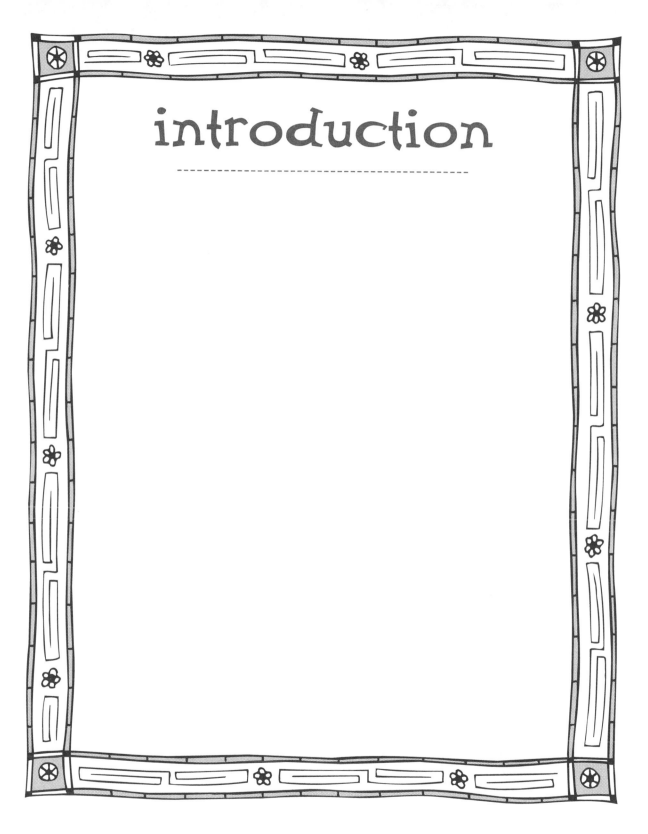

Our decision to leave Hong Kong proved more traumatic than I had expected. I felt alienated in quiet, ordered streets, missing the daily shove and jostle. Selecting packaged foods from neat rows in the supermarket made shopping for essentials a bland and unchallenging experience after the babble and barter of the markets. I even missed, for a while, the congested traffic and exhaust fumes that choked the city. But most of all I longed for the food: the crunch of a stir-fry; the strange gelatinous texture of a sliver of sea cucumber; the salty bean flavor of soy sauce; the joy of slurping noodles from a bowl of broth or shelling a fat steamed shrimp in a crowd of boisterous diners at a noisy seafood restaurant, surrounded by blue plastic tubs surging with live fish, eels, crab, shrimp in six sizes, clams, and turtles.

My local Chinese restaurant became my haven. A bowl of noodles would restore good humor and prompt a note in the diary of the likes: "Dinner at Sun Ruby last night. . . . Singapore Spicy Noodles, mmmm-mmmm!!!" What I termed my "noodle withdrawal" was painfully real to me for several years.

In Asia, noodles compete with rice as the staple food in every cuisine except Indian. As a snack food, noodles rule supreme, and noodle shops are the hub of activity in any city, town, or village. Some shops are gigantic, others minuscule, little more than a few wobbly wooden tables and stools beside a makeshift kitchen. On just about any street corner from northern China to Vietnam, you'll see a singlet-clad cook dunking his wire ladle of precooked noodles into huge pots of simmering water, emerging from the cloud of steam with deep bowls brimming with hot plump noodles and fragrant clear broth. In southern China, Singapore, and Malaysia, they'll be deftly shaking huge black woks over roaring flames which lick into the pan to give the noodles the elusive smoky flavor they call *wok hei*. In Japan, lights glow in tiny noodle shops before dawn and well into the night as *ramen* and *udon* are measured into bowls, splashed with broth, and passed across small counters with the appropriate shouted greetings.

Noodle shops ply a steady trade from the crack of dawn every day of the year. These are not places to linger in; they cater to a passing trade. Early-morning factory workers and produce merchants en route to the markets stop by for breakfast *mein* or *mee*. By day you see transport trucks lined up beside the noodle shops, a crush of factory or office workers squeezing in for their lunchtime bowl of *soba* or *somen*. Midmorning or midafternoon the shops offer a friendly ear, a bit of gossip, and a satisfying snack to tired shoppers and shopkeepers. They're a haven for the itinerant and a welcome respite for travellers, and they provide a comforting snack for day workers before the crush, jolt, and trauma of the evening ride home on public transport. After dark they're a solace for the night-shift worker and a necessary pit stop for late-night revellers. "Hand thrown" fresh noodles have a deliciously soft and satisfying texture that sets them apart from noodles that have been dried. In many parts of China, large tourist-oriented restaurants and small owner-operated noodle booths may have their noodle maker busy in a glassed-in compartment in full view of the diners or sidewalk traffic. He vigorously works a ball of flour-and-water dough on a marble slab, sprinkling on oil and water alternately until he has achieved just the right consistency, the gluten well warmed and elastic. He forms the dough into a sausage shape, which he coats thickly with flour. Then begins the soft switch and loop that stretches the dough into noodles. Holding each end of the roll of dough, he flicks the center away from him to bounce just above the surface of his worktable. Next, bringing the two ends together in one hand, he grasps the center of the loop in his free hand and swings the dough away again. Each swing stretches the noodle threads thinner and thinner until he is satisfied with the thickness of the strands. All he has to do now is to break off the ball of dough that holds the noodles together and—in just five minutes—he has a bundle of plump, soft, white noodles that will need just one minute in simmering salt water to be ready for the table. Japanese restaurant noodle makers also prepare thousands of pounds of fresh noodles a day, but their technique is more akin to the classic pasta preparation, with the dough rolled out and cut into strips.

Noodles, in their multifarious forms, are consumed by the ton in Asia every day. But as Americans' demand for noodles grows, we are catching up on their volume consumption. We have been eating noodles for years, but they've never tasted so good. Few of us are unfamiliar with the "Chinese noodle." Those thin egg and wheat-flour noodles sold in little tangled bundles or skeins have been around for ages. We cooked them with little care as *chow mein* and *lo mein* and slurped them from insipid clear soups under such familiar names as *sui min*. We accepted tasteless instant noodles in packets and tubs complete with flavor sachet ("Just add boiling water and wait two minutes") as a convenience food. We can do much, much better now.

The fast-food industry, ever vigilant to appropriate new trends, has

not ignored the demand for noodles. Nationally there are now thousands of containers of take-out noodles passing across countertops daily to meet a market that is here to stay.

New noodle restaurants like the Ollie's group in New York, specialty restaurants such as Noodles on 28th Street, and a proliferation of Japanese restaurants have acquainted us with noodles as they should be. Cold buckwheat noodles with soy and lime for dipping, flat rice noodles afloat in chili-hot, lemon-fragrant soups, and the tastes that characterize Vietnamese cooking—acrid fish sauce, minty herbs, lemon grass, and fragrant star anise—are no longer strangely exotic to the American palate.

Snacking is comforting and convenient in our busy world. Low-budget eating is mandatory for many, and discovering new tastes is a treat most of us enjoy. To me, noodles represent the ultimate in convenience food. They are inexpensive to buy and lightweight to carry home from the store, and nothing could be quicker or easier to cook.

The Noodle Shop Cookbook is the first to capture our hunger for noodles in a recipe book of favorites and a selection of my own innovations.

the noodles

Tradition, taste preference, aesthetics, and cooking require- ments all contribute to the choice of noodles used in a dish. The Chinese have traditionally enjoyed wheat-flour noodles made with egg; Vietnamese prefer rice noodles; the Japanese—avid noodle eaters—enjoy plump wheat noodles (*udon*) and the nutty-tast- ing buckwheat *soba*, and they can't resist the Chinese noodles they call *ramen*.

Certain noodles are best in liquid dishes, while others respond to frying in oil by crisping to a pleasing crunch. A chewy, meaty noodle serves some recipes best; others need no more than wisps of soft noo- dle for textural contrast. I have specified a particular style of noodle for each of these recipes, but I wouldn't discourage you from experiment- ing within the framework of the recipe.

If you store dried noodles in an airtight container in your pantry, they will keep for months. Fresh noodles have a short life span. Keep them refrigerated, and plan to use them within a few days.

Arrowroot noodles:

Semitransparent, buff-to-amber-colored noodles made from arrow- root starch. Used particularly in Sichuan province in China. Bean- thread vermicelli is a good replacement.

Bean-thread vermicelli:

Fine extrusions of a paste made from mung beans or broad (fava) beans. When cooked they are slippery and near transparent, with an enjoyable bite. Occasionally used in stir-fried dishes but more often in soups, hot pots, and braised dishes. They are extensively used in vege- tarian cooking. Also known as "bean threads," "glass noodles," and transparent vermicelli, they are sold in tight little bundles tied with cot- ton. Do not try to break them; when dry they are extremely tough and can pierce skin. Use a cleaver to cut them if you must.

Broad-bean noodles:

Similar to bean threads, but generally these are flat noodles about ⅛ inch in width. They can be used in any recipe for bean-thread vermi- celli and are excellent in hot pots.

Chinese thin egg noodles:

The classic Chinese noodle, a thin round strand of dough made from a flour-and-egg dough. They are sold in tightly furled bundles, which equate to one medium-size serving, or in larger skeins. Fresh thin noo- dles are sold by weight. Many commercial brands of Chinese noodles

are now made without eggs; they have the same taste and the same yellow color, acquired by adding lye to the water to form the dough, but the label stipulates "contains no egg." Fine egg noodles are used for soups and when stir-fried are served either soft (cooked and then bathed with gravy) or crisp (cooked and then deep- or shallow-fried).

Chinese fat egg noodles:

The main difference between thin and fat egg noodles is size; the fat ones are about ⅛ inch wide and therefore require slightly longer cooking. Strangely, although the preparation process is the same, they do have a slightly different flavor, which suits each type to different recipes. A recipe for homemade egg noodles is on page 15.

E-fu noodles: Thick, precooked, oiled, and dried egg noodles that are sold in large tangled bundles. Noodles labelled *pancit canton* can replace them in a dish, as can *Hokkien mee* or Shanghai noodles.

Hokkien mee: Thick egg noodles resembling spaghetti but colored a brighter yellow with food dye. They have a firm bite that suits certain dishes well. A substantial noodle that can be replaced, if necessary, by spaghetti. Fresh *Hokkien mee* is sold by weight and has been dipped in oil. Rinse with boiling water before adding to a dish.

Japanese noodles:

Many Japanese recipes can be made with the noodles of your choice. Most soup noodles are interchangeable.

Cha-soba: Buckwheat noodles flavored and colored by adding powdered green tea, which adds a subtle and memorable flavor. They could be used in most of the *soba* recipes in this book.

Hiyamugi: Fine white noodles similar to *miswa* or *somen* and used specifically in cold dishes.

Kishimen: Similar to *udon*, but wider and thicker. See my recipe for homemade *udon* noodles on page 18. They could be used in any *udon* recipe.

Shirataki filaments: The noodles used in *sukiyaki*. Made from a root vegetable that grows readily in Japan, they are produced by the same extrusion method applied to bean-thread vermicelli, which can replace them in a recipe. *Shirataki* noodles packed in water in a plastic tube are easy to use but less economical than dried noodles.

Soba: Round stick noodles, gray or buff in color, that are made from buckwheat flour. They have a pleasing taste and texture quite unlike other forms of noodle and are extremely popular in Japan in both hot and cold dishes. They are ideal in Asian-style salads. If they are unobtainable, use Japanese *somen* or other wheat-starch noodles.

Somen: Thin, white stick noodles made from hard-wheat flour, water, and oil. They are packed similarly to *soba*, in straight bundles bound with ribbon. They are quite breakable, so handle with care or they'll crumble. Substitute wheat-starch noodles, Spanish *fideua, miswa* from the Philippines, or a fine pasta called spaghettini.

Udon: Plump Japanese noodles made with hard wheat flour, salt, and water for use in soups and hot pots. Sold where Japanese foods are stocked; if you can't find them, make your own with my recipe on page 18.

Pancit canton: See *E-fu* noodles above.

Rice noodle dough sheets:

In the refrigerators of well-stocked Asian grocers you will find packages of rice noodle sheets. These can be cut to the width you require to make rice noodles. They can also be filled with a variety of ingredients for steaming as rice rolls. They will keep fresh for only a few days in the refrigerator.

Rice ribbon noodles, fresh: Sold chilled at Chinese grocery stores, they should be rinsed in hot water and require minimal cooking. See also my recipe for homemade rice ribbon noodles on page 17-18.

Rice sticks, dried:

In the pack they look like milky plastic extrusions; they turn soft and white when cooked. Sticks vary in width and marginally in taste from brand to brand. In Vietnam they are *banh pho* and in Thailand *sen mie*, and you will sometimes find those names on the label. Keep dry in storage, and do not overcook or they will fall apart. Narrow (thin) Vietnamese rice sticks are known as *bun* and are very white when cooked.

Rice vermicelli:

Sold in flat bundles, usually five to a pack. They are thin, cream-colored strands that turn white when soaked or cooked in water and expand dramatically to a frothy white cloud when deep-fried. Again, make sure they stay dry in storage.

Shrimp/seafood-flavored noodles:

Made from a wheat-starch-and-water dough with a puree of raw seafood added for flavor and texture. They are cut flat or thin in the same way as traditional egg noodles, which can replace them in any recipe. You can make your own, following my recipe for egg-and-milk noodles on page 16; also see my note on flavored and colored noodles on page 17.

Wheat-starch noodles, thin (*miswa*):

Very fine white extruded noodles.

Wheat-starch noodles, flat:

Noodles made with hard wheat flour, salt, and water. They are white in color and more fragile in texture than egg noodles, which they can replace in any recipe. Avoid overcooking them.

Wheat-starch noodles, wide ribbons:

Wheat-starch dough cut into noodles of ¼-inch width. They can be replaced with wide egg noodles or linguine or fettuccine in a recipe.

Vegetable noodles:

Made from egg or wheat-starch dough colored and flavored by adding pureed cooked vegetables. See my note on flavored and colored noodles, page 17.

the basics

Homemade Egg Noodles (recipe 1)

egg noodles

This standard egg noodle dough can be used to make fine Chinese-style noodles or wider ribbons of the fettucine type. It is also the recipe used for wonton skins (wrappers). A pasta machine makes rolling easier, but it is not a necessity.

This recipe makes 20 ounces of dough, which yields 2 pounds of cooked noodles. The vinegar helps to soften the dough and cannot be tasted, but it can be omitted if you prefer.

> 2½ cups all-purpose flour
> 5 medium eggs
> ⅔ teaspoon salt
> 1¼ teaspoons white vinegar

Sift the flour onto a worktop and make a well in the center. Beat the eggs together and pour into the well; add salt and vinegar. Carefully work the eggs into the flour, using your fingertips. Before all of the egg is incorporated, check the dough's consistency. If the dough looks like it will be dry and crumbly, add the remaining egg (and additional eggs, as necessary, or a sprinkle of cold water) and continue to work in. The dough should be firm but neither dry nor moist. It should be workable without sticking to the board. If additional egg or liquid is to be added, it is vital that it be done before the dough becomes too dry; otherwise, it will be impossible to work it in smoothly, leaving the dough hard and lumpy in patches. Knead for 7 minutes to make a smooth and elastic dough. Place in a bowl, cover with plastic wrap, and allow it to rest for at least 1 hour.

A good workout and then relaxation! That's the principle for perfect dough. When you make your own noodle dough don't cut short the kneading process, which should be a minimum of 7 minutes and an optimum 10 minutes. The longer you knead, the smoother and more elastic the dough. A perfect dough is soft and pliable yet does not stick to the fingers or worktop. Then it must rest—you'll probably want to as well after all that kneading. Shape it into a ball, dust slightly with flour, and wrap in plastic wrap or leave it to sit under an inverted mixing bowl for at least 1 hour at room temperature. Or you can wrap it and refrigerate overnight.

Homemade Egg Noodles (recipe 2)

This recipe gives a smoother-textured, whiter-looking noodle. I prefer it to straight egg dough. This recipe makes 18 ounces of dough, which yields about 1½ pounds of cooked noodles.

2 cups all-purpose flour
1¼ teaspoons salt
2 egg yolks
¼ cup milk at room temperature
¼ cup water

Sift the flour onto a worktop. Combine the salt, egg yolks, milk, and water. Make a well in the center of the flour, pour in the liquid, then slowly work it into the flour using your fingertips. Add extra liquid or egg at this stage, if needed. Knead until the dough is smooth and firm, adding additional flour if it is too moist.

Place in a bowl, cover with plastic wrap, and allow it to rest for at least 1 hour.

Making egg noodles with a pasta machine

Roll the dough into a sausage shape and flatten slightly. Set the pasta machine to its setting for the thickest extrusion. Pass the dough through. Dust lightly with flour. Decrease the setting and pass through again. Continue to decrease the setting until the sheet of dough is thin enough to be almost transparent. It may be necessary to dust with flour each time. Transfer it to the noodle cutter and cut to the required width.

Cutting egg noodles with a knife

On a lightly floured board or worktop, roll out the dough carefully, without creases, until quite thin. Dust with rice flour or cornstarch. Fold into thirds and then use a long, sharp knife to cut crossways into strips of the required width.

Cooking homemade egg noodles

Fresh noodles can be cooked immediately and require absolutely no more than 4 minutes' total cooking. If they are not to be used at once, spread them on a tray so they can slowly dry out. Do not cover, and do not wrap in plastic, which causes them to sweat and turn rancid. The longer they are left to dry, the longer the required cooking time. They can be stored, uncovered, in the refrigerator for up to 1 week. If they are to be held longer, make sure they dry out completely and store in an airtight container.

To make homemade wonton, dumpling, and egg-roll wrappers

Use freshly made noodle dough for dumpling and wonton skins. All you have to do is to roll it out paper thin, ensuring that there are no creases or tears. Dusting it with cornstarch or rice flour (brush off excess) gives the best results as it remains on the surface, not integrating with the dough as ordinary flour would do.

Cut the rolled dough into squares or circles of the desired size and stack together. Wrap unused wrappers in plastic cling wrap; these can be refrigerated for several days or kept in the freezer for several months. When forming your snacks, brush the edges of the wrappers with beaten egg and pinch them together to form a tight seal.

Flavored and colored noodles

For noodles with a difference, replace some of the liquid (egg, milk, or water) added to the dough with a puree of cooked vegetable or raw seafood.

rice noodles

I cannot see the point in making fresh rice noodles at home when dried noodles take just a few minutes to cook. I always buy dried rice vermicelli and rice sticks, but occasionally I make fresh rice ribbons. The noodles from this recipe are particularly good for a Malaysian *cha kway tiao* or *cha hor fun*, as they stand up well to rigorous tossing in a wok.

Rice Ribbon Noodles

Makes 1¼ pounds (3 to 4 servings)

> **2 cups rice flour**
> **¾ cup tapioca flour**
> **1¾ cups boiling water**

Measure the flours into a large bowl. It is essential that the water be virtually boiling when you add it to the flour, so measure quickly and have more standing by should you need it. Pour the boiling water over the flour and quickly work in with a wooden spoon. Turn onto a worktop and knead until the dough is smooth, about 1½ minutes. It will be quite hot, so it's best to work in gloves. Add a little extra rice flour if it seems too moist, a teaspoon or two additional water if too dry. But remember, it will smooth out as you knead. Pour a teaspoon of vegetable oil into the palm of your hand and wipe it evenly over the dough. Invert a bowl over the ball of dough and set aside for 10 minutes to cool. Roll out thin on a worktop dusted with tapioca flour. Cut into ¼-inch ribbons. Bring water to a boil. Add noodles and boil for about 45 seconds. Remove and spread on an oiled plate to partially dry before frying as required by the recipe you are using.

Japanese Udon Noodles

Makes 3 pounds, or 6 to 8 servings

6 cups hard bread flour
2 small egg yolks (optional)
2 tablespoons salt
1½ cups cold water

Sift the flour onto a worktop. In a bowl beat the egg yolks, salt, and water together. Make a well in the center of the flour, pour in the liquid, then slowly work it in with your fingertips until it is completely incorporated and you have a soft dough. Add a sprinkle more flour or water, as needed. Clean the worktop of dough crumbs, dust lightly with flour, and knead the dough for 8 minutes until soft and pliable. Return to the bowl, cover with plastic wrap and then a kitchen towel, and set aside for about 3 hours. This allows the gluten in the flour to relax, softening the dough to make it more tender when cooked.

When ready, dust the worktop with flour and roll out to ⅛-inch thickness. Cut into narrow strands. If not being used immediately, noodles may be kept in the refrigerator in a plastic bag for up to three days, but preferably no longer.

I have given specific instructions for cooking the noodles in most of these recipes. The principles are simple: Use plenty of water, do not let the water boil too fiercely, taste frequently so you can retrieve the noodles as soon as they are done—*al dente*, of course. If noodles are to be cooked a second time (stir-fried, deep-fried, etc.), make sure they are undercooked to begin with. Drain noodles well, and rinse if they are starchy. You can cook all noodles in advance and reheat in the Asian manner by placing them in a deep wire basket and immersing into a pot of briskly boiling water. Or, if you prefer, put them in a microwave-proof dish, cover with plastic wrap and microwave on high, until heated through. It is advisable to sprinkle a little cold water over the surface of the noodles before heating by microwave.

B ring a large pan of water to a boil, with or without salt as you prefer. When the water is briskly bubbling, add the noodles with 2-3 teaspoons of vegetable oil to prevent them sticking together. Stir with chopsticks to untangle them. Return the water to a brisk boil, begin to time cooking at this point, and slightly reduce the heat so the water continues to boil, but is not bubbling fiercely.

Cook, testing frequently, to the right degree of doneness, then pour the contents of the pan into a strainer. Rinse with hot water from the tap if the water is very clouded with starch, and set the noodles aside to drain.

It is impossible to be absolutely accurate when recommending cooking times, as the quality of packaged dried noodles varies considerably and will affect times. Fresh noodles rarely require more than 3½ minutes to cook, unless they have been allowed to dry out, when they will need longer.

The Japanese have a special technique for cooking their *udon* and *soba*, described below, which is also suitable for wheat-starch noodles. You may follow this method or simply cook your noodles by the standard method that applies to egg noodles, above.

Japanese method for cooking udon *and* soba

Bring 2 quarts of water to a brisk boil. Add the noodles and stir slowly to prevent them from sticking. When the water returns to a boil, add ½ to 1 cup cold water and bring to a boil again. Add another ½ to 1 cup cold water and bring back to a boil again. Reduce heat and cook the noodles for about 2½ minutes. They should be *al dente*. Drain, pour the noodles into a pan of cold water, and stir to arrest cooking and remove starch. Drain and set aside. Reheat before serving by placing in a deep wire-mesh basket and immersing in boiling water, or pour a kettle of boiling water over them.

Reheating noodles

Japanese method for cooking wheat-starch noodles (flat ribbons or somen)

Bring 1½ quarts of water to a boil. Add the noodles, bring back to a boil, and cook for 30 seconds. Add ½ cup cold water and bring back to a boil. Do this two more times (using 1½ cups cold water in all), each time bringing the water back to a boil. Then cook until the noodles are *al dente*. Drain in a colander.

Wheat-starch noodles cooked in this way should be used at once. Do not soak in cold water or they will lose their texture.

Soaking noodles

Bean-thread vermicelli, rice vermicelli, and fresh rice ribbons or rice noodle sheets do not need to be boiled. They are simply soaked to soften, in hot or boiling water.

Place the noodles in a bowl, pour on the water, and set aside until the noodles have softened to the required consistency. Noodles that are to be cooked (usually stir-fried) or added to a hot soup should still be slightly firm when they come out of the water.

See the soaking times in the table given on page 22.

Storing noodles

Dried noodles will keep indefinitely if stored in an airtight container in your pantry.

If you buy fresh noodles, plan to use them within two to three days, and keep them stored in the refrigerator in the meantime. This particularly applies to the thick, round, yellow noodles that have been coated with oil. Storage encourages rancidity, spoiling the taste and creating a health risk.

Homemade fresh noodles can be allowed to dry in baskets—uncovered, in the refrigerator in warmer weather. Their subsequent cooking time will increase according to how long they have been stored before cooking.

Cooked noodles freeze well. Pour drained noodles into plastic bags, each containing one or two servings. Then freeze. Heat in boiling water or in a microwave oven on high.

Table of cooking times to al dente *texture (calculated from when water returns to a boil after adding the noodles):*

Dried (Chinese) egg noodles (thin/regular); also *ramen*, shrimp, or flavored noodles	3½ minutes
The above, if in tight bundles	4 to 4½ minutes
Dried (Chinese) egg noodles (medium-fine)	5 minutes
Dried (Chinese) egg noodles, flat	6 to 8½ minutes, depending on thickness
Dried *soba* noodles	3 minutes (or refer to cooking details given above)

(continued on next page)

Dried *udon* noodles	5½ to 6 minutes
Dried rice sticks (narrow)	3 minutes
Dried rice sticks (medium to wide)	3½ to 4½ minutes
Dried rice vermicelli	1½ minutes
Bean-thread vermicelli	1½ minutes
Bean noodles—arrowroot, broad bean, etc.	5½ minutes
Dried, very fine wheat-starch noodles (*somen, miswa*)	1½ to 2 minutes
Dried, flat wheat-starch noodles (narrow)	3 to 3½ minutes
Dried, flat wheat-starch noodles (wide)	6 minutes
Fresh egg noodles (narrow)	2 to 2½ minutes
Fresh egg noodles (flat, wide)	3½ to 4 minutes
Fresh rice ribbon/rice-stick noodles	30 seconds
Fresh *hokkien mee*	3 to 4 minutes
Fresh *udon*	2½ minutes

For some recipes, bean-thread and rice vermicelli are soaked, not cooked.

In hot water	9 minutes
In boiling water	3 to 4 minutes
In cold water	25 minutes

basic stocks

Because the cooking times of many of their dishes are quite short, Asian cooks rely on well-flavored stocks to give soups and sauces the required depth and complexity of taste. Make stock with care, cooking it slowly and skimming accumulated residues from the surface to avoid clouding. Because it is a task that shouldn't be rushed, I usually make stock in large quantities when I feel like spending a few hours in the kitchen. You can freeze stock in convenient 1 to 2 cup quantities so you always have a ready supply. It can be thawed in the microwave, or overnight in the refrigerator.

Among Chinese and Malaysian cooks, a rich pork stock and a deeply flavored chicken stock are most important; the Vietnamese cook needs these, plus an intense beef stock, fragrant with anise and cassia or lemon grass. The Japanese cook needs only *dashi*.

DASHI

This infusion of dried fish and seaweed, the base of most Japanese soups and sauces, is one of the most important flavorings in the Japanese cuisine, contributing largely to the unique taste of Japanese food.

Ichiban dashi   dashi stock no. 1

The *premier cru* of Japanese stocks, this is the light and subtle first infusion of *kombu* (dried kelp) and *katsuobushi* (dried bonito shavings). It can be likened to the first pressing of olives for extra-virgin olive oil, or grapes for a premium wine. *Ichiban dashi* is used for clear soups, when clarity of color and a delicate but well-defined taste are required. Some sauces also call for this first infusion.

Makes 1 quart, or 4 servings of soup

   1 quart cold water
   ¼ ounce **kombu** *seaweed*
   ½ ounce dried bonito flakes

Pour the water into a saucepan and add the *kombu*. Bring slowly to a boil, removing the *kombu* just before the bubbles begin to break. Retain the *kombu* for further use. Add the bonito flakes, bring quickly to a boil, then remove immediately from the heat. Allow the bonito to settle in the stock for 1 minute, then strain through a sieve lined with a piece of fine cloth. Reserve the bonito for making Dashi Stock No. 2. It you do not need to use it immediately, it can be sealed in a plastic bag and frozen, though with some loss of flavor.

Niban Dashi   Dashi Stock no. 2

This heavier stock is used for strong-flavored soups, sauces, and simmered dishes and is the base for *miso* soup. *Kombu* and bonito are expensive ingredients but can be reused here from the *ichiban dashi* recipe.

Makes 1¼ quarts, or 4 to 6 servings of soup

> **1½ quarts cold water**
> **Reserved** kombu *and bonito from* ichiban dashi *(page 23)*
> **Additional ½ ounce dried bonito flakes**

Place the previously used bonito and *kombu* in a saucepan with the water. Bring just to a boil, then reduce heat and simmer uncovered for 15 minutes. The stock will reduce by about one-fourth.

Add the dried bonito flakes and immediately remove from the heat. Allow the bonito to settle in the stock for 1 minute, then strain through a sieve lined with a piece of fine cloth. This time, discard the bonito and *kombu* as they will no longer have enough flavor to impart to another stock.

Noodle Broth

Makes 2 quarts

> **2 quarts Dashi Stock No. 1 *(page 23)***
> **2½ tablespoons dark soy sauce**
> **¼ cup tamari or light soy sauce**
> **2 tablespoons sugar**
> **2½ tablespoons mirin *(Japanese sweet rice wine)***
> **Salt to taste**

Combine all ingredients in a large saucepan and bring to a boil. Simmer for 1 minute, then strain. Use immediately, or make in advance and refrigerate for 2 to 3 days.

Aromatic Beef Stock

Makes about 2¼ quarts

2 medium onions, unpeeled
2 cloves garlic, unpeeled
2 pounds gravy beef, cut into 2-inch cubes
2 pounds beef bones, preferably ribs
2 ham hocks
3 quarts water
3 whole star anise
3 pieces cassia bark or 1 cinnamon stick
One 2½-inch piece fresh ginger, peeled and quartered

Preheat the oven to 400°F. Place the onions, garlic, beef, and beef bones on a large oven tray. Place it in the oven to roast for 25 to 30 minutes.

Bring a pot of water (enough to cover the hocks) to a boil. Set the hocks in a bowl, pour on the water, and steep for 5 minutes, then drain.

Transfer the hocks to a large stewpan or stockpot and add the contents of the oven tray. Pour on the 3 quarts of water and add the spices and ginger. Bring to a boil, reduce the heat, and skim the surface. Place a lid on the pot, allowing a very small opening for steam to escape.

Simmer with the water barely bubbling for at least 2¾ hours. Strain into containers and cool quickly over ice water, then refrigerate or freeze.

A Good Beef Stock

Makes 1¾ to 2 quarts

3 pounds shin beef and bones
6 scallions, trimmed, green part only
One 2-inch piece fresh ginger, peeled
1 teaspoon black peppercorns
2½ quarts water
2 pieces dried mandarin orange peel or fresh peel of ½ orange

Blanch the beef in enough boiling water to cover for 5 minutes, then drain. Place all of the ingredients in a deep stockpot and bring the water to a boil. Reduce the heat, skim the surface, then cover the pan, allowing a small opening for steam to escape. Simmer for 2½ to 3 hours without allowing the water more than an occasional bubble. Strain and chill over ice water, then pour into containers to refrigerate or freeze.

Pork Stock

Makes 1¾ to 2 quarts

> *2 ham hocks*
> *1½ pounds pork bones*
> *One 1-inch piece fresh ginger, peeled*
> *2 whole scallions, trimmed*
> *2 lemon grass stems, halved lengthwise (see note)*
> *2½ quarts water*

Bring a kettle of water, enough to cover the ham hocks, to a boil. Place the hocks in a dish, pour on the water, and steep for 5 minutes. Add the pork bones and blanch for a few minutes, then drain. Beat the ginger with a meat mallet or rolling pin to release its juices. Transfer the bones to a stewpot with the ginger and remaining ingredients.

Bring the liquid to a boil, skim the surface, then reduce heat to medium-low. Cover the pan, leaving a small opening for steam to escape. Cook with the water barely bubbling for 2¾ to 3 hours. Strain into containers, cool quickly over ice water, then refrigerate or freeze. Note: Add lemon grass if to be used for Thai or Vietnamese dishes.

Chicken Stock

Makes 2½ quarts

> *3 pounds chicken trimmings—bones, necks, backbones, carcasses, wing tips, and feet (if available).*
> *5 whole scallions, trimmed*
> *One 2½-inch piece fresh ginger, peeled and quartered*
> *3 quarts water*

Blanch the chicken trimmings in 1½ quarts of boiling water for 2 minutes, then drain. Place in a deep stockpot or stewpan with all of the other ingredients. Bring to a boil, then skim the surface and partially cover the pan. Reduce the heat to medium-low and simmer, without allowing the stock to bubble, for about 35 minutes. Strain, then chill quickly (see note) and refrigerate or freeze.

Note: Chicken stock can develop salmonella bacteria in a very short time if allowed to stay warm. For safety, chill it over ice and refrigerate at once.

Wing tips and feet help to make the stock slightly gelatinous, which improves the texture.

Rich chicken stock: Chinese cooks also prepare a supreme stock, slow-cooking several whole boiling chickens along with trimmings for deep, intense flavor.

They may also add a pork hock to increase the flavor. If you wish to do so, proceed as directed but cook over very low heat, with the pan tightly covered, for several hours.

Fish Stock

It is vital that fish stock not be allowed to boil, or it turns milky and the clean, fresh seafood flavor is lost.

Makes 1¾ quarts

4 pounds fish heads and carcasses (see note)
2 quarts water
1 small onion, quartered
One 1½-inch piece fresh ginger, peeled and quartered

Rinse and drain the fish heads and carcasses and place in a large pot. Pour on the water and add the onion and ginger. Heat the liquid, and when the first bubble appears, reduce heat to medium-low to prevent it from reaching a boil.

Simmer for about 12 minutes. Strain the stock through a fine nylon strainer, or a coarser strainer lined with cheesecloth. Cool very quickly and refrigerate or freeze.

Note: Select only white-fleshed or non-oily fish for stock.

Vegetable Stock

Save vegetable peelings from carrots and washed potatoes, pumpkin trimmings, etc., for making vegetable stock. Add diced celery, onion, and turnips, and brown the ingredients in 1½ tablespoons oil until they have acquired a light color and good aroma.

Cover generously with water, then add salt, a few peppercorns, and ½ bay leaf. Simmer for 20 minutes, then strain. Allow to cool, then refrigerate.

a word on oils

Asian cooks prefer to use oil rather than animal fats for their cooking. Bland polyunsaturated vegetable oils like safflower and sunflower, and stronger-tasting peanut and palm oils, are used for deep-frying. Sesame is preferred as a flavor additive. The distinct taste of virgin and extra-virgin olive oil is not compatible with Asian flavors, but the refined, blander types of olive oil are acceptable. For stir-frying, Asian cooks prefer to use an oil that has been used before for deep-frying. This "cooked" oil has lost the raw taste associated with fresh oil and imparts more flavor to a dish. If frying oil is filtered after each use—a paper coffee filter works well—it can be used several times for deep frying. Store it away from light, and use within a few weeks of purchase.

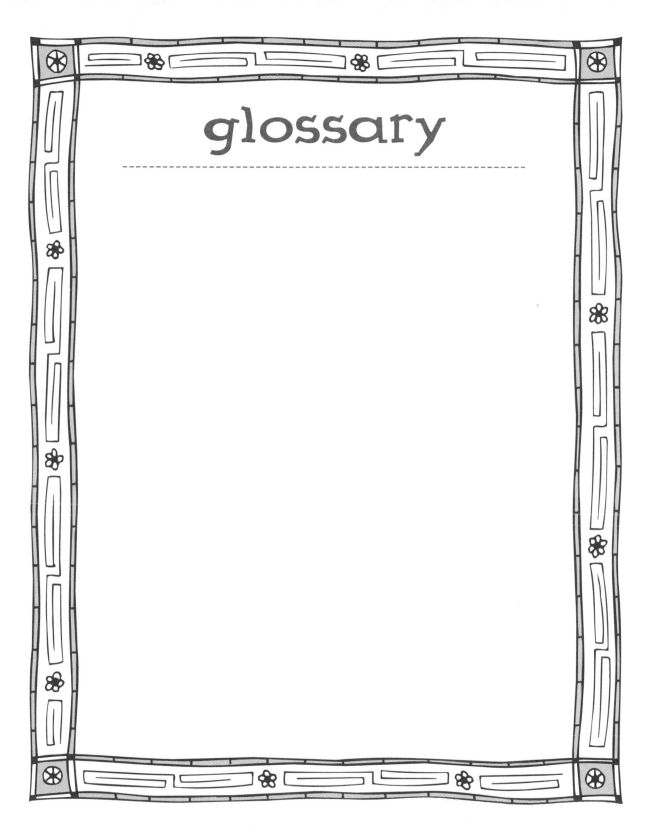

glossary

Aburage, fried tofu/bean curd (Japan):

Thin slices of tofu, about 2¼ inches square, deep-fried to golden on the surface. They will keep for weeks in the refrigerator, loosely wrapped with plastic. Before use, rinse in boiling water to remove the surface oil. They are usually simmered in a sweetened soy sauce.

Bamboo shoots:

Canned sliced bamboo shoots suffice for most of these recipes, but some call for winter bamboo shoots which are long and slender with a more pronounced flavor. Store what you don't use in the refrigerator, in a covered container with fresh water. If you change the water daily they should keep for at least a week.

Banh trang, rice paper sheets (Vietnam):

Round discs of rice batter, which look and feel like semitransparent pale-gray plastic. When softened by immersing in cold water, they are used to wrap traditional foods for eating from the fingers, in the same way as egg roll and spring roll wrappers.

Bean curd/tofu:

aburage: see separate entry

Compressed (firm): Tofu (bean curd) weighted to press out water, giving a firmer texture that slices well and does not break up during cooking. Compressed yellow tofu cakes, brushed with yellow food coloring, are favored by Malaysian and Indonesian cooks. In their absence, use plain compressed (firm) tofu.

Fresh (soft) tofu (bean curd): Made from the coagulated puree of dried soybeans and water, sold in cakes of about 3 ounces each. Store in the refrigerator and use within two days, for maximum freshness.

Fried cubes: 1½-inch cubes of soft tofu (bean curd) that have been deep-fried in oil until the surface is firm and golden. It can be stewed or refried; keeps for several weeks in the refrigerator.

Silk tofu (bean curd): The finest tofu, it is extremely soft and fragile, has a delicate flavor, and must be handled with care. It will keep for only a few days in the refrigerator.

Tofu (bean curd) skins/sticks: The firm, thin layers that congeal on the top of a tub of bean curd as it begins to cool and set. Dried, the skins become edible food wrappers for snacks, particularly in Chinese vegetarian cooking. The sticks are simply skins that have been bundled into sticklike shapes; they are used mainly in braised dishes and hot pots.

Soft tofu (bean curd): see Fresh tofu

Bean paste:

see hoisin sauce

Bean sauce, yellow *taucheo*:

Salt-fermented soya beans in a thin, salty liquid. Sold in cans and jars, it keeps well, preferably refrigerated in hot weather. White *miso* (see page 36) is a good substitute, although less salty.

Bean sprouts:

Sprouts of the mung bean. These should be blanched and refreshed in cold water before using, preferably even when using in salads. Store fresh bean sprouts in a perforated plastic bag or vegetable "stay fresh" bag in the vegetable compartment of the refrigerator for up to 4 days.

Blacan/trassi:

Compressed shrimp paste, an important seasoning in Malaysia and Indonesia. Its pungent smell is best trapped within an airtight jar, and it should preferably be stored away from light and heat. For best results cook it before use by wrapping in aluminum foil and placing in a hot oven or on the stove for a few minutes.

Black beans, salted:

Salt-fermented and dried soya beans, used as a flavoring in Chinese-style dishes. They should be rinsed, dried, and chopped before use. Chili and garlic form an unbeatable partnership with black beans.

Black fungus (wood ears/tree ears):

An edible fungus with a crunchy, slightly gelatinous texture. The crinkly dried fungus should be soaked for half an hour before use; it will soften and expand to several times its original volume. Make sure that it remains dry in storage.

Bok choy:

One of the most popular of the Chinese greens, with fleshy white stems that are eaten along with the dull green leaves. The smaller these cabbages are, the better the flavor, so choose bok choy that are no more than 3 to 4 inches long. They cook in minutes and are best blanched or parboiled before stir-frying.

Bonito flakes:

see *Katsuobushi*

Brown peppercorns:

Aromatic red-brown, peppery berries from the prickly ash tree, which grows extensively in China's Sichuan province. You might also know them as Chinese or Sichuan peppercorns. Use with discretion as an excess has an unpleasant numbing effect on tongue and lips. Grind it fine to make peppercorn powder to sprinkle over dishes.

Chili-bean paste:

Salted soybeans that are mashed with chili, plenty of salt, and occasionally other ingredients (often garlic). This richly flavored seasoning is added to stir-fries and braised dishes. Readily available from Chinese stores.

Chili oil:

An infusion of vegetable oil with chili. It is fiercely hot, so use with care as a seasoning or condiment.

Chili sauce:

There are so many types of chili sauce available that it is impossible to recommend one. Select your favorite, or better still, have several types for different flavor effects.

Chilies:

Dutch red chilies are the most commonly used in Asia, except in Thailand, where chili growing is an art form that has produced a variety of fiery fruits. Seeding them decreases their heat; if you prefer this option, slit them along their length and use the point of a small knife to scrape away the seeds as well as the fleshy filaments that cling to the inside of the chili pod. Shreds of red or green chili decorate many Asian dishes, and chili flowers (see sidebar, page 107) are an attractive garnish that can be made in minutes. It is best to wear gloves when handling chilies to prevent skin irritation.

Cilantro:

A small, aromatic herb, also known as fresh coriander or Chinese parsley, which is indispensable in all Asian countries except Japan and Korea. Its leaves are used for garnish and in sauces, stems and cream-colored roots in curry pastes, seeds in curry-spice mixtures like the Indian *garam masala*. It is easily propagated but must be replanted frequently as it goes to seed in just a few weeks.

Coconut milk:

White coconut flesh, grated to a paste and diluted with water to yield one of the creamiest curry or soup bases imaginable. Its flavor is unique, and Asians simply could not live without it. Fortunately we have ready access by way of cans, compressed blocks, and powdered coconut milk, but none of these compare to the rich, nutty taste of coconut milk fresh from the grater.

***Daikon* (Japan):**

The giant white or icicle radish sold in larger supermarkets and all Asian stores that stock vegetables. One of the mildest of all radishes, it turns almost sweet and bland when cooked. It will keep for at least a week in the refrigerator.

Dashi:

Japanese stock; see pages 23-24.

Fish sauce, *nam pla* (Thailand) and *nuoc mam* (Vietnam):

These two countries use fish sauce as the Chinese do soy, splashing it into almost every dish, dipping into it at the table, and marinating foods in it beforehand. It's salty, pungent, even offensive to the nose, but it imparts a flavor that nothing else can imitate. Keep a bottle on hand, but do keep it tightly capped.

Fish/seafood balls:

A pureed paste of seafood that is formed into bite-size balls and poached. Look for them in the frozen-foods department, and keep a stock on hand for quick noodle soups. See sidebar on page 82 for a recipe.

Five-spice powder:

An aromatic Chinese spice combination used in cooking and mixed with salt as a condiment.

Gai larn:

A popular Chinese green of the cabbage family. The whole plant is eaten, the stems requiring longer cooking than the leaves. Recognize it by its round, straight stems with a cluster of leaves at the top and tiny yellow flowers. Its close cousin, *choy sum*, has white leaves. They have a characteristic slightly bitter taste which is very pleasing. Oyster sauce over poached greens is a flavor match made in heaven.

Galangal, *kha* **(Thailand) and *laos* (Indonesia):**

A version of ginger that may be known to you as Thai ginger. It has smooth skin and straight pink sprouts, and if not sold fresh, it may be located in the frozen-foods department of well-stocked Asian stores. Dried and ground to powder, it's usually labelled *laos*, and 1 teaspoon gives the intensity of a ⅓-inch piece of the fresh root.

Garlic chives:

Deep green, flat-stemmed members of the onion family, which have the distinct flavor of garlic. Thai cooks are particularly fond of them, but a dish does not suffer too noticeably from their absence.

Gingerroot:

This root spice is indispensible in Asian cooking. Choose fresh young ginger, when possible, for its softer, less fibrous texture. Fresh ginger is readily available, but if a substitute is necessary, go for one of the bottled Japanese or Chinese products. Dried ginger does not equate with fresh in most Asian recipes.

Golden needles:

The slender, golden brown flowers of a type of day lily. Sold dried, they give a pleasing musky taste to braised dishes and occasionally soups. Keep dry when storing.

Hoisin sauce:

A thick, deep brown, sweet sauce that is often served as a condiment with roast meats. Sold in bottles, it keeps indefinitely in the refrigerator. It may be labelled barbecue sauce.

Kaffir lime leaf:

An unusual double leaf that imparts a distinct lemon fragrance to many Southeast Asian dishes, particularly soups and curries from Thailand. It is available fresh or frozen from Asian specialty stores. The central rib should be trimmed away if the leaf is to be finely shredded as an edible garnish.

Kamaboko **(Japan):**

Ground fish formed into a thick paste, then steamed in small log shapes whose upper surfaces are characteristically painted with bright pink or yellow food dye. Sliced, it decorates many Japanese soups and hot-pot dishes. Find it in the refrigerator of Japanese food stores.

Kangkong **(Malaysia):**

see Water spinach

Katsuobushi **(Japan):**

Fine flakes of dried bonito fish which resemble wood shavings. Intensely flavored *katsuobushi* is an essential ingredient in Japanese stocks. Make sure it is kept completely dry in storage. See *Dashi*, page 23-24.

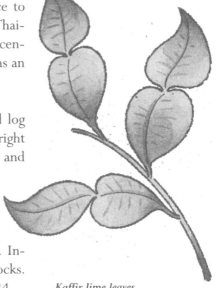

Kaffir lime leaves

Kecap manis **(Indonesia):**

The thick, sweetened soy sauce Indonesian cooks use liberally for a rich, deep color and flavor tones in their food. As a condiment, it is swirled over sate dipping sauces and stir-fries.

Kemiri **(Indonesia):**

A dry-textured nut also called a candlenut, used to thicken curries. Similar in taste to macadamias, which make an ideal substitute.

Kombu **(Japan):**

An enormous, tangled kelp that imparts an incomparable "of the sea" flavor to Japanese stocks and sauces. Japanese fishermen harvest thousands of miles of it annually to dry for use in the kitchen. It is usually sold in 4-inch squares, in packs of 6 or so pieces. Rinse surface salt before using. Store dry.

Lap cheong **(China):**

Hard, dry, sweet pork sausages that are sliced into rice dishes and fillings for dumplings, or added to braised dishes and soups. If they are very hard, steam for a few minutes before using them in a dish.

They keep indefinitely in the refrigerator.

Lemon grass:

A key ingredient in many Thai and other Southeast Asian dishes. Use only the lower 6 to 8 inches of the pale green lemon grass stem. To release its volatile lemon essence, slit the stem lengthwise, or bruise by beating with the side of a cleaver. Fresh lemon grass is available in good greengrocers and Asian stores. It keeps fresh in the fridgerator for 1 to 2 weeks and can be frozen. It grows easily in subtropical to tropical conditions. If you must resort to the dried ingredient, soak in boiling water for at least 15 minutes before using. It has a more peppery, less lemony character than the fresh.

Lime/lime juice:

Limes are the key to good Thai cooking. Don't resort to lemon juice unless you have absolutely no choice.

Mam ruoc **(Vietnam):**

see Shrimp paste

Mirin **(Japan):**

A clear, very slightly viscous liquor used in Japanese cooking. It may be labelled sweet rice wine. If it is unobtainable, a medium-dry sherry works in some recipes, but a closer approximation of flavor and effect would be achieved using *sake* lightly sweetened with sugar.

Miso:

This thick, salty ingredient used in Japanese soups and dressings is made from ground soybeans and salt. It varies from light yellow to a dark red-brown, with a corresponding increase in the intensity of its flavor. Sold in health food and Asian stores.

Mitsuba **(Japan):**

An herb resembling oversized parsley, which is easily grown in a home garden. As a garnish Italian flat-leaf parsley is a good alternative if you cannot obtain *mitsuba*, but in a dish the peppery taste of watercress is a better substitute.

Mushrooms:

Dried black/shiitake: You may simply call them Chinese mushrooms. The best have deep gray-brown caps with light cream ribbing beneath, and they should be plump and generous, not mean and thin. Soak for 25 minutes in warm to hot water to soften them before adding to all dishes except those in which they will slowly simmer. The hard stem should be trimmed close to the underside of the cap.

Enokitake (Japan): These slender, long-stemmed mushrooms are pale ocher in color, with tiny caps. They grow in clusters and are usually sold, fresh or canned, in that way. They require very brief cooking. Fresh *enokitake* do not last more than a day or two in the refrigerator.

Nameko (Japan): Small brown mushrooms with a unique clear, mucilaginous coating. They are sold canned and very occasionally fresh. If unavailable, substitute straw or oyster mushrooms or leave out of the recipe.

Oyster: Fragile albino mushrooms with flat caps and off-center stems, which grow in clusters. They have a subdued wild-mushroom flavor.

Straw: A deep gray mushroom with a round or pointed head that does not open into the traditional cap. Soft-textured and bland, it requires little cooking and is a common ingredient in many dishes. Champignons can be substituted. Sold in cans, straw mushrooms should be decanted into a refrigerator container for storage. Change their water every day if storing. If you are fortunate enough to find them fresh in your Asian market, use within 1 or 2 days of purchase.

Napa cabbage:

A large, pale green, tightly packed Chinese cabbage that is readily available. Common white cabbage can substitute, but its strong flavor will dominate a dish.

Nori (Japan):

Dark green sheets of compressed sea laver, which are used as edible wrappers around sushi and as a shredded garnish on many soup and noodle dishes. Store *nori* in an airtight container away from light, heat, and—more essentially—steam. Hold it briefly over a flame to crisp and brighten its color before using.

Orange peel, dried mandarin:

A seasoning that gives a perky flavor highlight to braised dishes. Buy from Chinese stores, or make you own by placing mandarin orange peels, scraped of white pith, in the hot sun or a low oven until completely dry. Grated lemon rind added to a dish at the last minute is a reasonable alternative.

Oyster sauce:

A thick brown sauce, an extraction of oysters, whose distinct sea flavor accentuates other flavors in a dish rather than overpowering them. It is also used as a condiment, particularly on Chinese green vegetables.

Palm sugar:

An aromatic, rich brown sugar, a vital ingredient in many Southeast

Asian dishes. It can be replaced with a good-quality dark sugar, but it is usually available in Asian stores and will keep for months, so do stock up on it.

Peanuts (groundnuts):

Roasted peanuts enrich many Asian sauces, and in Thailand you'll find them floating in sauces or scattered over dishes as a garnish. Shell the nuts, roast in a hot oven to loosen their pink or red inner skin, then rub in a kitchen cloth to remove it. Nuts roast well in the microwave.

Rice vinegar:

There are four main types of Chinese rice vinegar, all of which are distilled from fermented rice. White rice vinegar is used in cooking and as a flavoring in dips and sauces. Brown or black vinegar is mild in taste and is also used in cooking, particularly when an acidic flavor is required in a slow-cooked dish. Red vinegar is mostly used as a condiment and has a particular affinity with steamed dumplings and shark's fin. Sweet brown vinegar has specialist uses in Chinese cooking.

Rice wine:

Wine brewed from fermented cooked rice. It ranges from clear, potent liquid fire (*mao tai*) to more viscous, amber brews of lesser alcoholic content. *Shao hsing*, a pale golden rice wine, is the one most appreciated in cooking. Bottles labelled "cooking wine" are on sale at most Chinese food stores. In its absence, a very dry light sherry will suffice.

Roast duck sauce:

A sweet, thick condiment made from fermented soybeans, sugar, and spices. Served with roast Beijing (Peking) duck.

Sake:

A Japanese wine made from yeast fermented rice. It is clear and not strongly alcoholic.

Sambal ulek **(Indonesia):**

A condiment and seasoning made from mashed red chilies and salt, which adds fire to Indonesian dishes.

Sansai:

A fernlike indigenous Japanese vegetable, also known as "mountain vegetable." When cooked, it has a slightly bitter flavor and a pleasing tender texture. Young radish or beet greens are a good substitute.

Sesame oil:

An extract of sesame seeds. Its aromatic and nutty taste does wonders for many stir-fried dishes, but it's strongly flavored, so do not overdo it! Add it also to oil when deep-frying—2 teaspoons per cup.

Sesame paste (*tahini*):

A thick paste of ground roasted sesame seeds. It resembles unsalted peanut butter, which can be substituted, and is sold in health food and Asian stores.

***Shichimi* (Japan):**

A seven-spice mixture, probably Japan's most popular condiment. It is sold in small shaker bottles (see also sidebar, page 168).

Shrimp, dried:

Small peeled shrimp that are sun-dried to preserve and intensify their flavor. The best will be a bright peach-red color. Store in a covered container in the refrigerator to maximize freshness.

Shrimp paste, *mam ruoc* (Vietnam) and *kapi* (Thailand):

A smooth, strongly pungent, fermented shrimp paste used as a seasoning to accentuate other flavors. The Chinese version is a soft, sauce-like paste of a pink-gray color. It is known as *mam ruoc* in Vietnam and *kapi* in Thailand. Sold in jars, it should be kept tightly sealed, in the refrigerator. This differs from the harder, compacted shrimp paste known as *blacan*.

Sichuan chili-preserved cabbage/vegetables:

Cabbage, eggplant, and radish that have been preserved in brine with chili and usually garlic. This makes a strongly flavored pickle used as a between-meals snack, a condiment, and a seasoning. Sold in jars or cans (transfer to a glass container once opened), it should be refrigerated in hot weather.

Sichuan peppercorns/powder:

see Brown peppercorns

Sichuan sauce/hot sauce:

Mashed chili paste, similar to *sambal ulek*. You can substitute a strong chili sauce.

Soy sauce:

A salty, thin sauce produced from fermented distilled soybeans, used by Chinese cooks as a dip, condiment, and seasoning. Dark soy is less salty and gives color to a dish; light soy is clear, salty, and the one most commonly used. Sodium reduction has been taken into consideration, and now the Japanese tamari and other low-sodium soy sauces are available.

Soybean pastes:

Chinese cooks use seasoning sauces processed from salt-fermented soybeans. There are up to a dozen different types of soybean paste seasoned with chili, garlic, and spices to provide variations of flavor and pungency. Store bean pastes in the refrigerator in hot weather. Pour a film of vegetable oil over the surface of the paste to prevent its deterioration.

Sriracha (Thailand):
A scarlet chili sauce that is as hot as it looks. Keep this shake-and-squeeze bottle with your condiments.

Stocks:
see pages 22-28

Sugar candy:
Chunks of light-amber-colored sugar that are used as a sweetener by Chinese cooks. Sold in Chinese stores, it keeps for years in an airtight container. Crumble by smashing with the side of a cleaver before using.

Tahini:
see Sesame paste

Tamarind:
Tamarind pods contain several shiny black seeds surrounded by tart flesh. As a seasoning tamarind gives an appetizing citric tang to sauces and gravies. It is sold as whole seeds compressed into a block, which must be steeped in boiling water, mashed, and strained. As a strongly flavored liquid concentrate, it can be added directly to a dish. Look also for bottled tamarind sauce, which is a treat with fried Indian snacks like *pakoras* and *samoosas*.

Tororo (Japan):
A mountain yam, one of several types of edible tubers used in Japanese cooking. It has snowy white flesh which when grated develops a sticky, viscous texture not unlike lightly cooked egg white. It is said to be an excellent digestive. It can sometimes be purchased from Japanese specialty-food suppliers.

Wakame (Japan):
Curly kelp. This edible seaweed is delicately flavored with a pleasing crunch to it. It is used in salads, looks wonderful beneath a mound of freshly cooked seafood on a buffet table, and is delicious floating in Japanese soups. It is sold dried in small packets and swells to many times its dry volume when soaked in cold water. Mineral rich, it is an excellent addition to one's diet.

Wasabi (Japan):
A Japanese-style horseradish paste. It looks innocent enough, but

the pea-green condiment is volatile. Powdered *wasabi* must be reconstituted to a thick paste with water or *sake*, but it's also available in a squeeze-it-on plastic tube.

Water chestnuts:

Small, brown skinned bulbs with crisp white flesh. Canned are readily available. (They're also quite delicious eaten raw, chilled on ice, or in lightly salted water).

Water spinach:

A spinachlike vegetable that grows in watery habitats in Southeast Asian countries. It has triangular deep green leaves and long, hollow stems. Known as *kangkong* in Malaysia and Indonesia, *oong choy* in China, and *pak bung* in Thailand, it is sold where fresh Asian vegetables are marketed. Use like spinach, which you can substitute in any recipe.

Wonton skins:

Thin egg wrappers for dumplings. Sold fresh or frozen in packs. See the instructions for making homemade wonton skins on page 17. Well-wrapped skins may be stored in the refrigerator for a few days, or in the freezer indefinitely.

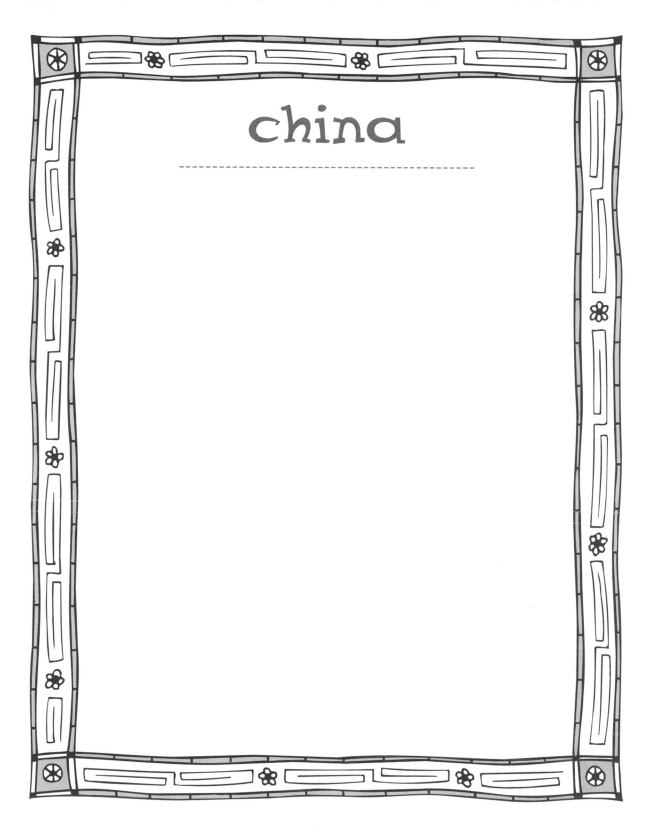

china

Nearly eight hundred years ago, Marco Polo showed that even an Italian could be lured by the multifaceted textures and tastes of Oriental noodles. He enthused about Chinese noodles, among myriad other well-documented culinary pleasures, during his visit to Hangzhou. It is said he compared preparation techniques for egg noodles with the methods employed in southern Italy, where pasta eating was already well established.

The cross-cultural *chow meins* and *lo meins* that were the precursors to genuine Chinese food in America are still with us today. We enjoy these friendly, reliable old favorites as much as some of the newer flavors associated with noodles—sesame and garlic chives, Sichuan pepper and bean paste. Noodles used to be merely an accompaniment to a Chinese meal and were usually listed in the back pages of the menu. Now, they rate restaurants of their own, casual places where diners come to eat noodles as a snack, a meal, a late-night supper, or a midmorning pick-me-up.

Egg noodles are synonymous with Chinese cooking. The Chinese serve them soft, floating in bland gravy flecked with wisps of shredded vegetables and meat, or crisp and wok-smoky in flavor-packed sauces. But they favor soft, fresh rice ribbons with seafood or meat shreds and broccoli, and they choose slippery, transparent bean threads when using the hot and powerful spices of central-western Sichuan. They like noodles cold, beneath creamy dressings of mustard and sesame, and steaming hot in bowls of broth to slurp noisily.

Chinese noodle manufacturers flavor noodles with seafood and color them with vegetable juices. Cooks improvise noodles from tofu (bean curd) sheets and flour from arrowroot and sweet potato, and sometimes they don't even bother to cut their dough into noodles but use it in sheets to wrap fillings, or in squares to make dumplings and wontons.

When soft tofu is handled, all too often it will collapse into a mush before it reaches the dish it was intended for. To cut it into even-sized cubes that can be easily slipped into the dish you're preparing, hold the cake in the palm of your hand and gently cut downward with a knife that is not excessively sharp. Slide the cubes from your hand directly into the wok or pan. In this way you can avoid the excess handling that causes tofu to break up.

Shanghai Chicken Noodle Soup

Serves 6, or more if sharing several dishes

2 pounds chicken parts
6 dried black mushrooms, rinsed and drained
One 2-inch piece fresh ginger
4 whole scallions
3 ounces dried, thick, wheat-starch noodles (or spaghetti)
1 4-ounce cake soft fresh tofu (bean curd)
Salt and tamari or light soy sauce

Rinse chicken under running hot water, drain, and place in a stewpan or stockpot. Add 2 quarts of water and place over medium heat.

Peel the ginger and cut into thick slices. Trim the scallions, setting aside the green tops from two of them for garnish. Place the mushrooms, ginger, the whole scallions, and 2 scallion whites in the pot, cover, and bring slowly to a boil. Reduce heat to low and simmer the chicken very gently with the pan covered, for 1 hour. Do not allow the broth to boil or it will become cloudy. Skim occasionally.

Bring 1 quart of water to a boil. Add the noodles and cook for approximately 5½ minutes until al dente. Drain and divide among six soup bowls.

Dip the bean curd into cold water to rinse, then cut into ½-inch cubes (see sidebar). Remove the chicken from the stock in a wire ladle. Drain for several minutes, then remove the skin. Tear the meat into thin shreds. Remove the mushrooms, drain, and trim stems close to the caps. Strain the stock, discarding ginger and scallions. Add salt and a splash of light soy sauce to taste.

Add several pieces of bean curd, a mushroom, and a portion of chicken to each bowl of noodles. Pour in the hot broth. Slice the reserved scallion greens, cutting them diagonally. Scatter onto the noodle soup and serve.

Bean-Thread Vermicelli and Chicken Mousse in Clear Mushroom Soup

This is my choice when I want an elegant, light soup.
Serves 6 to 8

> 12 to 18 dried black mushrooms, soaked for 15 minutes in cold water
>   and drained
> 2 pounds chicken parts, skinned and boned
> 2 scallions, whites and green tops separated
> 6 thick slices fresh ginger
> 2 ounces bean-thread vermicelli
> 4 ounces boneless, skinless chicken breast
> 12 snow pea shoots or spinach leaves
> Tamari or light soy sauce
> Salt

> SEASONING:
> 2 egg whites
> 1 tablespoon very finely minced scallion whites
> 1 teaspoon tamari or light soy sauce
> 1/3 teaspoon salt
> 2 1/2 tablespoons cold water

Place the mushrooms in a saucepan with 2½ quarts of water, the chicken pieces, the scallion whites, and the ginger. Bring to a boil, reduce heat to low, and cook very slowly for 30 minutes. Skim the broth from time to time. When done, strain and discard chicken parts, scallion, and ginger.

Bring a small pan of water to a boil, add the vermicelli, stir three times, and then drain in a colander. Finely slice the scallion greens diagonally and set aside for garnish.

Cube the chicken breast, place in a food processor with the seasoning ingredients, and grind to a smooth paste. Fill into a piping bag.

Trim the stems from the mushrooms and return the mushroom caps to the broth with the drained vermicelli. Reheat to boiling. Pipe small "sausages" of the chicken mousse into the soup. Add the snow pea shoots or spinach leaves, and season to taste with soy sauce and salt. Heat for 2 minutes. Transfer to a soup bowl or tureen and garnish with sliced scallion greens. Serve.

Dried black mushrooms have a wonderfully intense flavor, but they are also beneficial to your health, being particularly good for the respiratory system. Keep a supply of good-quality (price is usually the indicator) dried mushrooms on hand in a tightly sealed jar.

Remove the cream-colored seed pods and the tapering root ends from the bean sprouts by pinching off with the fingers to make "silver sprouts." Their flavor becomes more subtle, and the elegance they add to a dish makes it worth the few extra minutes' work.

Egg Flowers in Crab-Flavored Noodle Soup

Serves 4, or 6 sharing several dishes

4 ounces dried rice vermicelli (thin egg noodles or shrimp-flavored noodles can be substituted; see sidebar, page 49)
3 ounces fresh bean sprouts
8 ounces cooked crabmeat, flaked
3 teaspoons Chinese rice wine or dry sherry
1 teaspoon ginger juice (see sidebar, page 50)
2 scallions, white parts only, minced
Tamari or light soy sauce for the table
Chinese red vinegar for the table

BROTH:
6 cups chicken stock (pages 26-27)
1 ½ teaspoons salt
1 tablespoon tamari or light soy sauce
3 egg whites

Soak the rice vermicelli in warm water for about 8 minutes to soften. (If using thin egg noodles or shrimp-flavored noodles, cook in boiling water for about 5 minutes.)

Rinse the bean sprouts and pick over to make "silver sprouts" (see sidebar). Blanch in simmering water for 30 seconds, then refresh in cold water and drain.

Combine the crabmeat with the wine and ginger juice and set aside. Bring the stock to a boil in a nonaluminum pan, and add the salt and soy sauce. Reduce the heat so that the soup is no longer bubbling.

Beat the egg whites and strain to remove filaments. Stir the broth in a circular motion, then slowly pour the beaten egg in a thin stream into the broth. As it cooks it will form fine white threads in the soup.

Add the noodles, crabmeat, bean sprouts, and scallions and heat through. Invite your guests to add light soy sauce or Chinese red vinegar to their taste to complete this delicately flavored soup.

Shrimp Noodle Soup with Chinese Greens

Serves 4, or 6 to 8 sharing several dishes

> 4 ounces dried shrimp-flavored noodles
> 12 medium-sized fresh shrimp
> 4 ounces gai larn (Chinese broccoli)
> 1 tablespoon minced whole scallion
>
> BROTH:
> 5 cups chicken stock (pages 26-27)
> 1 tablespoon light soy sauce
> 1/8 teaspoon white pepper
> Salt to taste
>
> SEASONING:
> 1 1/2 teaspoons Chinese rice wine or dry sherry
> 1 teaspoon tamari or light soy sauce

Bring 1 quart water to a boil, add noodles, and boil 3 minutes. Pour into a colander to drain.

Shell the shrimp, cut deeply along the backs and devein, rinse in cold water, and dry. Place in a dish with the rice wine and 1 teaspoon soy sauce and set aside until needed.

Cut the broccoli stems into 2-inch pieces, setting the leaves aside. Heat a small pan of water and blanch the stems in simmering water for 2 minutes, then drain.

In a medium saucepan heat the chicken stock until it comes to a boil. Season with 1 tablespoon soy sauce and pepper. Add the broccoli stems and leaves and the noodles, and simmer for 1 1/2 minutes. Add shrimp and simmer an additional 30 seconds. Taste, adding salt if needed. Ladle into four bowls and garnish with the scallion.

There is a range of seafood-flavored noodles available at good Chinese grocery stores. Shrimp-flavored noodles give this soup a distinctive taste, or you could try fish or crab. But if you prefer a traditional taste, use fine Chinese egg or wheat-starch noodles.

Ginger juice is a more subtle seasoning than ginger flesh itself; it adds a hint of exotic flavor to seafood. To make it, grate fresh ginger onto a square of fine, clean cloth. Gather the edges of the cloth together so the grated ginger forms a ball in the center, then twist the cloth to extract the juice from the ginger. You will need a 1-inch piece of young, fresh ginger to make 1 teaspoon of juice. Older ginger—which is dryer, with a wrinkled skin and woody flesh—will yield less. Use a 2-inch piece and, if needed, moisten the grated flesh with warm water before squeezing.

Fish Two Ways in Noodle Soup

Serves 6, or more sharing several dishes

1 pound plus 6 ounces white fish, skinned
1 1/2 tablespoons plus 1/4 cup cornstarch
7 ounces fine wheat-starch noodles
7 cups fish stock (see page 27)
1 1/2 teaspoons salt
1/2 cup very finely shredded fresh ginger

Ginger juice

SEASONING FOR FISH:
1 teaspoon ginger juice (see sidebar)
2 teaspoons Chinese rice wine or dry sherry
1/2 teaspoon salt

SEASONING FOR FISH BALLS:
1 1/4 teaspoons finely grated fresh ginger
1/2 teaspoon salt

Cut the 1 pound of fish into thin slices. Sprinkle on the fish seasoning ingredients and set aside. Cube the 6 ounces of fish and grind in a food processor with the fish-ball seasoning ingredients, 1 1/2 tablespoons cornstarch, and 2 tablespoons cold water. With wet hands, form the mixture into small balls.

Bring a pan of lightly salted water to a boil, cook the noodles until barely tender, drain, and rinse in running cold water. Pour the fish stock into another pan and bring to a boil over medium-high heat. Drop in the fish balls and cook until they float to the surface, about 2 minutes. Add the salt and shredded ginger. Simmer briefly.

Mix the 1/4 cup cornstarch with 1/3 cup cold water, pour into the broth, and stir until it boils and begins to thicken. Add the sliced fish and poach in the hot broth until it turns white.

Reheat the noodles in boiling water and drain thoroughly. Divide among six bowls (or transfer to a soup tureen) and pour on the hot broth. Divide the sliced fish, fish balls, and ginger shreds evenly among the bowls.

Pork and Peas in Rice Vermicelli Soup

Serves 6

   12 ounces coarsely ground lean pork
   1½ cups frozen green peas
   5 ounces rice vermicelli
   1½ tablespoons vegetable oil
   1 tablespoon very finely shredded fresh ginger (see sidebar, page 63)

   SEASONING FOR PORK:
   1 tablespoon tamari or light soy sauce
   1 teaspoon dark soy sauce
   ⅓ teaspoon minced garlic
   2 teaspoons Chinese rice wine or dry sherry

   BROTH:
   6½ cups pork stock (page 26)
   Salt and white pepper
   ½ teaspoon sesame oil (optional)
   ⅓ cup sliced scallion greens

Place the pork in a dish and add the pork seasoning ingredients. Mix well and set aside for 1 hour (in the refrigerator in warm weather).

Cook frozen peas in lightly salted water until tender, and drain.

Soften the vermicelli in hot water for 8 to 9 minutes. Drain and place a bundle of noodles in each of six bowls.

Heat the oil in a wok or skillet over high heat and stir-fry the pork until it is lightly browned, about 4 minutes. Spoon over the vermicelli, and add the peas and ginger.

Bring the stock to a boil and season to taste with salt and pepper. Add the sesame oil. Pour carefully into the bowls, add scallion greens and serve.

Scallion greens add their jade green accent of color to innumerable Chinese dishes. As a garnish they are sliced diagonally at a quite extreme angle, and you can make them as fine or as wide as you like. Curled tangles of shredded scallion greens are attractive piled on the edge of a serving plate, with perhaps a flower decoration carved from a carrot or formed from a tomato skin. To make shreds, cut the scallion greens lengthwise into strips as narrow as you can manage, and chill them in ice water until they curl into a perky tangle.

Wonton skins are made from egg noodle dough. Prepare the dough on page 15 and roll out fairly thick, then cut into 4-inch strips. Feed these through a pasta machine set on the thinnest setting to extrude a sheet of dough so thin it is semi-transparent. If you do not have a machine, roll out the dough as fine as you can. Dust it with rice flour and cut into 2½- to 3-inch squares. See page 17 for ways to add flavor or color to your dumpling/wonton dough.

$hort and Oong $oup
(WONTON AND NOODLE SOUP)
Serves 6 to 8

Making wontons

WONTONS:
1 package (48 pieces) wonton skins (see sidebar)
4 ounces fatty pork
½ pound shelled and deveined shrimp
1 egg white
⅔ teaspoon salt
¼ teaspoon white pepper
⅓ teaspoon sesame oil
2 ounces water chestnuts, very finely chopped
1 ounce garlic chives, very finely chopped

BROTH:
2 ounces egg noodles
1½ quarts chicken stock (pages 26-27)
1 small bunch oong choy (water spinach) or leaves of other Chinese greens
⅓ teaspoon sesame oil
¼ cup sliced scallion greens
Tamari or light soy sauce and salt to taste

Cover the wonton skins with a cloth to prevent them from drying out. Have ready a small dish of water. In a food processor grind the pork, shrimp, egg white, salt, pepper, and sesame oil to a smooth paste. Add the water chestnuts and garlic chives and process briefly to combine.

Place a spoonful of the filling in the center of each wrapper and brush the edges with water. Fold to form a triangle, then bring the two outer points together and pinch to secure them.

Bring a pan of lightly salted water to a boil. Add the wontons in batches of 8 and poach until they float, then cook for another 2 minutes. Remove to a dish of cold water, using a slotted spoon. Cook the remaining wontons.

Boil the noodles in lightly salted water until tender, then drain. Bring the stock to a boil, season to taste with sesame oil, soy sauce, and salt, and reduce the heat slightly. Cut stems from spinach and discard or reserve for another recipe. Blanch leaves in boiling water for 10 seconds, drain, and add to the soup. Add the wontons and noodles, and heat through. Pour into a soup tureen or divide between bowls, add scallion greens, and serve.

Sichuan Fireball Dumplings

Dumplings in this fiery sesame chili sauce are a daily necessity in Sichuan. Make your own wrappers from a basic egg noodle recipe.

Serves 6, or up to 12 if sharing several dishes

SAUCE:

2 tablespoons sesame paste

2 tablespoons chicken stock (pages 26-27)

2 tablespoons chopped scallion or leek, white part only

1 tablespoon minced garlic

2 teaspoons minced fresh ginger

1 to 2 tablespoons chili oil

2 tablespoons sesame oil

1 tablespoon tamari or light soy sauce

1½ tablespoons dark soy sauce

1 tablespoon sugar

1½ to 2 teaspoons Sichuan peppercorn powder

DUMPLINGS:

1 package fresh or frozen wonton skins, or 1 recipe egg noodle dough (page 15)

8 ounces lean pork, finely ground, and 3 ounces pork fat, finely ground (or use one 14-ounce fat pork chop, deboned and finely ground)

1 leek (white part only), minced

8 water chestnuts, minced

3 dried black mushrooms, soaked for 30 minutes

1¼ teaspoons salt

Thaw frozen wonton skins and cover with a cloth to prevent them from drying out. If using egg noodle dough, prepare the dough according to directions and roll out into a ¼-inch-thick sheet. Cut into 4-inch strips and pass through the thinest setting on a pasta machine, or roll out thin on a lightly floured worktop. Cut into 2½- to 3-inch squares.

Combine the filling ingredients and squeeze through your fingers for 5 to 6 minutes until thoroughly amalgamated. If you like, place the ingredients in a food processor fitted with a metal blade and process to a smooth paste.

Place 1½ teaspoons of the filling in the center of each wonton skin. Brush the edges with cold water, fold into a triangle, and pinch the

Sichuan peppercorns are the fragrant red-brown berries harvested from the prickly ash tree. You may know them as brown peppercorns or Chinese peppercorns, or if you're botanically inclined, as Xanthoxylum piperitum. By whatever name, choose the rosiest ones when buying and store them whole in a spice jar. Lightly crush them if using whole, or grind them fine to sprinkle in moderation. They can be mouth-numbing taken in excess.

edges together to seal. Fold the dumplings around a finger, bringing the two outer points together, and pinch to seal.

Dilute the sesame paste with chicken stock, then add the remaining sauce ingredients, mix thoroughly, and set aside.

Bring a large pan of very lightly salted water to a boil. Add the dumplings and poach until they float to the surface, cook for about 2 minutes more, then retrieve with a wire ladle.

Divide the dumplings among soup bowls and pour on the sauce. Serve at once.

I learned from my Chinese cooking teachers to always sizzle soy sauce or rice wine onto the sloped inner surface of the hot wok rather than mix it in with the sauce ingredients. The heat of the pan brings out its fullest flavors, intensifying them and adding much to the aroma of the dish.

Yang Chow Soft Fried Noodles

Serves 2 to 3, or 4 to 6 sharing several dishes

6 ounces dried egg noodles (see note)
4 ounces skinless, boneless chicken breast
3 ounces shrimp, shelled and deveined
4 ounces gai larn (Chinese broccoli)
3 tablespoons vegetable or peanut oil
1 whole scallion, trimmed and cut into 1-inch pieces
¼ cup sliced bamboo shoots
¼ cup sliced straw mushrooms
½ cup sliced red bell pepper
¾ cup fresh bean sprouts
3 ounces cha siu (Chinese roast pork), thinly sliced
1⅓ tablespoons tamari or light soy sauce
1½ teaspoons dark soy sauce

SEASONING FOR CHICKEN:
1½ teaspoons tamari or light soy sauce
1 teaspoon Chinese rice wine or dry sherry
1 teaspoon cornstarch

SEASONING FOR SHRIMP:
1½ teaspoons Chinese rice wine or dry sherry
⅓ teaspoon salt
1 teaspoon cornstarch

⅓ cup chicken stock (pages 26-27)
¼ teaspoon white pepper
2 teaspoons cornstarch

Bring 1½ quarts of water to a boil. Add the noodles and return to a boil, then reduce heat and cook for 5 minutes, to *al dente*. Pour into a colander, drain, and rinse in hot water. Set aside to drain again.

Cut the chicken into small cubes, mix with chicken seasoning ingredients, and set aside. Place the shrimp in a dish with shrimp seasoning ingredients, mix well, and set aside for 10 minutes. Separate the *gai larn* stems and leaves. Cut the stems diagonally into 1½-inch-long pieces. Blanch the stems only in boiling water for 1½ minutes and drain.

Combine the stock, pepper, and cornstarch for the sauce in a small bowl.

Heat half the oil in a wok or large skillet over high heat. Stir-fry the chicken until it changes color, about 45 seconds. Add the shrimp and stir-fry briefly, then remove to a plate and keep warm. Reheat the wok over high heat, add the scallions, sliced bamboo shoots, mushrooms, pepper, and *gai larn* stems. Stir-fry for 1½ minutes over very high heat. Add the *gai larn* leaves, bean sprouts, and roast pork; cook briefly, then transfer to a plate. Rinse and wipe the wok or pan.

Reheat the pan over high heat and add remaining oil. When a haze of smoke floats over the pan, add the noodles and stir on high heat for 40 seconds. Sizzle the soy sauces into the pan and stir into the noodles. Give the stock mixture a stir and pour into the pan. Cook, stirring, until mixture thickens.

Return all the vegetables and meat to the pan and stir over high heat for 40 seconds. Check seasonings, adding salt and pepper if needed. Serve at once.

Note: This dish is usually made with flat, narrow egg noodles, but any kind of Chinese noodle will be suitable, with adjustments to cooking time.

Three Flowers on Soft Egg Noodles

Serves 3, or 5 to 6 sharing several dishes

½ *pound dried, thin egg noodles*
½ *pound cleaned fresh squid*
1 *medium carrot*
12 *small broccoli florets*
½ *rib of celery*
2½ *tablespoons vegetable oil*
4 *thin slices fresh ginger, cut into fine shreds*
1 *ounce sliced bamboo shoots*
4 *or 5 straw mushrooms, halved*
12 *small snow or sugarsnap peas*
2 *whole scallions, trimmed and cut into 1-inch pieces*
1½ *ounces fresh bean sprouts*
Salt and white pepper

SAUCE:
¾ *cup chicken stock (pages 26-27)*
3 *tablespoons tamari or light soy sauce*
1 *teaspoon Chinese rice wine or dry sherry*
2½ *teaspoons cornstarch*
1 *teaspoon salt*

Cutting squid tentacles from the head

Bring 1½ quarts of water to a boil, add the noodles, and return to a boil. Cook for 3½ minutes until barely tender, then drain.

To prepare a whole squid, first pull off the head, which will draw the stomach from the tubular body. Pull the skin from the body, then rinse under running cold water and set aside. Cut above the eyes and the hard "beak" to separate the tentacles from the head in one connected piece, and discard the head. Rinse the tentacles thoroughly. Prepare all of the squid in this way, then cut open each tubular body and press flat. Cut into 1½ (3.5cm) squares. Using a sharp knife, score the inside in a close criss-cross (see sidebar, page 57). Heat a

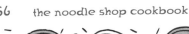

pan of water to boiling, add the squid pieces, and blanch for 15 seconds (they will curl attractively into "flowers"), then drain and set aside. Blanch the tentacles in the same way and drain.

Peel and slice the carrot. Using the point of a small knife, carve out four V-shaped grooves along the length of the carrot so that, when it is sliced, the pieces resemble flowers with four petals. Blanch the carrots and broccoli florets in boiling water for 2 minutes and drain.

Combine the sauce ingredients in a bowl and set aside.

Heat 2 tablespoons of the oil in a wok or skillet over high heat until a haze of smoke floats over the pan. Add the prepared squid and stir-fry over high heat for 30 to 40 seconds. Remove.

Reheat the pan over medium-high heat, then add the broccoli, carrots, and remaining vegetables and stir-fry until crisp-tender, about 1½ minutes. Return the squid to the pan with the ginger and stir-fry briefly, then pour on the sauce and cook until it thickens. Check seasoning, adding salt and pepper. Remove from the heat.

Immerse the noodles in boiling water to reheat, then drain. Spread on a serving plate and lightly stir in the remaining oil. Cover with the sauce and vegetables and serve at once.

To make squid curl into attractive pine cone shapes when cooked, cut open the cleaned tubular bodies and flatten out. Score the inside with a closely worked cross-hatch, holding the knife at a sharp angle. Do not cut all the way through the flesh. Do not overcook the squid, or it will toughen.

Scoring squid

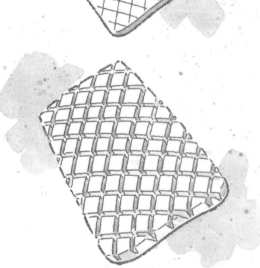

Crabmeat sauce is a favorite Chinese dressing for vegetable dishes, particularly broccoli and Napa cabbage. It is sublime over large scallops that have been wok-seared with scallions.

Chicken in a Creamy Crabmeat Sauce over Egg Noodles

Serves 2 to 3, or 4 to 6 sharing several dishes

7 ounces flat egg noodles
1½ tablespoons vegetable oil
5 ounces skinless, boneless chicken breast
2 whole scallions, trimmed and cut into 1-inch pieces
5 ounces cooked crabmeat or surimi crab, flaked

SEASONING FOR CHICKEN:
1 teaspoon tamari or light soy sauce
1 teaspoon Chinese rice wine or dry sherry
2 teaspoons cornstarch

SAUCE:
1¼ cups chicken stock (pages 26-27)
2 teaspoons nam pla (Thai fish sauce) or tamari soy sauce
1 teaspoon Chinese rice wine or dry sherry
2½ teaspoons cornstarch
Salt and white pepper

Bring 1½ quarts of water to a boil. Add 1 teaspoon salt and the noodles and bring back to a boil. Cook for 5½ to 6 minutes, until *al dente*.

Pour into a colander to drain. Transfer to a bowl, stir in 2 teaspoons of the vegetable oil, and set aside.

Cut the chicken into small dice and mix with the chicken seasoning ingredients. Set aside for 20 minutes. Combine the sauce ingredients in a bowl and set aside.

Heat the remaining vegetable oil in a wok or skillet over high heat and stir-fry the chicken until it turns white, about 45 seconds. Add the scallions and stir-fry for 30 seconds.

Add the crab and stir over high heat for another 45 seconds. Stir up the premixed sauce, pour into the pan, and cook, stirring, over medium-high heat for about 2½ minutes, until thickened.

Reheat the noodles by immersing in boiling water, drain, and spread on a platter. Pour on the sauce and serve at once.

Chicken and Garlic Chives on Fried Noodles

Serves 2, or 4 sharing several dishes

5 ounces fine Chinese noodles
6 ounces boneless, skinless chicken breast
¼ cup vegetable oil
1 tablespoon shredded fresh ginger
12 garlic chives
Salt and white pepper
Oyster sauce

SEASONING FOR CHICKEN:
2 teaspoons tamari or light soy sauce
1 teaspoon Chinese rice wine or dry sherry
1½ teaspoons cornstarch

SAUCE:
¾ cup chicken stock (pages 26-27)
2 teaspoons tamari or light soy sauce
⅓ teaspoon sugar
3 teaspoons cornstarch

Bring 1½ quarts of water to a boil. Add the noodles and 1 tablespoon vegetable oil. Return to a boil, then reduce the heat so the water is barely bubbling. Stir the noodles to untangle them, then cook for 3¼ minutes. Drain well and spread on a large plate to partially dry.

Slice the chicken thin and cut into fine shreds. Combine the chicken seasoning ingredients in a bowl, add the chicken, and mix well. Set aside for 15 minutes. Combine the sauce ingredients in a bowl and set aside.

Cut the garlic chives into 1-inch pieces. Heat 2½ tablespoons of the oil in a wok or large, heavy skillet over medium-high heat. Spread the noodles in an even layer in the pan and cook until the underside and the outer edge of the noodle layer is crisp. Turn in one piece and cook the other side, then lift onto a serving plate.

Add the remaining oil, if needed, and reheat the pan over high heat. Stir-fry the chicken until it turns white, about 40 seconds. Add the ginger and garlic chives and stir-fry for 30 seconds, mixing with the chicken. Stir up the sauce, pour into the pan, and cook, stirring

Garlic chives combine the subtle taste and texture of scallion with a pronounced garlic flavor. Recognize them at the market as deep green, flat-leafed shoots that give off a strong garlic aroma when rubbed between the fingers.

continuously, until it thickens. Season with salt and pepper. Pour over the noodles.

Pour several thin streams of oyster sauce over the dish and serve at once.

With its distinct, nutty taste and powerful aroma, sesame oil makes its presence felt in a dish. Used appropriately, it adds a luxurious flavor note, but do not be tempted to splash it on willy-nilly without thought for the consequences. Do add a shake or two from the bottle into your oil when deep-frying—Japanese cooks wouldn't dream of leaving it out of their tempura frying oil.

Soy-and-Sesame-Flavored Duck on Noodles

Serves 4, or 6 to 8 sharing several dishes

> ½ duck (about 1½ pounds)
> 2 tablespoons sesame oil
> ¼ cup dark soy sauce
> ¾ cup Chinese rice wine or dry sherry
> 3 cups water
> 1½-inch piece fresh ginger, peeled
> 9 ounces fine wheat-starch noodles or somen
> ½ pound baby bok choy (small Chinese white cabbage)
> 1 teaspoon salt

Using a cleaver to cut through the bones, chop the duck into 1¾-inch pieces. Heat the sesame oil in a heavy saucepan over high heat and fry the duck until the skin is evenly browned. Add the soy sauce, rice wine, and water to the pan. Cut the ginger into thick slices, add to the pan, cover, and bring to a boil. Reduce the heat and simmer until duck is tender, about 35 minutes.

Bring a pan with 2 quarts of water to a boil. Add the salt. Add the noodles and cook for 3 minutes, until tender, and drain. Bring another small pan of water to a boil. Rinse the bok choy, drain well, and cut in half lengthwise. Boil for 3 minutes until crisp-tender and drain.

Divide the noodles among six bowls. Place the duck and vegetables on the noodles and spoon some of the broth over them.

beef and "five shreds" on soft noodles

Serves 3, or up to 5 sharing several dishes

    6 ounces thin Chinese noodles
    5 ounces beef tenderloin (or lean lamb)
    4 dried black mushrooms, soaked for 25 minutes in warm water
    1 rib of celery
    1 medium carrot, peeled
    1 small cucumber or chayote, peeled and seeded
    1/2 red bell pepper, seeded and trimmed
    1 medium yellow onion
    3 tablespoons vegetable oil
    1/2 teaspoon minced garlic

SEASONING:
2 1/2 teaspoons tamari or light soy sauce
1 1/2 teaspoons Chinese rice wine or dry sherry
1 teaspoon cornstarch
1/2 teaspoon salt

SAUCE:
1 cup beef stock (pages 25-26)
1 1/2 tablespoons tamari or light soy sauce
2 teaspoons dark soy sauce
2 teaspoons chili bean sauce, mashed smooth
1/2 teaspoon sugar
3 teaspoons cornstarch

Bring 2 quarts of water to a boil. Add the noodles and return to a boil. Reduce the heat and simmer for 3 1/2 minutes, until noodles are firm-tender, perfectly *al dente*. Pour into a colander to drain, rinse under running hot water, and set aside to drain again.

    Slice the beef or lamb very thin. Stack the slices and cut into narrow shreds. Combine the season-

Chinese cooks are masters of the cleaver. They keep their "choppers" razor sharp, traditionally by rubbing the blade over the unglazed base of a pottery bowl. I knew a cook who could slice meat so thin that through a slice he could read the name of the cleaver's maker, imprinted on the blade. You probably won't be as good as Ah Chan, but it will help.

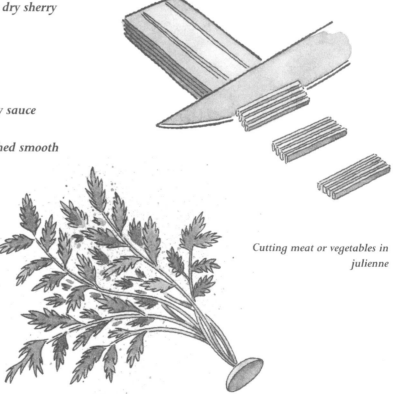

Cutting meat or vegetables in julienne

ing ingredients in a dish, add the meat, mix well, and set aside for 20 minutes. Combine the sauce ingredients in a bowl and set aside.

Drain the mushrooms and squeeze out excess water. Trim the stems and cut the caps into narrow strips. Cut the vegetables into julienne strips.

Heat half the oil in a wok or large skillet over high heat and stir-fry the vegetables on high for 2 minutes. Remove from the pan and set aside, keeping warm. Reheat the pan over high heat. Stir-fry the beef or lamb on very high heat for 1½ minutes, add the garlic, and stir-fry a further 30 seconds. Set aside with the vegetables.

Wipe out the wok, pour in the remaining oil, and reheat over high heat. Stir-fry the noodles for 40 seconds. Stir the sauce, pour over the noodles, and cook for 2 minutes, stirring frequently. Add the vegetables and beef, stir to mix well, and cook for 1 minute on high heat. Serve.

You'll find few dishes from Sichuan that don't use chili—and many that call for quantities that you would think were beyond human tolerance. Sichuan cooks add chilies directly to a dish, dried and fresh, roasted and pickled. But for good measure, they also pack a chili punch into their seasoning ingredients. Fermented soya bean sauces can be incendiary, and salt-pickled vegetables—which they love in this part of China—often come fired up with chili.

"dan dan" Spicy Peddler's Noodles

"Dan Dan" noodles have been one of the favorite streetside noodle snacks in Sichuan province for centuries. You can still find peddlers hawking noodles from their ingenious makeshift kitchens on a cart or bicycle.
Serves 4 to 6, or more if sharing several dishes

> *1 pound dried wheat-starch noodles*
> *1 tablespoon sesame oil*
> *4 ounces pork liver, sliced (optional)*
> *Sichuan peppercorn powder*
> *1 tablespoon toasted sesame seeds*

> DRESSING:
> *2½ ounces canned or bottled Sichuan chili-preserved cabbage or pickled Sichuan vegetables*
> *⅔ cup tamari or light soy sauce*
> *¼ cup sesame paste*
> *2 teaspoons sugar*
> *1½ tablespoons sesame oil*
> *¼ cup vegetable oil*
> *¼ cup chili oil (or to taste)*
> *2 tablespoons finely chopped scallion*

Bring 1½ quarts of water to a boil. Add the noodles, return to a boil, and

cook for 45 seconds. Add 1 cup cold water and bring the water back to a boil again. Add another cup of cold water, return the water to a boil, and cook until noodles are tender. Drain and divide among bowls.

Heat a wok or skillet over high heat and add 1 tablespoon sesame oil. Fry the liver until cooked through but not overdone. Remove and let cool, then cut into very small dice and scatter over the noodles.

To make the dressing, very finely chop the chili-preserved cabbage. Combine the soy sauce, sesame paste, sugar, and 1½ tablespoons sesame oil until smooth. Add the vegetable oil and chili oil and beat until very smooth and well emulsified. Stir in the chili-cabbage and scallions.

Pour the dressing over the noodles and stir in lightly. Season with Sichuan peppercorn powder and sprinkle on the sesame seeds. Serve.

Shanghai Shrimp in Tomato Sauce on Wheat-Starch Noodles

Serves 2 to 3, or 4 to 5 sharing several dishes

9 ounces shrimp, shelled
2 scallions
1 medium yellow onion
1 rib of celery
6 ounces fine wheat-starch noodles or somen
2½ tablespoons vegetable oil
1½ tablespoons very finely shredded fresh ginger (see sidebar)
1 tablespoon tamari or light soy sauce

SEASONING:
2 teaspoons nam pla (Thai fish sauce)
2 teaspoons cornstarch

SAUCE:
½ cup chicken stock (pages 26-27)
3 tablespoons ketchup
2 teaspoons rice or cider vinegar
1 teaspoon Thai sriracha or hot chili sauce
½ teaspoon sugar
½ teaspoon sesame oil
Freshly ground black pepper
2 teaspoons cornstarch

Ginger and seafood have a natural affinity. Chinese cooks like to toss finely shredded fresh ginger into many of their seafood dishes for an unexpected zap of gingery fire. Choose a young, fresh root (it will have a smooth, cream-buff skin), peel it closely with a paring knife, then cut into transparent-thin slices. Stack the slices and cut them into very fine shreds. Shred one whole piece of ginger at a session and wrap small bundles tightly in plastic wrap to freeze for later use. See also the sidebar on page 50 about ginger juice.

Make a deep cut in each shrimp down the center of its back so it will curl during cooking. Remove and discard the intestinal veins. Rinse the shrimp, drain, and dry on paper towels. Mix with the seasoning ingredients and set aside for 10 minutes.

Trim the scallions, cut the white parts into ¾-inch pieces, and slice the green tops for garnish. Set aside. Peel the yellow onion and cut into narrow wedges (see sidebar, page 68). Cut the celery into thin diagonal slices.

Combine the sauce ingredients in a bowl. Bring 1½ quarts of water to a boil, add the noodles, and cook for just a few minutes, until tender. Drain.

Heat half the oil in a wok or large skillet over medium-high heat. Stir-fry the shrimp with half the ginger until the shrimp curl and turn pink, then remove and set aside. Add the white parts of the scallions, celery, and onion wedges and stir-fry over medium-high heat until softened but not browned. Sizzle the soy sauce over them and cook briefly. Remove to a plate and set aside.

Reheat the remaining oil in the wok over high heat. Stir-fry the noodles on very high heat for 1 minute, then spread on a serving plate. Rinse out the wok and reheat over medium-high heat. Stir the sauce and pour into the wok. Stir until it boils, then lower the heat and simmer for 1½ minutes. Add the scallion, celery, and onion and heat through for 1 minute, then add the shrimp and heat briefly, mixing well. Pour over the noodles, garnish with the sliced scallion greens and ginger shreds, and serve at once.

Chinese Celery, Leeks, and Beef with Noodles in a Spicy Sauce

Serves 3 to 4, or up to 6 sharing several dishes

> *9 ounces fine dried wheat-starch noodles or somen*
> *3 ribs Chinese celery*
> *1 large leek*
> *1 pound ground beef*
> *3 tablespoons vegetable or peanut oil*
> *2 tablespoons minced scallion*
> *1 tablespoon minced fresh ginger*

½ teaspoon minced garlic
1 tablespoon minced Sichuan pickled vegetable (jarred or canned)
Sichuan peppercorn powder
Tamari or light soy sauce, on the side
Chili oil, on the side

SAUCE:
1½ tablespoons dark soy sauce
1 to 2 teaspoons chili oil
⅓ cup rich chicken stock (see sidebar, page 27)

BROTH:
3 cups rich chicken stock
1½ tablespoons cornstarch

Chili oil is a great ingredient to keep in the pantry. Like Tabasco, it has a good life-span, since you only need a few drops at a time—"one bottle per marriage" was the acid observation of a several-times-wed colleague.

Bring 2 quarts of water to a boil, add the noodles, and return the water to a boil. Add ½ cup of cold water, bring back to a boil, then reduce the heat slightly and cook the noodles for just a few minutes until tender. Test them frequently to avoid overcooking. Drain and cover with cold water, then set aside.

Cut the celery into 2-inch lengths and then into fine julienne strips. Trim the leek by cutting off the base and the dark green leaves. Cut into 2-inch pieces, then cut in half lengthwise and shred into fine julienne strips.

Combine the sauce ingredients in a bowl. Make the broth by stirring the cornstarch into the chicken stock, and set aside.

Heat half the oil in a wok or skillet over medium-high heat, stir-fry the celery and leek over medium-high heat until very well softened and very lightly browned, and remove. Reheat the wok with the remaining oil and stir-fry beef until it changes color, breaking it up with the edge of a spatula. Add the scallion, ginger, garlic, and pickled vegetable and stir-fry on high heat for 2 to 2½ minutes, until cooked. Add the sauce ingredients, return the leek and celery to the pan, and cook, stirring frequently, until the liquid has been absorbed.

Bring the broth to a boil, stirring until it becomes slightly thick and translucent, about 5 minutes. Drain the noodles and immerse in boiling water to reheat, drain again, and divide noodles among deep bowls. Pour on the broth. Add the spicy beef and leek sauce and season generously with Sichuan peppercorn powder. Invite your guests to add soy sauce and chili oil to taste.

Asian cooks often season their frying oil by cooking ingredients such as chilies, garlic, shallots, and peppercorns in it before they begin frying. It gives an added burst of flavor to the dish and teases the nostrils wondrously. They rarely use fresh vegetable oil for stir-frying, preferring "cooked oil"—oil that has been previously used for deep frying—for the flavors that it adds.

Beijing Noodles

Serves 2 to 3, or 6 sharing several dishes

> **6 ounces lean pork, coarsely ground**
> **½ pound fine wheat-starch noodles**
> **¼ cup vegetable oil**
> **2 teaspoons Chinese brown peppercorns**
> **2 cloves garlic, peeled**
> **4 ounces fat pork, finely ground**
> **2 tablespoons minced scallion**
> **1½ teaspoons minced fresh ginger**
> **1 cup chicken stock (pages 26-27)**
> **1 tablespoon cornstarch**
> **Salt and pepper**
> **Hoisin sauce (sweet bean paste) on the side**

> SEASONING FOR PORK:
> **1½ tablespoons tamari or light soy sauce**
> **3 teaspoons hoisin sauce (sweet bean paste)**
> **2½ teaspoons sugar**

Place the lean pork in a small dish with the pork seasoning ingredients and mix well. Set aside for 20 minutes.

Bring 1½ quarts of water to a boil, add the noodles, and return the water to a boil. Add ½ cup of cold water, bring the water back to a boil again, then cook the noodles until tender, testing frequently after the first 2 minutes. Drain in a colander and set aside.

Heat the oil in a wok or skillet over high heat until a haze of smoke floats over the pan. Add the peppercorns and garlic, reduce the heat to medium-low, and cook for 1½ minutes over medium heat. Remove peppercorns and garlic with a wire ladle and discard (see sidebar).

Increase the heat to high. Add the seasoned pork and fat pork and stir-fry on high heat 3 minutes, until cooked, using a spatula or metal spoon to break up the meat. Add the scallion and ginger and stir-fry briefly.

Combine chicken stock and cornstarch, pour into the pan, and cook on high heat, stirring constantly, until thickened. Season to taste with salt and pepper.

Divide the noodles among shallow bowls and spoon on the sauce. Dilute extra Hoisin sauce with a little cold water to serve on the side.

Pork Lo Mein

Serves 2 to 3, or 6 sharing several dishes

½ pound coarsely ground pork
1 small onion, peeled
½ red bell pepper
1 rib of celery
2 whole scallions
8 fresh oyster mushrooms
¼ cup vegetable or peanut oil
4 ounces sliced bamboo shoots
1 pound fresh, thick egg noodles or 10 ounces dried e-fu noodles
1 tablespoon sesame oil
1 teaspoon Chinese black vinegar
2 tablespoons oyster sauce
1 teaspoon salt

SEASONING FOR PORK:
2 teaspoons grated fresh ginger
2 cloves garlic, minced
3 teaspoons tamari or light soy sauce
3 teaspoons cornstarch
1 teaspoon sugar
Pinch of white pepper
1 tablespoon vegetable or peanut oil

SAUCE:
1¼ cups chicken stock (pages 26-27)
1 tablespoon cornstarch
1½ tablespoons oyster sauce

Combine the ground pork and pork seasoning ingredients in a bowl, mix well, and set aside for 30 minutes.

Peel the onion and cut into narrow wedges (see sidebar, page 68). Remove the inner ribs and seeds from the pepper and cut into strips. Slice the celery thin, on the diagonal. Trim the scallions and cut into 1-inch pieces. Cut the larger mushrooms in half.

Bring 2 quarts of water to a boil, add the noodles, and bring the water back to a slow boil. Cook for about 2½ minutes (7 minutes if using dried noodles), until *al dente*. Transfer to a colander to drain. Have an-

To make neat slices of onion for stir-frying, try the Chinese technique. Peel the onion and turn on its side. Cut the bottom end off cleanly to remove the root section. Cut a similar slice from the top, removing the stem end. Turn the onion onto its base and then use the point of a small, sharp knife to cut vertically into narrow wedges, taking the knife only to the core of the onion. Work your way around the onion in this way, then separate the layers. You will have tidy, curved, shell-like pieces that will keep their shape during cooking.

other pan of simmering water ready for reheating the noodles later.

Combine the sauce ingredients in a bowl.

Heat 2 tablespoons vegetable oil in a wok or large skillet over high heat and stir-fry the prepared vegetables and bamboo shoots for 2 to 3 minutes until crisp-tender. Remove and keep warm. Add the pork and stir-fry on high heat until evenly browned, breaking it up with the edge of a spatula. Return the vegetables to the pan.

Stir the sauce, pour into the pan, and stir on medium heat until it begins to thicken. Transfer to a dish and set aside, keeping warm. Rinse and dry the wok or pan.

Immerse the drained noodles in the simmering water to reheat. Transfer to a colander to drain well. Heat remaining vegetable oil in the wok. Stir-fry the noodles on high heat for 1 minute. Add the sesame oil, vinegar, oyster sauce, and salt and stir-fry until each strand is coated with the seasonings. Return the cooking sauce and reheat with the noodles, mixing in evenly. Serve.

Cutting onion wedges

Red-Cooked Beef on Egg Noodles

Serves 4, or 6 to 8 sharing several dishes

> One 1¾-pound piece of beef skirt or round, or use 2½ pounds of beef
>   short ribs cut into 2-inch pieces
> 1⅓ cups cold water
> 9 ounces thick egg noodles or wheat-starch noodles
> ½ pound baby bok choy (small Chinese white cabbage)
> 6 cups beef stock (pages 25-26)
> 1 tablespoon tamari or light soy sauce
> 1 teapoon sesame oil
> 1½ tablespoons diagonally sliced scallion greens (see sidebar, page 51)

SEASONINGS FOR BEEF:
> ¾ cup dark soy sauce
> 3 tablespoons Chinese rice wine or dry sherry
> 1½-inch piece fresh ginger, peeled and quartered
> 1 garlic clove, peeled
> 1½ star anise
> 3 tablespoons crushed Chinese sugar candy
> 2 teaspoons sesame oil

If you bought a whole bunch of bok choy or other Chinese greens for a recipe and used only a few ounces, store the remainder, wrapped in paper, in the vegetable compartment of your refrigerator—ideally for no more than 2 days. To cook Chinese greens as a vegetable, dunk them into a pan of boiling water to cook for about 3½ minutes until crisp-tender. Drain well, stack on a serving plate, and use kitchen shears to cut into manageable lengths. Pour oyster sauce in thin lines over them and serve hot.

Place the piece of beef or the ribs in a saucepan with a heavy base and tight-fitting lid. Add the water and beef seasoning ingredients and bring to a boil. Cover, reduce the heat to very low, and simmer for 2 hours, uncovered, turning the beef occasionally. It should be very tender when done. Remove the beef with a heavy wire skimmer and set aside. Continue to simmer the broth until well reduced.

Bring 2 quarts of water to a boil. Cook the noodles for 5 to 7 minutes until *al dente* and drain well.

Cut each cabbage in half lengthwise. Pour the beef stock into a saucepan, bring to a boil, and season with soy sauce and sesame oil. Add the cabbage, simmer for 3 minutes, and remove. Place noodles in the same cooking liquid and heat through. Remove noodles and divide among four soup bowls; discard the broth.

Cut the beef into bite-sized cubes (ribs can remain as they are). Arrange the beef or ribs on the noodles, add cabbage, and ladle on some of the reduced, rich red stock. Garnish with the scallions and serve. Offer a chili condiment, such as the Japanese *shichimi*.

$hanghai $rown-$auce Noodles

Napa cabbage keeps well, unwrapped, in the vegetable compartment of the refrigerator. If you have any left over from a recipe, use it up in stir-fries, or poach it until tender and serve with a sauce of flaked crabmeat in chicken stock thickened with cornstarch.

Serves 2 to 4

10 ounces fresh, thick noodles
½ pound Napa cabbage
½ pound boneless chicken breast, skin on if possible
3 tablespoons vegetable oil
2 teaspoons grated fresh ginger
2 tablespoons dark soy sauce
2 tablespoons hoisin sauce (sweet bean paste)
2 cups chicken stock (pages 26-27)
1 teaspoon sesame oil
White pepper

SEASONING FOR CHICKEN:
1 tablespoon tamari or light soy sauce
1 teaspoon dark soy sauce
2 teaspoons Chinese rice wine or dry sherry
1 teaspoon cornstarch

Bring 2½ quarts of water to a boil, add noodles, and cook for 1 minute. Drain and spread on a tray to dry.

Finely shred the white, thick cabbage stems, and cut the leaves into ¾-inch slices. Cut the chicken into thin slices, then into shreds, place in a dish with the chicken seasoning ingredients, and set aside for 10 minutes.

Heat half the oil in a wok over high heat and stir-fry the chicken for 1½ minutes. Remove, add the cabbage and ginger, and stir-fry for 1 minute or until cabbage is wilted. Remove.

Add the remaining oil to the wok and stir-fry the noodles for 2 minutes. Add the dark soy sauce and hoisin and stir-fry 1 minute. Pour in the stock and simmer for 5 minutes. Return the chicken and cabbage to the wok and stir to thoroughly mix. Heat through, tossing the noodles for 2 minutes.

Transfer to a serving plate and sprinkle on the sesame oil and white pepper.

Chiu Chou Noodles in Sesame Sauce

(SESAME NOODLES)

Serves 3 to 4, or up to 6 sharing several dishes

4 bundles (7 ounces) fine Chinese noodles
2 dried black mushrooms, soaked for 30 minutes
2 ribs of celery
12 small lettuce leaves, finely shredded
3 scallions
3 ounces lean pork, preferably tenderloin
1 ½ tablespoons vegetable or peanut oil
1 ½ teaspoons sesame oil

SESAME SAUCE:
2 tablespoons tahini (sesame paste)
1 ½ teaspoons soft, fresh shrimp paste
1 teaspoon Chinese rice wine or dry sherry
¼ teaspoon sugar
1 ½ cups chicken stock (pages 26-27)
5 teaspoons cornstarch
Salt and white pepper

Tahini (sesame paste) gives a tantalizing nuttiness to a sauce for hot noodles. But it is equally appealing drizzled over cold noodles, especially when countered by the hot-fresh taste of a mustard or Japanese horseradish sauce.

Bring 1 ½ quarts of water to a boil. Add the noodles and bring back to a boil, add ½ cup of cold water, and bring the water back to a boil again. Stir to untangle the bundles, add another ½ cup of cold water, and return to a boil. Reduce heat and cook noodles until tender but not soft, about three minutes. Drain and set aside.

Drain the mushrooms, trim the stems, and shred the caps fine. Trim the celery and scallions and cut into fine julienne strips. Combine the sauce ingredients in a small saucepan and bring to a boil. Stir over medium heat for 2 minutes, until thickened, and keep warm.

Slice the pork thin, stack the slices together, and cut into fine shreds.

Heat the oils in a wok over high heat until the pan is smoking. Stir-fry the pork for 1 ½ minutes, then push to the side of the pan and add the mushrooms, celery, and scallions. Stir-fry for 1 minute. Pour on the sauce and stir in, cooking briefly. Remove from the heat.

Immerse the noodles in boiling water to reheat; drain well.
Divide noodles among bowls, add the shredded lettuce, and spoon the pork and vegetable sauce evenly over the noodles. Serve at once.

There is a simple trick to deveining a shrimp. Hold up a shelled shrimp, pressing top and tail together so the body arches upward. Insert the point of a small skewer or cocktail pick into the center, push it under the vein, then gently lift it upward, easing out the vein.

Deveining shrimp

Seafood Rice Ribbons

Serves 3 to 4, or 6 sharing several dishes

> 1⅓ pounds fresh rice ribbon noodles
> 1 pound fresh seafood (scallops, shrimp, squid, crabmeat or surimi crab, white fish)
> 3 scallions
> 12 small spinach leaves
> 2½ tablespoons vegetable oil
> 1 red chili pepper, seeded and sliced
> 2 tablespoons chopped cilantro (Chinese parsley)

> SEASONING FOR SEAFOOD:
> 2 teaspoons minced fresh ginger
> 1½ tablespoons tamari or light soy sauce
> ¾ teaspoon salt

> SAUCE:
> ¾ cup chicken stock (pages 26–27)
> 1 teaspoon cornstarch
> Salt and white pepper

Bring 2½ quarts of water to a boil, add the noodles, and immediately pour into a colander to drain. Cover with cold water and set aside.

Clean the seafood as needed and cut into bite-sized pieces (see sidebar for deveining shrimp). Place in a dish with the seafood seasoning ingredients and mix well. Set aside for 20 minutes.

Trim the scallions; cut white parts in half lengthwise and then into 1-inch pieces. Shred some of the green tops for garnish. Combine the sauce ingredients in a bowl. Blanch the spinach in a small pan of boiling water for 30 seconds and drain.

Heat half the oil in a wok or skillet over high heat. Stir-fry the seafood until it changes color. Add the scallions and stir-fry for 40 seconds. Add the seasoned seafood and stir-fry for 1½ minutes or until the seafood is cooked. Remove to a plate.

Drain the noodles thoroughly. Rinse and dry the wok, add the remaining oil, and reheat. Stir-fry the noodles until each strand is glazed with the oil. Stir the sauce and pour over the noodles, cook for 1½ minutes, then return the seafood and add the red chili and spinach leaves. Stir-fry 1 minute more.

Season to taste with salt and pepper, arrange on a platter, and garnish with the cilantro and scallion greens.

Broccoli Stems and Lamb on Rice Ribbon Noodles

Serves 2 to 3, or 4 to 6 sharing several dishes

4 ounces lamb tenderloin (or use venison, beef or veal tenderloin, or sirloin steak)
1 pound broccoli stems
1 pound fresh rice ribbon noodles
3½ tablespoons vegetable oil
2 scallions, trimmed and cut into 1½-inch pieces
Salt and white pepper
½ teaspoon sesame oil
½ teaspoon salt

SEASONING FOR LAMB:
2 teaspoons dark soy sauce
2 teaspoons Chinese rice wine or dry sherry
2 teaspoons cornstarch
2 teaspoons vegetable oil
½ teaspoon sesame oil

SAUCE:
2 teaspoons dark soy sauce
2 tablespoons oyster sauce
1 cup chicken stock (pages 26-27)
1 teaspoon sugar
1 tablespoon cornstarch

Broccoli is one of my favorite vegetables. The stems have a superb texture and flavor reminiscent of asparagus. Our greengrocers like to sell up a sizable piece of stem with each broccoli head, and it's a pity to throw them away. My family loves broccoli florets stir-fried, steamed briefly in the manner described in the recipe, then stir-fried again with finely shredded fresh ginger and a sprinkle of sugar.

Slice the meat very thin and cut into strips 2 inches long and ¾ inches wide. Combine the lamb seasoning ingredients in a dish, add the meat, mix well, and leave for 30 minutes.

Peel the tough outer skin from the broccoli stems with a paring knife. Cut wide stems crosswise into thin slices; cut slender stems lengthwise into 1½-inch pieces. Bring a small pan of water to a boil, add the broccoli stems, blanch for 1 minute, and drain.

In a bowl, combine all the sauce ingredients except the soy sauce and 1 tablespoon of the oyster sauce. Set aside. Place the noodles in a colander, pour on boiling water to rinse and soften, and set aside to drain well.

Heat 1 tablespoon of the oil in a wok or large skillet over medium-high heat and stir-fry the broccoli stems for 2 minutes. Add 1 tablespoon of water, cover the pan, and steam for 1 minute, until the water has evaporated.

Add a little extra oil and the scallions. Cook briefly, then remove the vegetables and keep warm. Reheat the wok over very high heat, add another tablespoon of oil and heat until a haze of smoke appears over the pan. Add the meat and stir-fry over high heat until the meat changes color. Sizzle in the reserved soy sauce.

Stir the sauce mixture and pour into the pan. Cook quickly until the sauce thickens. Return the vegetables to the pan and stir to glaze with the sauce. Season with salt and pepper to taste and remove from the heat.

Rinse the wok and reheat over high heat. Add another tablespoon of vegetable oil and the sesame oil, and when a haze of smoke floats over the pan add the noodles and ½ teaspoon salt. Stir-fry for 1 minute, or until heated through and crisp on the edges. Spread the noodles evenly over a serving plate.

Spread the meat and vegetables with their sauce evenly over the noodles. Drizzle the reserved oyster sauce in thin streams over the top. Serve.

Heavenly Lamb Shreds

Serves 2, or 4 sharing several dishes

1 pound lean lamb
1 quart oil for deep-frying
2 ounces rice vermicelli
1 medium yellow onion
2 tablespoons vegetable oil
1 ½ teaspoons sesame oil
1 ⅓ tablespoons hoisin sauce
2 teaspoons Chinese hot chili sauce or Thai sriracha chili sauce

⅓ teaspoon salt
1 tablespoon finely shredded orange peel
1 tablespoon finely sliced scallion greens

SEASONINGS:
3 teaspoons Chinese rice wine or dry sherry
1 teaspoon brown sugar
1 tablespoon hoisin sauce

Slice the lamb very thin, then cut into fine shreds. Place in a bowl with the seasoning ingredients, mix well, and cover. Marinate for 2 hours.

In a fryer, large wok, or skillet, heat the oil for deep-frying to medium, 375°F. Carefully slide the vermicelli into the hot oil and cook just long enough for it to expand into a white cloud. Turn quickly—it should not be allowed to color—and cook the other side. Lift into a colander lined with several layers of paper towel and set aside.

Peel the onion and cut into narrow wedges (see sidebar, page 68).

Heat the 2 tablespoons vegetable oil and the sesame oil together in a wok or skillet over high heat until a haze of smoke floats over the pan. Add the onion and stir-fry for about 2 minutes, until well cooked. Remove or push to the side of the pan.

Add the lamb and stir-fry for 2 minutes. Add the hoisin sauce, chili sauce, and salt and cook another 20 seconds. Remove from the heat.

Spread the crisp-fried vermicelli on a platter. Spoon the spicy lamb over the noodles and garnish with the orange-peel shreds and scallion greens. Serve at once.

Quick-cooked Asian dishes often require meat that is cut into fine shreds. To make this easier, partially freeze the meat until it is firm enough not to "wriggle" as you slice it, then stack the slices in piles of four or five and cut across the stacks to give you fine shreds. The finer the slices are, the more tender when cooked and the more they will absorb the flavor of marinades and seasonings.

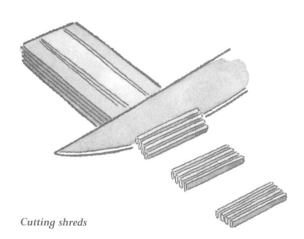

Cutting shreds

Deep-frying at home can be unnerving. A wok sitting firmly on a wok stand over your highest heat source is one of the safest and most effective ways to deep-fry. The curve of the wok's sides insures that the deepest oil is in the center, the shallowest at the edges. So if the oil begins to rise in a mass of steaming hot-oil bubbles, the edges will cool, preventing it from boiling over to sure disaster. But I repeat, make sure your wok is sitting firmly on its stand before you begin.

Sweet and Sour Seafood on a Cloud

Serves 2, or more sharing several dishes

6 cups vegetable oil for deep-frying
2¹/₂ ounces rice vermicelli
5 ounces white fish filets
2 ounces small scallops
2 ounces cleaned squid
6 medium-sized shrimp, shelled and deveined
Cornstarch for coating
1 rib of celery, thinly sliced diagonally
¹/₃ cup (2 ounces) sliced bamboo shoots
1 small onion, cut into narrow wedges (see sidebar, page 68)
1 small carrot, thinly sliced diagonally

FOR THE SAUCE:
³/₄ cup chicken stock (pages 26-27)
¹/₂ cup sugar
¹/₃ cup rice vinegar
2 teaspoons shredded fresh ginger
¹/₂ teaspoon chopped garlic
3 tablespoons ketchup
1 tablespoon cornstarch
¹/₂ teaspoon salt
¹/₃ teaspoon sesame oil
Red food coloring (optional)

In a fryer or wok, heat the oil over medium-high heat to 375°F. Add the vermicelli in a single piece. It should expand into a puffy white cloud within seconds. Turn to cook the other side, making sure all has been exposed to the oil and is therefore crisp and white. Lift onto a rack over a double thickness of paper towel to drain. Set aside.

Combine the sauce ingredients in a bowl and set aside.

Cut the fish into thin slices, then into 1½-inch squares. Halve the scallops horizontally and cut the squid into flowers (see pages 56-57) or rings. Coat the fish, squid, scallops, and shrimp very lightly with cornstarch.

Pour off all but ½ cup of the oil from the pan and reserve for another use. Reheat over high heat until a haze of smoke floats over the pan. Stir-fry the seafood for 2 minutes until firm; remove and set aside.

Discard this oil and add another 1½ tablespoons of the oil used for frying to the pan. Reheat over medium heat. Stir-fry the celery, bamboo shoots, onion, and carrots for about 1½ minutes. Stir the sauce, pour into the pan, and bring to a boil. Cook, stirring often, for 2 to 3 minutes.

Return the seafood to the pan and heat gently for 2 minutes. Place the noodles on a serving platter and crush lightly with the back of a wok spatula. Ladle the sauce over the noodles and serve.

Bean Threads Stir-Fried with Sichuan Spiced Beef

Serves 3 to 4, or 6 to 8 sharing several dishes

½ pound dried bean-thread vermicelli
10 ounces lean beef (or use pork or lamb)
½ red bell pepper
½ green bell pepper
1 medium onion
3 tablespoons vegetable oil
Cilantro (Chinese parsley) to garnish

SEASONING:
1 teaspoon minced fresh ginger
1 teaspoon minced garlic
1 teaspoon dark soy sauce
2 teaspoons Sichuan hot sauce
1½ teaspoons sugar
2 teaspoons Chinese black vinegar
2 teaspoons sesame oil

SAUCE:
¾ cup chicken stock (pages 26-27)
1 to 1½ teaspoons chili oil
2 teaspoons Chinese rice wine or dry sherry
1½ tablespoons tamari or light soy sauce
¾ teaspoon salt
1 to 1⅓ teaspoons Chinese black vinegar
1½ teaspoons cornstarch

The Chinese are old masters at making vinegar. They've been doing it for more than five thousand years. The mildly flavored black or brown vinegar is used in stir-fries and braised dishes; a good-quality white rice vinegar is superior to its distilled counterpart for sauce; and red vinegar is favored as a condiment, for dipping and splashing into soups and sauces at the table.

Bring 1½ quarts of water to a boil, add the vermicelli, and remove from the heat. Let stand for 1 minute, then drain and cover with cold water.

Cut the beef into very thin slices, then stack the slices and cut across them into fine shreds. Combine the seasoning ingredients in a bowl, add the beef shreds, mix well, and leave for 20 minutes.

Remove the inner ribs and core of the peppers and cut into fine shreds. Peel the onion and cut into thin wedges (see sidebar, page 68).

Heat 1 tablespoon oil in a wok or skillet over high heat until a haze of smoke floats over the pan. Add the peppers and onion, stir-fry for 40 seconds, and remove.

Add another 1 tablespoon of the oil. Add the beef and stir-fry on high heat, tossing and stirring continuously, for 1½ minutes. Return the peppers and onions, mix well, and remove from the wok.

Drain the noodles thoroughly. Combine the sauce ingredients in a small bowl. Rinse and dry the wok, then heat the remaining oil over high heat. Stir-fry the noodles briefly, add the sauce, and cook until the sauce is absorbed. Add the beef and vegetables and stir in thoroughly. Garnish with cilantro and serve.

If you find a tub of fresh bam-boo shoots at your Chinese greengrocer, buy one or two to en-joy their fresh flavor and wonder-ful crunch. If they are still in their leaves, peel these away to reveal the tender shoot and boil it for 30 minutes to soften before using as you would the canned variety. Recognize winter bamboo shoots by their distinct resinous aroma, deeper yellow color, and long thin stems. They taste quite different from common bamboo shoots and add much more flavor to a recipe.

Red-Hot Bean Threads

Serves 2 to 3, or 4 to 5 sharing several dishes

> 1 ounce dried shrimp
> 8 dried black mushrooms
> 5 ounces bean-thread vermicelli
> 1 large yellow onion
> 2 tablespoons vegetable oil
> 1½ teaspoons sesame oil
> 2 ounces fresh bean sprouts
> 1½ ounces fresh bamboo shoots, finely chopped (see sidebar)
> 1 to 2 red chili peppers, seeded and chopped
> 1½ tablespoons tamari or light soy sauce
> ⅓ to 1 teaspoon chili oil
> ½ teaspoon salt
> ¾ cup chicken stock (pages 26-27)

2 teaspoons minced fresh ginger

2 teaspoons minced garlic

1 tablespoon Chinese black vinegar

Soak the dried shrimp and mushrooms separately in boiling water for 15 minutes. Bring 1½ quarts of water to a boil, add the vermicelli, and remove from the heat. Drain after 1½ minutes, or when tender.

Peel the onion and cut into narrow wedges (see sidebar, page 68). Drain the shrimp and mushrooms, trim the mushroom stems, and cut the caps into thin slices.

Heat the vegetable and sesame oils in a wok or skillet over medium-high heat. Stir-fry the onion until softened, about 1½ minutes. Add the seasoning ingredients, shrimp, mushrooms, bean sprouts, bamboo shoots, and chili and stir-fry for 2 minutes on high heat.

Sizzle the soy sauce into the pan, add chili oil, salt, stock, and the noodles, and stir and toss the ingredients in the pan over high heat for about 2 minutes; most of the liquid will be absorbed by the noodles. Transfer to warmed plates and serve.

Stir-Fried Transparent Noodles with Beef and Mushrooms

Serves 2, or 4 sharing several dishes

6 ounces arrowroot or broad-bean noodles

8 ounces beefsteak

1 large yellow onion

5 dried black mushrooms, soaked for 20 minutes in hot water

2 tablespoons vegetable oil

2 teaspoons toasted sesame seeds

SEASONING FOR BEEF:

2 teaspoons minced fresh ginger

1½ teaspoons minced garlic

1 tablespoon Chinese rice wine or dry sherry

1½ teaspoons chili-bean paste

1 tablespoon tamari or light soy sauce

2 teaspoons sesame oil

They love noodles in Sichuan, and make them with all sorts of starchy ingredients. In their markets you'll find freshly made bundles of gray and pink sweet potato starch noodles; semi-transparent extruded noodles from broad-bean and mung-bean flour, and also a type similar to the clear filaments used in sukiyaki. Closer to home, you can find both arrowroot and sweet potato noodles in well-stocked Asian grocery stores, and bean-flour noodles that go under names like "glass," "transparent," and "bean-thread" are readily available.

¼ cup beef stock
1 teaspoon cornstarch
½ teaspoon salt

Bring 1½ quarts of water to a boil, add the noodles, and bring almost back to a boil. Cook for 3½ to 4 minutes without allowing the water to boil again. The noodles should be tender while retaining their texture. Drain, rinse with hot water, and drain again.

Cut the beef into thin slices, then stack the slices and cut into shreds. Combine the seasoning ingredients in a bowl, add the beef shreds, and mix well. Set aside for 20 minutes.

Combine the sauce ingredients in a small bowl.

Peel the onion and cut into narrow wedges (see sidebar, page 68). Drain the mushrooms, squeeze out the water, trim the stems close to the caps, discard stems and shred the caps (see sidebar, page 170).

Heat the oil in a wok or skillet over medium-high heat and stir-fry the onion to a golden brown, about 2 minutes. Add the mushrooms and stir-fry briefly. Remove and reserve the onion and mushrooms.

Reheat the pan and stir-fry the beef shreds over very high heat until cooked. Return the onions and mushrooms to the pan. Stir the sauce and pour into the pan. Cook, stirring, until the sauce has thickened. Check seasonings and adjust to taste.

Add the noodles and heat through, stirring thoroughly. Transfer to a platter, scatter on the sesame seeds, and serve.

"Crossing the Bridge" Noodles

Serves 4 to 6

FOR THE NOODLES:
14 ounces fresh Chinese egg noodles (page 15)
2 ounces young spinach leaves
4 ounces boneless chicken breast
3 ounces white fish
3 ounces shrimp, shelled and deveined

SEASONING:
1 teaspoon Chinese rice wine or dry sherry

½ teaspoon tamari or light soy sauce
½ teaspoon salt

BROTH:
7 cups chicken stock (pages 26-27)
6 thin slices fresh ginger
Salt to taste
⅓ cup rendered chicken fat (see sidebar, page 94)

Bring 2½ quarts of water to a boil. Add the noodles and reheat the water until it begins to bubble again, then reduce the heat to medium and cook the noodles for about 1½ minutes. Drain, transfer to a deep bowl, and cover to keep warm.

Cook the spinach for 2 minutes in lightly salted water, then drain. Slice the chicken, fish, and shrimp very thin (so they can cook in the hot broth) and arrange on a plate. Sprinkle on the seasonings. Arrange the spinach around the edge of the plate.

Bring the stock to a boil, add the ginger, salt to taste, and chicken fat. Pour into a soup tureen.

Take the noodles, plate of meat, and spinach to the table. Bring in the piping-hot broth and in front of your guests add the noodles and other ingredients to the broth. Cover and leave for 5 minutes before spooning carefully into large soup bowls.

*L*ike so many dishes from China, this classic noodle soup from Yunnan province in central China has an interesting story to go with its name.

A rich merchant's son had repeatedly failed to pass the imperial examinations. His frustrated father sent him to live and study undisturbed in their garden cottage, separated from the family by a small river crossed by an arched bridge. The family cook found the only way to deliver hot meals to the son was to take the noodles and broth separately. He floated melted chicken fat on the surface of the richly flavored broth to retain the heat.

Beijing Noodle Hot Pot

Serves 6 to 10 sharing several dishes

6 ounces flat wheat-starch noodles
²⁄₃ cup (4 ounces) chicken leg meat, diced
4 ounces prepared fish or squid balls (see sidebar)
6 small dried black mushrooms, soaked for 25 minutes in ¹⁄₂ cup hot water
3 baby bok choy (Chinese white cabbage) or other Chinese greens
¹⁄₂ cup sliced straw mushrooms or champignons
¹⁄₃ cup sliced bamboo shoots
3 small tomatoes, quartered
2 scallions, trimmed and cut into 2-inch lengths
2 4-ounce cakes tofu (soft bean curd), cubed

SEASONING FOR CHICKEN:
2 teaspoons Chinese rice wine or dry sherry
1 teaspoon ginger juice (see sidebar, page 50)

BROTH:
6¹⁄₂ cups chicken stock (pages 26-27)
2 tablespoons tamari or light soy sauce
1¹⁄₂ teaspoons salt
¾ teaspoon sugar

Cook the noodles in a pan of simmering water until *al dente*, then drain. Pour into a clay pot or a casserole and set aside.

Place the diced chicken in a bowl and add the chicken seasoning ingredients, mix well, and leave for 10 minutes. Cut the fish or squid balls in half. Drain the black mushrooms, reserving the liquid, and remove stems. Bring a small pan of water to a boil. Cut the cabbages in half or shred coarsely, as preferred. Parboil until crisp-tender, about 2¹⁄₂ minutes, and drain.

Arrange the meat, vegetables, and tofu over the noodles. Combine the broth ingredients in a saucepan. Strain the reserved mushroom liquid, add to the pan, and bring to a boil. Pour into the casserole and place over medium heat to simmer gently for 10 minutes. Serve in the casserole.

singapore, malaysia, and indonesia

The three countries at the southernmost tip of Southeast Asia have many dishes in common. Their cuisines have elements of Chinese cooking, Indian influences, and ingredients that reflect local ethnic food preferences. The result is a polyglot, where coconut milk is as important as soy sauce, where ginger is a dominant taste, where spices give richness and herbs lend clarity to sauces of ingenious combination. Flavors can be hot, for chili is no stranger here. They can be deep and mysterious, for this region's cooks call on the full range of Chinese bean-based seasonings, plus their own pungent shrimp paste, *blacan*, and *kecap manis*, a thick, sweet soy sauce.

All kinds of noodles go into *woks* and *wajans* here: plump yellow *Hokkien mee* as thick and chewy as spaghetti al dente, flat and thin egg noodles, wheat-starch noodles as white and fine as cotton threads. But the noodles that best characterize these cuisines are the fresh rice ribbons called *kway tiao* or *mei fun* and the finer dried rice vermicelli called *behoon* or *laksa*.

Hokkien mee hits the pan with a sizzle and a host of accompanying ingredients to be tossed and turned until crisp at the edges, redolent of smoke and about as tasty as you could ever dream. At the other end of the flavor spectrum is *laksa*, floating soft and creamy-white in a coconut curry gravy as rich as a spice merchant's purse, and so aromatic you can smell it a block away.

Mei fun rice noodles are steamed sheets of rice dough that can be used whole as a wrapper, torn into fragments, or cut into noodles of any width. Their bland flavor makes them an excellent foil for seasonings, sauces, and well-spiced meats in stir-fried dishes and soup pots.

Cha siu (Chinese roast pork) is easy to make at home, using a premixed package of marinade from your Chinese grocer. Or try this recipe, which I have been using for years:

For 12 ounces of pork tenderloin, trimmed of fat and surface tissue, combine 2 teaspoons dark soy sauce, 1 tablespoon light soy sauce, 2 teaspoons white sugar, 2 teaspoons rice wine, 2 teaspoons Hoisin sauce, ½ teaspoon five-spice powder, and a pinch of powdered red food coloring. Brush the mixture over the pork and marinate for 45 minutes, uncovered, in the refrigerator in warm weather. Place on a wire rack in a roasting pan and roast at 425°F for 20 to 25 minutes until the surface is flecked with brown but the meat is still pink and moist inside.

When I'm in a hurry, or when I want an intensely flavored fish-seafood stock for a soup, I use a powdered or granulated Japanese dashi broth base. One teaspoon, or a dash more for stronger taste, stirred into hot water is all you need, and it's ready in a flash.

Fine Vermicelli in Clear Soup with Cha Siu

Serves 6

> ½ *pound fine wheat-starch* (misua) *vermicelli*
> 10 *ounces* cha siu *(Chinese roast pork), thinly sliced*
> 6 *dried black mushrooms, soaked for 20 minutes in warm water*
> 7 *cups chicken stock (pages 26-27)*
> 1 *tablespoon rice wine or dry sherry*
> 4 *thin slices fresh ginger, finely shredded*
> 3 *stems* choy sum *or* gai larn *(Chinese greens), cut into 2-inch pieces*
> 1½ *tablespoons light or tamari soy sauce*
> *Salt and white pepper*
> 2 *to 3 tablespoons scallion greens, sliced diagonally*

Bring 1½ quarts of water to a boil and salt it sparingly. Add the noodles and return to a boil. Reduce the heat and simmer until the noodles are tender, about 1½ minutes. Drain, then distribute the noodles evenly among six deep soup bowls and set aside.

Drain the mushrooms and remove and discard the stems. In a large saucepan bring the stock to a boil, add the wine, ginger, mushrooms, and green vegetables, and simmer for 5 to 7 minutes until the vegetables are tender. Season with soy sauce and add salt and pepper to taste.

Pour over the noodles, placing equal amounts of vegetables in each bowl. Arrange the sliced pork over the noodles and garnish with scallion greens. Serve.

Miswa Soup Noodles

Serves 4 to 6

> 6 *ounces* miswa *(fine wheat-starch vermicelli)*
> 5 *ounces fresh, cleaned squid*
> 4 *ounces raw shrimp, shelled and deveined*
> 4 *ounces poached boneless, skinless chicken or boiled pork*
> 6 *cups fish stock (page 27)*
> 1 *teaspoon sugar*
> 1 *cup fresh bean sprouts*

1 cup shredded Napa cabbage
2 to 3 teaspoons tamari or light soy sauce
½ cup finely sliced scallion greens
Small sprigs of cilantro (Chinese parsley)
Lime wedges

Bring 1½ quarts of water to a boil, add the noodles, and cook for about 1 minute. Remove from heat and let them stand for 1 minute more, then drain.

Cut the squid into rings or score and cut into squares (see sidebar, page 57). Slice the shrimp in half lengthwise. Slice the chicken or pork, stack the slices together, and cut into fine shreds.

Bring the stock to a boil, add the sugar, squid, shrimp, bean sprouts, and cabbage, and cook for 2 minutes. Season with soy sauce. Add the noodles and heat through, then ladle into bowls.

Arrange a little stack of the shredded meat on the noodles, garnish with the scallion greens and cilantro, and serve with lime wedges for squeezing into the soup to taste.

Five-Minute Noodle Soup with Chinese Sausage

Serves 4

4 ounces dried rice vermicelli
5½ cups broth (made from stock on hand, or your favorite instant stock powder)
2 to 3 lap cheong (Chinese sausage)
1 ounce canned, salt-preserved vegetables (turnip or Shanghai cabbage)
1 tablespoon tamari or light soy sauce
2 tablespoons minced scallion greens

Soak the vermicelli in warm water to soften. Drain. Place the sausages in a steamer to steam for 2 to 3 minutes. Remove and slice diagonally.

Bring the broth to a boil in a 2-quart pot and add the sausage. Finely shred the vegetables and add to the broth with the noodles and soy sauce. Serve in deep bowls, garnishing with minced scallions.

Lap cheong are firm, chewy, pure pork sausages flavored with Chinese spices and sugar. Like a good salami, they will keep for months in the refrigerator, or in cool climates you can safely hang them in the kitchen. Steaming softens and plumps them, making them even more delicious. Keep some on hand to toss, thinly sliced on the diagonal, into stir-fries, stuffings, and vegetable dishes.

When roasted, dried chilies acquire a pleasing nutty taste. To make roasted chili flakes, wrap several large dried red serrano chilies in a piece of aluminum foil. Place in a hot oven, over a low gas flame, or in a small, heavy pan over medium heat. Cook until the chilies are dry, crisp, and well browned. Crush in a mortar, cool, and store in an airtight spice jar. For roasted chili powder, grind the roasted chilies in a blender or spice grinder.

Combination Soup Noodles

Serves 4, or 6 to 8 sharing several dishes

6 cups pork stock (page 26)
1 fresh red chili pepper, seeded
2 teaspoons vegetable oil
2 tablespoons tamari or light soy sauce
1 teaspoon sugar
¾ teaspoon salt
⅓ teaspoon pepper
4 ounces dried Hokkien mee (thick yellow noodles), or 1 pound fresh noodles
2 ounces rice vermicelli
5 ounces fresh bean sprouts
2 ounces fresh spinach or water spinach leaves
½ pound raw shrimp, shelled and deveined
3 ounces cleaned squid, cut into rings
3 ounces boiled or roasted pork, thinly sliced
1½ tablespoons chopped cilantro (Chinese parsley)
2 tablespoons fried onion flakes (see sidebar, page 89)
Roasted chili flakes (see sidebar)

Measure the stock into a pan and add the chili and oil. Simmer over medium heat for 5 to 6 minutes, covered. Add the soy sauce, sugar, salt, and pepper, reduce the heat to low, and keep the soup hot until needed.

Bring 1 quart of water to a boil. Cook the *mee* to *al dente* and pour into a colander to drain. Rinse under running cold water and drain again. Leave in the colander.

Cover the rice vermicelli with hot water to soften, let stand for 7 minutes, then drain. Bring a kettle of water to a boil. Pour over the *mee* to reheat through, drain, and divide among soup bowls. Place a portion of the rice vermicelli on top.

Bring the broth to a boil, add the bean sprouts and spinach and blanch for 30 seconds, then add the shrimp, squid, and pork and heat thoroughly. Pour over the noodles and sprinkle on the cilantro, fried onion flakes, and chili flakes.

$ingapore $eafood ∩oodle $oup

Serves 4, or 6 to 8 sharing several dishes

   ½ pound white fish
   2 fish heads and carcasses, or 12 ounces shrimp heads and shells
   1 scallion, trimmed and cut into 2-inch pieces
   One 1-inch piece fresh ginger
   7 cups water
   1½ teaspoons salt
   4 ounces fine egg noodles or shrimp-flavored noodles
   3 ounces fresh, cleaned squid
   3 ounces raw shrimp, shelled and deveined
   2 baby bok choy (Chinese white cabbage)
   1 cup sliced Napa cabbage
   4 thin slices fresh ginger, finely shredded
   1½ teaspoons sesame oil
   ½ cup diced seedless cucumber
   ½ teaspoon five-spice powder
   1 tablespoon tamari or light soy sauce
   5 ounces cha siu (Chinese roast pork; see sidebar, page 86)
   3 ounces fresh bean sprouts
   ¼ cup fried onion flakes (see sidebar)
   Cilantro (Chinese parsley)

To prepare the broth, cut the fish into cubes, place in a pan with the fish heads and carcasses or shrimp heads and shells, sliced scallion, the 1-inch piece of ginger, 7 cups of water, and salt, and bring it barely to a boil. Reduce the heat and simmer, covered, for 10 minutes. Do not allow the water to bubble, which will cloud the broth. Strain into another pan and keep hot.

Bring 1½ quarts of water to a boil, add the noodles, and cook until tender, about 5½ minutes. Drain, rinse in hot water, and drain again.

Cut the squid into 2-inch squares (see sidebar, page 57). Cut the bok choy in half lengthwise, blanch for 2 minutes in lightly salted water, and drain.

Add the squid and shrimp, bok choy, cabbage, shredded ginger, and sesame oil to the broth and simmer for 5 minutes. Stir in the cucumber, five-spice powder, soy sauce, noodles, sliced roast pork, and bean sprouts. Cook another 2 minutes, then ladle into large bowls. Garnish with the fried onion flakes and sprigs of cilantro.

To make fried onion flakes, peel 8 ounces of shallots and slice them very thin, cutting lengthwise. Heat 2½ cups of vegetable or peanut oil in a wok or deep skillet over high heat until a haze of smoke appears over the pan. Add the onions and cook for 1 minute, then reduce the heat slightly and continue to fry until the onions are a deep golden brown, taking care not to burn them. Remove with a slotted spoon or wire skimmer and drain on a double thickness of paper towel. When completely cold, store in an airtight jar in the refrigerator. Given the chance, they will keep for many months, but they're so delicious sprinkled over noodles, rice, or curries that they usually don't last more than a few days.

Sweet, thick, glossy kecap manis *gives a rich color and deep soy-caramel flavor to any dish it's added to. The Indonesians drizzle it lavishly, as does my daughter Isobel, on just about any dish that needs a little zing.*

Indonesian Shrimp Noodle Soup
(Soto Udang)

Serves 4 to 6

> **5 ounces rice vermicelli**
> **8 ounces fresh bean sprouts**
> **1 1/4 cups vegetable oil**
> **1 to 3 dried red chilies, seeded**
> **1/2 cup shelled peanuts**
> **1 1/4 pounds fresh shrimp, in their shells**
> **6 cups water**
> **1 teaspoon minced garlic**
> **1 teaspoon minced fresh ginger**
> **2 teaspoons minced lemon grass**
> **2 tablespoons kecap manis** *(sweet soy sauce; see sidebar)*
> **2 tablespoons tamarind concentrate (or lemon juice)**
> **1 tablespoon soft brown sugar**

Soak the vermicelli in hot water for 7 minutes, then drain. Blanch the bean sprouts in simmering water for 40 seconds, refresh in cold water, and drain.

Heat the oil over high heat until smoking, then reduce the heat to medium. Fry the chilies until crisp and well browned, remove from the oil, and drain on a paper towel. Add the peanuts to the oil and fry to golden, then remove and cool. Chop fine and set aside.

Place the shrimp in a saucepan with the 6 cups water, garlic, ginger, and lemon grass. Bring to a boil and simmer for 6 minutes. Lift out the shrimp with a slotted spoon. Set aside to cool for a few minutes, then remove the heads and shells and return these to the stock. Simmer a further 10 minutes. Strain the broth into another pan and season with the *kecap manis*, tamarind concentrate, and sugar.

Slice each shrimp in half lengthwise. Distribute the noodles, bean sprouts, and shrimp evenly among four to six bowls. Pour on the broth. Crush the fried chilies and sprinkle chili flakes and peanuts over each bowl of noodle soup.

Hokkien Mee Soup

Serves 6

> 1 pound round or skirt beef, cut into 2-inch cubes
> 2½ tablespoons vegetable oil
> ½ pound fresh **Hokkien mee** (thick yellow noodles)
> 4 ounces firm tofu (bean curd)
> 1½ teaspoons minced garlic
> 1 rib of celery, thinly sliced diagonally
> 1 fresh red chili
> 4 ounces raw shrimp, shelled
> 6 ounces fish balls (see sidebar, page 82)
> ½ cup diagonally sliced scallion greens
> 3 ounces **oong choy** (water vegetable or spinach leaves)
> Salt and white pepper
> Tamari or light soy sauce

Brown the beef in a heavy pan with half the vegetable oil over high heat. Add 2 quarts water and bring to a boil. Simmer, partially covered, until the meat is tender, about 1 hour. Strain the broth (there should be about 6 ½ cups) and keep hot. Cut the beef into small cubes.

Bring 1½ quarts of water to a boil. Add the noodles and cook for 2 to 2½ minutes, drain, and divide the noodles among six soup bowls. Top with the beef cubes.

Cut the tofu into thin slices, stack the slices together, and cut across them to make narrow strips.

In a small pan heat the remaining oil over medium-high heat. Stir-fry the garlic, tofu, celery, and chili for 2½ minutes. Add the shrimp and fish balls and cook a further 1½ minutes, until the shrimp turn pink. Pour on the hot broth, add the scallion greens and *oong choy*, and heat through. Add salt and pepper to taste, pour over the noodles, and serve with soy sauce.

Note: The broth can be made ahead of time and refrigerated or frozen until needed. The remaining ingredients will take just a few minutes to prepare.

*O*ong choy *has tender leaves similar to spinach. If you have some left over from this recipe, cook it the following night in a wok, stir-frying with masses of minced garlic, or with a spoonful of Chinese shrimp paste, the soft, fresh, pink-gray variety that Chinese cooks favor over the more intensely pungent* blacan *used in Malaysia.*

Most Malaysian and Indonesian dishes begin with an aromatic blend of fresh herbs and dried spices, ground by hand in a stone mortar. This is the rempah, the secret to the wonderful depth of flavor found in these dishes. Many a clever young girl has won herself a good husband by carefully selecting herbs and refining her technique of pounding the rempah to just the right consistency for perfect results.

Indonesian Chicken Noodle Soup

(MEE SOTO)

Serves 4, or 6 to 8 sharing several dishes

3 pounds chicken thighs

3 cups water

2 thick slices fresh ginger

Salt and white pepper

1¼ pounds **Hokkien mee (thick yellow noodles)**, or 12 ounces spaghetti

6 ounces fresh bean sprouts, blanched

2 tablespoons diagonally sliced scallion greens

2 tablespoons fried onion flakes (see sidebar, page 89)

REMPAH:

2 tablespoons coriander seeds

1 teaspoon cumin seeds

½ teaspoon aniseed or caraway seeds

1 tablespoon chopped **galangal** or fresh ginger

3 tablespoons chopped French shallots or yellow onion

3 large cloves garlic, peeled

2 tablespoons chopped macadamia nuts

3 tablespoons peanut or vegetable oil

Place the chicken in a saucepan with the 3 cups water and ginger. Bring to a boil, reduce the heat to low, and leave to simmer while the *rempah* is made.

To make the *rempah*, toast the coriander, cumin, and aniseed in a dry pan over medium heat until aromatic. Transfer to a spice grinder and grind to a powder. Add the *galangal* or ginger, shallots, garlic, and macadamia nuts and grind to a reasonably smooth paste (add a little of the oil to the spice grinder if it begins to clog). Heat the oil in another pan over medium heat and fry the spices for about 4 minutes, until aromatic.

Remove the chicken from the broth. Drain briefly, then fry with the *rempah* until well colored. Strain the broth into another pan, add the chicken, and continue to cook until the chicken is very tender, about 30 minutes. Skim the fat from the broth (the fat can be reserved for another use; it adds wonderful flavors to a stir-fry, for example). Remove the chicken, debone, and tear into pieces. Season the broth with salt and pepper to taste.

Cook the fresh noodles in boiling water for about 2½ minutes (if using spaghetti, cook for 12 to 13 minutes). Drain well. Divide among soup bowls and place chicken on top. Pour on the sauce and add bean sprouts. Garnish with the scallions and onion flakes. Serve a hot chili sauce on the side.

Seafood Coconut Curry Soup

Serves 4 to 8

10 ounces firm white fish
4 ounces cleaned squid
4 ounces fresh scallops or clams
4 ounces shelled and deveined raw shrimp or crab meat
7 ounces rice vermicelli
1½ cups fresh bean sprouts
5 scallions, trimmed and finely sliced
Cilantro leaves (Chinese parsley)
Mint or basil leaves, or Vietnamese mint
2 to 3 tablespoons freshly squeezed lime juice (or tamarind water) to taste

COCONUT CURRY SOUP:
2 large onions, finely sliced
3 tablespoons vegetable oil
1½ teaspoons minced garlic
2 teaspoons minced fresh ginger
1½ teaspoons Chinese shrimp paste
½ cup mild Malaysian curry sauce
1 to 2 fresh green chilies, seeded and finely sliced
1½ cups thick coconut milk (coconut cream)
5 cups water
Salt and freshly ground pepper

To make tamarind water, soak 3 to 4 teaspoons of tamarind pulp in 3 tablespoons of boiling water. Mash with the back of a spoon, then strain off the liquid.

Cut the fish into ¼-inch cubes and the squid into rings or scored squares (see sidebar, page 57). Slice the scallops in half horizontally. Clams can be left in their shells after a thorough scrub with a brush. Cut the crab claws in half diagonally and leave in the shell.

Soften the noodles in hot water to cover for 3½ minutes and drain well. Bring a small pan of water to a boil, add the bean sprouts, blanch

for 30 seconds, and drain. Refresh in cold water, drain again, and set aside.

To make the soup, sauté the sliced onions in the oil over medium heat until soft and translucent, remove and reserve half, and continue cooking the remainder until well browned. Add the garlic, ginger, and shrimp paste and cook, stirring, for 1 minute. Pour in the curry sauce, add the chilies, and cook over medium heat for 5 minutes, stirring. Pour in the coconut milk and bring to a boil, stirring. Reduce the heat and cook gently for about 12 minutes.

Add the 5 cups water, bring to a boil again, and simmer on reduced heat for 10 minutes. Return the reserved onions and add the seafood. Bring to a boil and simmer slowly for a few minutes. Check seasoning, adding salt and pepper to taste.

When ready to serve, bring about 2 quarts of water to a boil. Place the scallions, cilantro, and mint (or basil) in little dishes, the lime juice (or tamarind water) in small bowls. Set on a tray.

Place the noodles in a strainer and pour on the boiling water to re-heat the noodles, drain well, and divide evenly among soup bowls. Place some bean sprouts on top of the noodles. Pour on the hot soup, distributing the seafood evenly among the bowls. Serve with the condiments, for each diner to add according to preference.

This fragrant chicken broth can be used in many of the recipes in this book. Skim off the fat and pour the stock into freezer containers—it's best to freeze it in small lots for easier use later. Frozen stock can be added directly to the pan—no thawing is required. The skimmed fat can be saved to be used in stir-fries.

Chicken Shreds in Two Dressings on Noodles

This would make a delightful appetizer before a Chinese or Thai meal. It's also a good dish for eating outdoors. For a picnic, pack it in a chiller container, with the soy-chili dressing packed separately.

Serves 4 as a main course, or 6 as an appetizer

> 1 3-pound chicken
> 5 thick slices fresh ginger
> 6 scallions
> 1½ teaspoons salt
> 1 teaspoon sesame oil
> 2 tablespoons crushed, roasted peanuts
> 3 tablespoons vegetable oil

4 ounces rice vermicelli, or ½ pound fresh egg noodles (page 15)

SOY-CHILI DRESSING:
1 fresh red chili
1 tablespoon vegetable oil
2 tablespoons tamari or light soy sauce

Cut the chicken in half, place in a stewpan with the ginger, and add water to barely cover. Trim the scallions; cut two in half and place in the pan along with 1 teaspoon salt. Cover and bring almost to a boil, reduce the heat immediately, and cook the chicken slowly for 45 minutes. The water should not be allowed to boil during cooking.

Remove the chicken to a plate and allow to cool. Brush with the sesame oil, then debone and tear the chicken into narrow strips. Reserve the broth for another recipe (see sidebar, page 94).

Mince the remaining scallions. Heat the oil in a wok over medium heat and fry the scallions for 2 minutes until very well cooked. Add the peanuts and heat through.

Combine the soy-chili dressing ingredients in a small bowl.

Cook the vermicelli in boiling water for 45 seconds (if using fresh egg noodles, boil in water with 1 tablespoon vegetable oil and remaining ½ teaspoon salt for 3 minutes). Drain thoroughly and spread on a plate. Arrange the chicken evenly over the noodles and top with the peanut-and-scallion mixture. Serve at room temperature with the soy-chili dressing on the side.

⟡enang ⟡aksa

Serves 4 as a generous main course, or 6 to 8 sharing several dishes

12 ounces rice vermicelli
1 pound firm white fish
1½ pounds fish heads and bones
1 lemon grass stem
4 slices galangal (Thai ginger; see sidebar) or ¾ teaspoon laos powder
4 slices fresh ginger
6 French shallots
4 scallions
5 to 6 fresh red chilies
2 teaspoons blacan (dried shrimp paste)
1 teaspoon ground turmeric
3 tablespoons concentrated tamarind
2½ teaspoons sugar
Salt and freshly ground black pepper

ACCOMPANIMENTS:
1 cup diced pineapple
1 cup diced cucumber
2 cups shredded lettuce
¼ cup sliced pickled shallots or garlic
Small sprigs of fresh herbs (mint, cilantro, and basil)
Fresh red and green chilies, seeded and finely sliced
Kapi (fresh shrimp paste) or the pink-gray, smooth, moist Chinese shrimp paste

Prepare the accompaniments, arrange on a platter, cover with plastic wrap, and refrigerate until needed. The shrimp paste should be diluted with warm water to a creamy consistency and served in a small dish. Keep well covered to prevent the odor from permeating the refrigerator.

Prepare the noodles by soaking in hot water to cover for 7 minutes, until tender. Drain and transfer to a deep serving dish or divide among four bowls. Cut the fish into 1-inch cubes.

Bring 2 quarts of water to a boil, add the fish heads and bones and the cubed fish, and cook for 5 minutes without allowing the water to bubble energetically. Remove the fish cubes with a slotted spoon and place on top of the noodles. Continue to simmer the bones a further 5 minutes.

In a food processor, blender, or mortar, grind the lemon grass, *galangal*, ginger, shallots, scallions, and chilies to a paste. Add the shrimp paste and turmeric. Fry in 3 tablespoons oil until very fragrant, about 5 minutes. Add the tamarind. Strain the fish broth and add to the mixture, bring to a boil, then reduce heat and simmer for 6–7 minutes. Check seasonings, adding the sugar, and salt, and pepper to taste.

Pour the piping-hot broth over the noodles and add the fish. Take to the table with the platter of accompaniments.

Laksa Lemak

Serves 4

> *7 ounces shrimp, shelled and deveined*
> *6 ounces squid balls, halved (see sidebar, page 81)*
> *7 ounces rice vermicelli*
> *6 ounces fresh bean sprouts*
> *1 small cucumber*
> *1 to 3 fresh chilies, seeded and chopped*
> *3 fresh Kaffir lime leaves (optional)*
>
> SAUCE:
> *5 dried red chilies*
> *1 tablespoon coriander seeds*
> *1 teaspoon cumin seeds*
> *1 tablespoon chopped macadamia nuts*
> *1 teaspoon ground turmeric*
> *2 teaspoons* blacan *(shrimp paste)*
> *6 slices fresh ginger*
> *4 slices* galangal *(optional)*
> *1 lemon grass stem, trimmed and chopped*
> *1 tablespoon chopped cilantro stems (Chinese parsley) and roots*
> *3 tablespoons vegetable oil*
> *2 cups thin coconut milk*
> *1 cup thick coconut milk*
> *Salt, pepper, and sugar*

To make the sauce, first toast the chilies and coriander and cumin seeds in a dry pan over medium heat until they are very aromatic, about 2

Kaffir lime leaves are used to give a characteristic lemony taste and tempting aroma to many dishes in Southeast Asia, particularly curries and soups with a coconut milk sauce. Fresh leaves should be scored with the point of a knife to release the flavor, and added about halfway through the cooking. Dried leaves must be reconstituted in hot water before adding to a dish. As a garnish, which is frequently how they appear, the leaves should be very finely shredded. Fold in half and trim away the central rib first. Then cut across the leaf into very thin pieces. Scatter over the dish to delicious effect.

Kaffir lime leaves

minutes. Pour into a spice grinder and grind to a fine powder. Add the nuts and turmeric and grind again. Toast the shrimp paste (see sidebar, page 141) or fry it in a little vegetable oil over medium heat for 40 seconds.

Add the shrimp paste, ginger, *galangal*, lemon grass, and cilantro to the spices and grind to a paste, adding a little of the oil if needed to prevent the blades of the grinder from clogging.

Heat the oil (or remaining oil) in a medium-sized, heavy pan and gently fry this paste, known as *rempah* (see sidebar, page 92) for about 4 minutes over medium heat until it is very aromatic. Pour on the thin coconut milk and bring to a boil, stirring.

Reduce the heat and simmer, partially covered, for about 12 minutes, then pour in the thick coconut milk. Check seasonings, adding salt, pepper, and a little sugar to taste.

Add the shrimp and squid balls to the sauce and cook for 5 to 6 minutes. Meanwhile, blanch the vermicelli in boiling water for 30 seconds, drain, and blanch again. Drain thoroughly.

Divide the vermicelli among four deep bowls. Blanch the bean sprouts in boiling water and drain. Cut the unpeeled cucumber in half, scoop out the seeds, and cut across into thin slices. Place the cucumber and bean sprouts on the noodles and pour on the sauce, distributing the shrimp and squid balls evenly.

Add a little of the chopped chilies to each bowl. Scatter the shredded lime leaves (see sidebar, page 97) over the top. Serve the remaining chilies in a small dish.

Beehoon

Serves 3 to 4

4 ounces small raw shrimp, shelled and deveined
4 ounces boneless chicken breast, cubed
2 teaspoons minced fresh ginger
2 teaspoons tamari or light soy sauce
1 teaspoon rice wine or dry sherry
1½ teaspoons cornstarch
10 ounces rice vermicelli
8 dried black mushrooms, soaked in cold water for 20 minutes
4 ounces cleaned fresh squid
1½ cups vegetable oil
4 ounces fresh firm tofu (bean curd)
2 eggs, lightly beaten
2 medium yellow onions, finely sliced
½ green or red bell pepper, seeded and julienned
1 to 2 fresh red chilies, seeded and minced
4 ounces fresh bean sprouts
3 scallions, trimmed and cut into 1-inch pieces
Salt and freshly ground black pepper

SAUCE:
⅔ cup chicken stock (pages 26-27)
1 tablespoon tamari or light soy sauce
¾ teaspoon salt
½ teaspoon hot chili powder
1 teaspoon minced garlic
1 teaspoon minced fresh ginger
1½ teaspoons ground coriander
½ teaspoon ground turmeric

Marinate the shrimp and chicken with the minced ginger, soy sauce, rice wine, and cornstarch until required. Soak the vermicelli in warm water for 5 minutes to soften and untangle. Drain and spread on a tray to partially dry.

Drain the mushrooms, squeeze out excess water, and trim the stems close to the caps. Shred the caps fine and set aside. Cut the squid into rings, or cut into squares and score (see sidebar, page 57). Set aside.

To prepare the sauce, combine the chicken stock, soy sauce, salt, and

Indonesian cooks like to drape fine shreds of egg crepe over their dishes as a garnish, with perhaps a few shreds of green and red chili. In Thailand they do the same, adding roasted peanuts and garlic chives as well.

To make an egg crepe, beat eggs and strain through a fine nylon sieve. Heat 1 teaspoon of oil in a sauté pan or wok, or heat a nonstick pan, then rub the inside of the pan with a balled-up piece of paper towel to make the surface very smooth. When the pan is quite hot but not overly so, pour in the egg and tilt the pan to swirl the egg over as wide a surface as possible. Cook until the edges loosen, then flip and briefly cook the other side. Remove to a board to cool, then roll up and cut crosswise into very fine shreds.

chili powder in a small bowl. Combine the garlic, ginger, coriander, and turmeric in another bowl and set aside.

Heat the oil in a wok or skillet over very high heat until a haze of smoke appears over the pan. Cut the tofu into small dice and fry until crisp on the surface (see sidebar, page 135). Remove with a wire strainer or slotted spoon. Pour most of the oil into a metal dish and set aside, leaving a light coating of oil in the pan. With the heat on high, add the vermicelli, stir-fry for 1 minute, remove, and set aside.

Make the egg crepe as directed in the sidebar.

Reheat the pan again with 1 tablespoon of the reserved oil and stir-fry the onions on high heat until very lightly browned. Add the peppers and stir-fry until softened, then remove.

Add a little more oil and stir-fry the marinated shrimp, squid, and chicken until cooked, 1½ to 2 minutes. Return the vegetables to the wok, add half the chili, the bean sprouts, and the scallions, and stir-fry for 1½ minutes. Remove. Return the noodles to the wok, adding a little extra oil if necessary. Stir in the reserved ginger-and-garlic mixture and cook on high heat, stirring continuously for 30 seconds. Add the stock mixture and continue to cook on high heat, stirring continuously, until the liquid is absorbed and the noodles are reasonably dry again.

Return the cooked ingredients (except egg) to the wok and cook over high heat, tossing and stirring, until thoroughly combined. Check seasonings, adding salt and pepper to taste, then transfer to a large platter. Scatter the shredded egg crepe over the noodles with the remaining chili.

Cutting an egg crepe into shreds

Fried Beehoon Noodles with Fish

Serves 2 to 3, or more sharing several dishes

 6 ounces fine rice vermicelli
 3 ounces fresh bean sprouts
 1/2 pound firm white fish, cubed (see sidebar)
 1 tablespoon minced fresh ginger
 2 1/2 tablespoons vegetable oil
 1 1/2 teaspoons minced garlic
 1 1/2 ounces sliced straw mushrooms or champignons
 1 to 2 red chilies, seeded and finely sliced
 2 scallions, white part only, cut into 1-inch pieces
 2 large eggs, beaten lightly
 1 1/2 to 2 teaspoons tamari or light soy sauce
 Salt and white pepper
 Chili shreds and cilantro sprigs for garnish

Flat, firm-textured fish of the John Dory or pompano family are the ones most likely to be used in Southeast Asia for a dish of this type. Sea bass, snapper, or codfish would also do.

Soak the vermicelli in boiling water for 1 minute, drain, and spread on a plate to partially dry. Blanch the bean sprouts in simmering water for 40 seconds and drain. Place the ginger on a piece of fine, clean cloth.

Add 1 tablespoon water and squeeze the liquid through the cloth onto the fish.

Heat the oil in a wok or skillet over medium heat and fry the garlic until golden. Increase the heat, add the fish, cook until barely done, and remove. Add the mushrooms, chili, and scallion to the pan and stir-fry for 1 minute. Push to the side of the pan, or remove. Reheat the pan to very hot and stir-fry the drained vermicelli for 30 seconds. Push to the side of the pan. Add the bean sprouts and stir-fry briefly, until wilted.

Make a space in the center of the pan. Pour in the eggs and cook until firm. Break up with the edge of a spatula, then stir into the noodles.

Return the other cooked ingredients to the wok and stir-fry on medium heat until the dish is well mixed and heated through. Add the soy sauce and check seasonings, adding salt and pepper to taste. Garnish with chili shreds or sprigs of cilantro.

Fried Rice Ribbon Noodles

(CHA KWAY TIAO)

Serves 2 to 4

4 ounces boneless chicken, thinly sliced
2 ounces lean pork, thinly sliced
1 tablespoon plus 2 tablespoons tamari or light soy sauce
$\frac{1}{3}$ teaspoon black pepper
$1\frac{1}{2}$ pounds fresh rice ribbon noodles
$3\frac{1}{2}$ tablespoons vegetable or peanut oil
4 ounces raw shrimp, shelled and deveined
2 lap cheong (Chinese sausages), thinly sliced diagonally
3 ounces cleaned squid, sliced
2 teaspoons sesame oil
2 teaspoons dark soy sauce
$\frac{1}{2}$ cup diagonally sliced scallions
1 cup fresh bean sprouts, blanched for 40 seconds
1 cup loosely packed spinach or kangkong (water vegetable) leaves
Salt and freshly ground black pepper
Sugar
Red and green chilies for garnish

Marinate the chicken and pork with 1 tablespoon of the tamari and the black pepper for 10 minutes. Soak the noodles in cold water for 2 minutes, drain thoroughly, and spread on a tray until required.

Heat $1\frac{1}{2}$ tablespoons of the vegetable oil in a wok or heavy skillet over very high heat and stir-fry the pork and chicken for 2 minutes. Add the shrimp, sausage, and squid and stir-fry for $1\frac{1}{2}$ minutes more over high heat. Remove from the pan.

Add the remaining 2 tablespoons of vegetable oil and the sesame oil. Add the noodles and stir-fry for about 3 minutes over the highest heat your stove can produce, until they acquire a delicious smoky aroma and taste (see sidebar).

Sizzle the remaining 2 tablespoons tamari and the dark soy sauce onto the sides of the pan and stir into the noodles. Add the cooked ingredients plus the scallions, bean sprouts, and spinach or water vegetable and stir-fry for 2 minutes. Check the seasonings, adding salt, pepper, and a dash of sugar to taste. Serve on a large platter.

The usual garnish for this dish is fine shreds of egg crepe (see sidebar, page 99) and strips of green and red chilies.

Stir-Fried Rice Ribbon Noodles, Singapore Style

(CHA HOR FUN)

Serves 2 to 3

10 ounces lean pork

1 tablespoon taucheo *(salted yellow bean sauce)*

5 ounces dried wide rice noodles, or 1¼ pounds fresh rice ribbon noodles, or rice dough sheets cut into ½-inch noodles (see sidebar)

3 tablespoons vegetable oil

4 ounces shrimp, shelled and deveined

2 ounces sliced champignons or straw mushrooms

2 ounces sliced bamboo shoot

4 ounces spinach or kangkong *(water spinach)* leaves

1 cup rich-flavored chicken or beef stock (pages 25-27)

1 tablespoon cornstarch

1 tablespoon dark soy sauce

2½ teaspoons white sugar

2 tablespoons chopped cilantro (Chinese parsley)

2 tablespoons scallion greens, sliced diagonally

Rice dough sheets—round, thin sheets of steamed rice dough—can be purchased in Asian food stores and in some well-stocked Chinese noodle shops. To use, they must be cut into ribbons of about ¼ inch wide, and they require very minimal cooking.

Cut the pork into thin slices across the grain, then stack the slices and cut into ½-inch strips. Mash the yellow bean sauce with 1 tablespoon water, pour over the pork, and marinate for 30 minutes.

Bring 1½ quarts of water to a boil, add the dried noodles, and cook for about 4 minutes, until tender. If using fresh noodles, soak in cold water for 2 minutes, then drain.

Heat half the oil in a wok or large, heavy skillet over very high heat until a haze of smoke appears over the pan. Stir-fry the pork for about 1½ minutes, then remove. Add the shrimp, mushrooms, and bamboo shoots and stir-fry for 1 minute. Add the spinach or water vegetables and stir-fry until they wilt. Remove from the pan.

Rinse out the pan and reheat with the remaining oil over your highest heat. Add the drained noodles and stir-fry for 2 to 2½ minutes until they have acquired a smoky aroma (see sidebar, page 102).

Combine the stock and cornstarch. Sizzle the soy sauce down the sides of the pan, add the sugar, and pour in the stock. Cook, stirring, until the sauce glazes the noodles. Return the cooked ingredients to the wok and heat through. Stir in half the cilantro and scallions, transfer to a platter, and garnish with the remainder. Serve at once.

Chow Fun Noodles with Beef and Chinese Greens

Serves 2 to 3, or 4 to 6 sharing several dishes

> *1¼ pounds fresh rice dough sheets (see sidebar, page 103)*
> *½ pound beef filet or sirloin steak*
> *½ pound gai larn or chow sum (Chinese green vegetables)*
> *⅓ cup sliced button or straw mushrooms*
> *2 tablespoons plus 1 tablespoon vegetable oil*
> *1 teaspoon sesame oil*
> *1½ teaspoons minced fresh ginger*
> *1 scallion, cut into 1-inch pieces*

> SEASONING:
> *½ teaspoon minced garlic*
> *1 tablespoon tamari or light soy sauce*
> *2 teaspoons dark soy sauce*
> *1 tablespoon rice wine or dry sherry*
> *2 teaspoons cornstarch*
> *1 teaspoon fine white sugar*

> SAUCE:
> *⅓ cup chicken stock (pages 26-27)*
> *1 teaspoons tamari or light soy sauce*
> *2 tablespoons oyster sauce*
> *¾ teaspoon sugar*
> *1 teaspoon cornstarch*
> *White pepper*

Cut the rice dough sheets into noodles ¼ inch wide, rinse in cold water, and set aside to drain. Slice the beef very thin, stack the slices, and cut into ribbons ¾ inch wide. Combine the seasoning ingredients in a wide, shallow dish. Add the meat, mix well, and set aside for 30 minutes.

Cut the Chinese greens into 1½-inch pieces. Bring 3 cups of lightly salted water to a boil. Blanch the vegetable stems for 2 minutes, add the leaves and cook briefly, then cool under running cold water and drain well. Set aside.

Combine the sauce ingredients in a bowl and set aside. Heat 2 tablespoons vegetable oil and the sesame oil in a wok or large skillet over very high heat. When a haze of smoke appears over the pan, add the noodles and cook, tossing and stirring constantly, until they are slightly charred at the edges and smell deliciously smoky, about 3 minutes. Remove to a plate.

Add the remaining 1 tablespoon oil to the wok, stir-fry the Chinese greens and mushrooms for 1 minute, and remove. Stir-fry the ginger, scallion, and marinated meat on very high heat until barely cooked, about 1½ minutes. Add a little extra oil or a splash of sesame oil, if needed.

Return the noodles, green vegetables, and mushrooms to the wok. Add the sauce and stir until all ingredients are well combined and heated through. Serve on a large platter.

Rice-Stick Noodles with Chicken Curry Sauce
(DENGAN KUAH AYAM)
Serves 3 to 4

1 lemon grass stem
2 to 4 fresh green chilies, seeded and sliced
¼ cup macadamia nuts or almonds
1 teaspoon ground turmeric
1 teaspoon minced garlic
1 teaspoon minced fresh ginger
3 tablespoons vegetable oil
1¾ pounds chicken parts (with bones)
Salt and freshly ground black pepper
½ cup sliced French shallots
1½ tablespoons tamari or light soy sauce
2½ cups coconut milk
4 dried curry leaves or 1 bay leaf
12 ounces raw shrimp, shelled and deveined
1½ pounds fresh rice-stick noodles or dough, or 10 ounces dried rice
    sticks

GARNISH:
3 to 4 basil sprigs
1 hard-boiled egg, sliced
1 tablespoon fried onion flakes (page 89)

To prepare the *rempah* (see sidebar, page 92), place the lemon grass, chilies, nuts, turmeric, garlic, and ginger in a spice grinder, mortar, or blender and grind to a paste. Heat 1 tablespoon of the oil in a medium saucepan with a heavy base over medium-high heat. Fry the *rempah* for about 2 minutes, stirring frequently.

Season the chicken pieces with salt and pepper, add the chicken and shallots to the pan, and fry on medium-high heat until the chicken is lightly browned.

Add the soy sauce, the coconut milk, 1½ cups water, and the curry leaves and bring to a boil. Immediately reduce heat and simmer, partially covered, for about 45 minutes, until the chicken is tender. Add the shrimp and cook for 3 minutes. Season to taste with salt and pepper.

When the chicken is almost done, bring 2½ quarts of water to a boil and salt sparingly. Add the fresh noodles and cook for 40 seconds, then drain immediately. (If using dried noodles, cook for about 3¼ minutes, until tender, and drain.) Divide the noodles among three or four deep bowls, or place in a tureen.

Remove the chicken pieces with a slotted spoon and place one piece into each bowl, or debone and tear the meat into strips. Pour the sauce over the noodles and chicken. Garnish each bowl with a sprig of basil, a slice or two of egg, and the onion flakes. Serve at once.

Spicy Singapore Noodles

Serves 4

> 12 ounces dried rice vermicelli
> 5 tablespoons peanut or vegetable oil
> 1 large onion, very thinly sliced
> 1 medium-large carrot, peeled and julienned
> 2 teaspoons minced garlic
> 2 ribs of celery, julienned
> 1 red bell pepper, cored, seeded, and julienned
> 6 ounces fresh bean sprouts
> 2 tablespoons mild curry powder
> Salt and white pepper
> 3 tablespoons finely shredded crystallized ginger or Chinese sweet

> mixed pickles (which contain watermelon rind or papaya, shallot,
> ginger, carrot, cucumber, and Oriental pear)
>
> 2½ teaspoons fine white sugar
> 3 tablespoons soy sauce
> ¾ cup chicken stock (pages 26-27)
> ½ pound cha siu (Chinese roast pork), thinly sliced
> Curled scallion greens for garnish (see sidebar, page 51)

Bring 1½ quarts of water to a boil. Place the vermicelli in a bowl, pour on the water, and let sit for 1 minute, then drain and cool under running cold water. Drain again thoroughly and spread on a plate until needed.

Heat 2½ tablespoons of the oil in a wok or large skillet over high heat and sauté the onion and carrot for 2 to 3 minutes, until softened. Add the garlic, celery, and pepper and sauté on medium-high heat until crisp-tender, then add the bean sprouts and sauté briefly. Remove from the pan.

Heat the remaining 2½ tablespoons of oil in the pan, add the noodles, and stir-fry on high heat, adding the curry powder, salt, pepper, ginger, and sugar. Stir-fry for 1 minute.

Return the vegetables to the pan. Add the soy sauce and stock and cook, covered, for 1½ minutes, until the liquid is absorbed. Continue to stir-fry on high heat until the noodles are done, about 1½ minutes. Stir in the sliced pork and transfer to a serving dish. Garnish with scallion greens.

Decorate a spicy noodle dish with chili flowers. Using the point of a small paring knife, make 6 or 7 parallel slits the length of a long, thin, fresh red chili, cutting right through at the tip but leaving ½ inch uncut at the base. Separate the petals, then carefully pare or scrape away the white fibers clinging to the inside and separate them from the seed stamen. Chill in ice water until the petals curl. Store in the refrigerator in a plastic container until needed.

Cutting chili flowers

If you find "winged beans" (square, pale green beans with a little frill running along each rib) at your Asian market, buy them for this dish. Use in exactly the same way as long beans. They have a taste that is reminiscent of asparagus, which would also be superb in this recipe.

Pork and Long Beans on Soft Fried Egg Noodles

Serves 3 to 4, or 6 to 8 sharing several dishes

> ½ **pound pork tenderloin**
> 2 **tablespoons tamari or light soy sauce**
> 1 **teaspoon white sugar**
> ½ **pound long (snake) beans or green beans**
> 1 **medium yellow onion**
> 12 **ounces thin egg noodles**
> 3 **tablespoons vegetable oil**
> 6 **slices fresh ginger, finely shredded**
> 1 **teaspoon minced garlic**
> 1 **cup chicken stock (pages 26-27)**
> 2½ **teaspoons cornstarch**
> 1½ **tablespoons oyster sauce**

Cut the pork across the grain into very thin slices and place in a dish. Add 1 tablespoon of the soy sauce and the sugar, mix well, and set aside while the remaining ingredients are prepared.

Cut the beans into 1½-inch pieces. Peel the onion, cut a slice from top and bottom, then cut into narrow wedges, separating the layers (see sidebar, page 68).

Bring 2 quarts of water to a boil and salt sparingly. Add the noodles and bring back to a boil. Reduce heat slightly and cook for 3½ minutes, until *al dente*. Drain in a colander.

Heat 1 tablespoon of the oil in a wok or skillet over medium heat and stir-fry the beans for 30 seconds. Add 1 tablespoon of cold water, cover the pan, and cook for 1½ to 2 minutes. Remove to a plate.

Rinse and dry the pan. Reheat over high heat with 1 more tablespoon of the oil and stir-fry the onion until barely tender. Remove.

Heat the remaining oil over very high heat. Add the noodles and stir-fry until each strand is glazed with the oil. Transfer to a serving plate.

Stir-fry the pork in the oil remaining in the pan, adding the ginger and garlic. When the pork changes color, after about 1 minute, sizzle the remaining tablespoon of soy sauce onto the sides of the pan. Return the beans and onions to the pan and stir-fry for 30 seconds.

Combine the stock and cornstarch and pour into the pan. Cook, stirring, over high heat until the sauce glazes the meat. Arrange over the noodles, pour the oyster sauce in thin lines over the dish, and serve at once.

bakmi goreng indonesia

Serves 2 to 4

10 ounces flat egg noodles
4 ounces boneless, skinless chicken breast
4 ounces lean pork
3 tablespoons tamari or light soy sauce
¾ cup vegetable or peanut oil
1 large yellow onion, thinly sliced
2 teaspoons minced garlic
2 teaspoons minced fresh ginger
2 teaspoons sambal ulek (Indonesian chili sauce; see sidebar)
4 ounces shrimp, shelled, deveined, and chopped
2 cups shredded Napa cabbage
3 whole scallions, trimmed and cut into 1-inch pieces

SAUCE:
¾ cup chicken stock (pages 26-27)
1 teaspoon sugar
1 teaspoon salt

GARNISHES:
2 eggs made into crepe shreds (see sidebar, page 100)
1 tablespoon fried onion flakes (see sidebar, page 89)
1 tablespoon chopped roasted peanuts
Sprigs of basil and cilantro (Chinese parsley)
Kecap manis *(sweet soy sauce)*

Sambal ulek is useful for adding the zip of chili to dishes and sauces. Made of fresh chilies mashed with salt, it is a fresh ingredient that should be refrigerated once opened. Indonesians love this fiery sambal so much they're quite happy to stir it into their rice. I tried that once. . .ONLY!

Bring 2½ quarts of water to a boil. Cook the noodles until tender, about 5 minutes, and drain thoroughly.

Cut the chicken and pork into thin slices, then into narrow strips. Sprinkle with 1 tablespoon soy sauce and set aside. Combine the sauce ingredients in a bowl and set aside. Prepare the garnishes.

Heat 1½ tablespoons of the oil in a wok or large skillet over high heat until a haze of smoke appears over the pan. Stir-fry the meat for 1 minute and remove. Add the onion to the pan and stir-fry for 1½ minutes, adding a little extra oil if needed.

Return the meat to the pan along with the the garlic, ginger, and *sambal ulek* and stir-fry briefly. Add the shrimp, cabbage, and scallions and stir-fry for about 1½ minutes. Sizzle the remaining 2 tablespoons soy sauce onto the sides of the pan and stir over high heat as it runs into the ingredients.

Stir the sauce, pour into the pan, and cook, stirring, until it thickens and glazes the ingredients. Remove from the heat.

Pour the remaining oil into another pan and heat to 375°F. Add the noodles and fry until golden on the underside, then turn and fry the other side for about 30 seconds. Lift up and allow to drain, then place on a serving plate.

Reheat the topping and pour over the noodles. Add the prepared garnishes and serve at once.

It takes only a little longer to make this dish with fresh, homemade egg noodles. Follow the directions on page 15, pass through your pasta machine to cut into narrow strips or flour the rolled dough, roll it up, and cut across the roll into fine noodles. They will cook in about 2½ minutes.

$weet Pork and Onions on Noodles

Serves 1 to 2

> **6 ounces pork tenderloin**
> **1 medium yellow onion**
> **4 tablespoons vegetable oil**
> **5 ounces thin Chinese noodles**
> **2 teaspoons rice wine or dry sherry**
> **1 tablespoon hoisin sauce (sweet bean paste)**
> **2 teaspoons tamari or light soy sauce**
> **¼ red bell pepper or 1 large red chili, seeded and finely shredded**
> **½ cup chicken stock (pages 26-27)**
> **Salt and white pepper**
> **1⅓ teaspoons cornstarch**
>
> SEASONING FOR PORK:
> **2½ teaspoons tamari or light soy sauce**
> **1 teaspoon rice wine or dry sherry**
> **1 teaspoon cornstarch**

Cut the pork into paper-thin slices, then into 2-inch-by-1-inch strips. Place in a bowl and add the pork seasoning ingredients, mix well, and set aside for 20 minutes to marinate.

Peel the onion and cut into thin wedges (see sidebar, page 68, for the Chinese technique).

Bring 1½ quarts of lightly salted water to a boil with 1½ teaspoons of the oil. Add the noodles and reheat to boiling, stirring to untangle the bundles. Reduce the heat until the water is slowly bubbling and cook the noodles for about 3 minutes to *al dente*. Drain and set aside.

Heat half of the remaining oil in a wok over high heat. Stir-fry the noodles for 30 seconds, keeping them constantly moving. Transfer to a plate.

Heat the remaining oil in a wok over high heat until a haze of smoke appears over the pan. Add the onion and stir-fry until softened, about 1 minute. Push to the side of the pan. Add the pork slices and stir-fry on high heat until they change color, about 1 minute.

Sizzle the 2 teaspoons rice wine onto the sides of the wok, then add the Hoisin sauce and the 2 teaspoons of soy sauce. Add the bell pepper or chili and stir-fry until the meat is glazed with the sauce.

Combine the stock, salt, pepper, and cornstarch, add to the pan, and stir until the sauce thickens and clears. Pour over the noodles and serve at once.

Fried Malaysian Noodles

Serves 2 to 4, or more sharing several dishes

1 pound fresh egg noodles (page 15)
4 ounces beef tenderloin or sirloin
2 teaspoons plus 2 tablespoons tamari or light soy sauce
1 teaspoon rice wine or dry sherry
4 ounces boneless, skinless chicken breast
⅓ teaspoon white pepper
4 ounces small shrimp, shelled
3 slices bacon, or 3 ounces ham
4 tablespoons vegetable or peanut oil
2 large eggs, lightly beaten
3 cloves garlic, minced
1 cup shredded kangkong (water spinach) or Napa cabbage
1 cup fresh bean sprouts
2 whole scallions, trimmed and cut into 1-inch lengths
1 teaspoon minced fresh ginger
2½ teaspoons salted yellow soybean sauce, mashed
¾ cup chicken stock (pages 26-27)
Fresh herbs for garnish

Bring 2 quarts lightly salted water to a boil. Add the noodles and cook for 3 minutes, drain, rinse with cold water, and set aside to drain again.

Slice the beef thin, then cut into ½-inch strips. Sprinkle with 2 teaspoons soy sauce and wine and set aside. Cut the chicken into narrow strips and set aside. Devein the shrimp and make deep cuts along the center of their backs to butterfly. Cut the bacon or ham into narrow strips.

Heat 2 teaspoons of the oil in a wok or large skillet over medium-high heat and pour in half the beaten egg. Cook into a thin crepe, remove from the pan and cook remaining egg in the same way (see sidebar, page 100). Add another 2 teaspoons oil to the pan and sauté the bacon or ham until crisp, then add the garlic and cook until golden. Remove to a small dish and set aside.

Add 1 tablespoon oil to the pan and reheat over very high heat. Stir-fry the beef and chicken together until they change color, about 2 minutes. Add the pepper and shrimp and stir-fry briefly. Remove.

Rinse the pan, wipe dry, and reheat with the remaining oil. Stir-fry the noodles for 2 minutes until well coated with the oil, then remove from the pan to a plate.

In the same pan, stir-fry the cabbage, bean sprouts, and scallions with ginger and mashed yellow bean sauce for 1½ minutes, stirring constantly. Return all of the cooked ingredients, except the noodles and egg crepes, to the pan and cook, stirring constantly, on high heat for about 40 seconds.

Pour in the remaining soy sauce and the chicken stock, return the noodles to the pan, and cook until the liquid is absorbed. Transfer to a large platter. Stack the two crepes together and roll up, cut into fine shreds, and scatter over the noodles, adding sprigs of fresh herbs to garnish.

Malay Mee

This makes a generous one-bowl meal for at least six hungry guests. Substitute pork or lamb for the beef, if preferred, and add your own choice of accompaniments—crisp-tender steamed green beans or broccoli, sliced cucumber, blanched Napa cabbage, sliced lettuce, and so on.

Serves 6

2 pounds lean round or skirt beef

1 medium onion, quartered

1 cinnamon stick

¾ teaspoon black pepper

3 tablespoons peanut or vegetable oil

1½ tablespoons ground coriander

1½ teaspoons ground cumin

2 teaspoons chili flakes

1 tablespoon almond meal or ground macadamia nuts

3 teaspoons minced fresh ginger

2 teaspoons minced garlic

¼ cup grated onion

1 tablespoon soybean paste

1½ pounds mee (thick yellow noodles) or 12 ounces spaghetti

6 ounces fresh bean sprouts

Salt (or soy sauce) and sugar to taste

Asians enjoy the slurp and splash of noodle eating. If you're more conscious of dry cleaning bills, snip noodles into shorter lengths with kitchen shears before serving.

(continued on next page)

(continued from previous page)

ACCOMPANIMENTS:

1½ cups vegetable oil
1½ cups finely sliced French shallots
2 tablespoons finely sliced garlic
1 cup finely sliced firm tofu (bean curd)
2 large eggs, made into omelette shreds (see sidebar, page 100)
¼ cup sliced whole scallion
½ cup finely sliced celery
1 to 4 red and green chilies, seeded and finely sliced

Place the beef in a saucepan with quartered onion, cinnamon stick, and pepper. Add 2 quarts water and bring to a boil. Skim, then cover, reduce the heat, and simmer gently for about 1 hour. The meat will be very tender and the liquid reduced to 5 to 6 cups. Remove the meat and tear into shreds, place in a dish with a little broth to moisten, and set aside. Also set aside the broth.

Heat the oil in a medium saucepan over medium-high heat. Make a paste of the coriander, cumin, chili, nuts, ginger, garlic, and grated onion *rempah* (see sidebar, page 92). Fry in the oil for 4 minutes, stirring constantly. Moisten with a little of the broth if it begins to stick to the pan. Add the meat and cook for 3 to 4 minutes, until coated with the spices. Add the soybean paste and cook 1 minute more.

Pour in the broth and bring to a boil. Reduce the heat and simmer for 10 minutes. Check for seasonings, adding salt or soy sauce and a little sugar to taste.

In the meantime, bring two pans of water (2½ quarts and 3 cups) to a boil. Add the noodles to the larger one and cook for 1½ minutes (or boil spaghetti for 12 minutes), then drain. Add bean sprouts to the other pan of boiling water and drain immediately.

To prepare the accompaniments, heat the oil in a wok or skillet and add the sliced shallots. Cook for about 4 minutes until well browned. Remove with a slotted spoon. Add the garlic and fry until deeply browned, taking care it does not burn, and remove. Last, add the tofu and cook until golden.

Arrange all of the accompaniments on a platter.

Drain the noodles and divide among six deep bowls. Pour on the broth and meat and add bean sprouts. Serve with the accompaniments.

Stir-Fried Hokkien Mee

Serves 2 to 4

> 1 pound Hokkien mee *(plump yellow noodles)*
> 2 tablespoons dried shrimp, soaked for 25 minutes in boiling water
>   *(see sidebar)*
> 4 ounces long (snake) beans or green beans
> 4 ounces gai larn, choy sum, or bok choy *(Chinese green vegetables)*
> 3 ounces fresh bean sprouts
> 3½ tablespoons vegetable or peanut oil
> 1 medium yellow onion
> 4 ounces small shrimp, shelled
> 4 ounces boneless chicken breast, cubed
> 1½ ounces (¼ cup) sliced water chestnuts
> 2 ounces (½ cup) sliced champignons or straw mushrooms
> 4 ounces soft tofu (bean curd), cubed

SAUCE:
> 1 medium yellow onion, very finely sliced
> 1¼ tablespoons vegetable oil
> 1 cup chicken stock (pages 26-27)
> 1½ tablespoons tamari or light soy sauce
> 1½ teaspoons dark soy sauce
> ½ teaspoon sugar
> ¼ teaspoon white pepper
> 1 tablespoon cornstarch

Bring 2½ quarts of lightly salted water to a boil. Add the noodles and return to a boil. Reduce the heat slightly and cook for 2½ to 3 minutes, until *al dente*. Drain.

Drain the dried and soaked shrimp, dry on a paper towel, and chop roughly. Cut the beans into 1-inch pieces, slice the vegetable stems thin, and cut the leaves into 1-inch strips. Blanch the bean sprouts and drain. Cut the onion into narrow wedges (see sidebar, page 68) and separate the layers.

To prepare the sauce, sauté the sliced onion in oil over medium heat until very well cooked, about 5 minutes. Add the remaining sauce ingredients and bring to a boil. Simmer for 2 minutes, then remove from the heat and set aside.

In a wok or large skillet heat half the vegetable or peanut oil over

Seafood seasonings and dried seafood are the magic, surprise ingredient in many Asian dishes. The intent is to enhance other flavors by their presence, not to make the dish taste of seafood; the impact is subtle, but effective. Dried shrimp should be bright pink, with a pleasing aroma. Store in a sealed jar in the refrigerator to retain freshness.

high heat until a smoky haze appears over the pan. Stir-fry the onion and dried shrimp for 2 minutes. Remove. Reheat the pan and stir-fry the beans for 1 minute. Add greens, bean sprouts, water chestnuts, and champignons and stir-fry briefly, then remove.

Reheat the pan over high heat, adding a little more oil if needed, and stir-fry the chicken and fresh shrimp until cooked, about 1 minute. Add the cubed tofu and stir-fry briefly. Remove.

Wipe the pan and reheat with the remaining oil over intensely high heat. Stir-fry the noodles until each strand is glazed with the oil. Pour in the sauce and cook until it is partially absorbed into the noodles, about 1 minute. Return the other ingredients to the pan, mix well, and serve.

I keep a bottle of ginger wine ever-ready to splash into stir-fries and to marinate chicken and seafood. If your liquor merchant doesn't stock it, combine 2 parts Japanese mirin with 1 part pickled pink ginger shreds. It can be kept for months, the flavor and aroma developing over time.

$eafood ₪o ₪ein

Serves 2 to 4

1¼ *pounds fresh, thick egg noodles (or cooked spaghetti)*
3 *whole scallions*
6 *small cleaned squid*
6 *clams or scallops*
3 *ounces white fish (sea bass, snapper, codfish)*
6 *medium shrimp, shelled and deveined*
1½ *tablespoons ginger wine (see sidebar)*
1 *rib of celery*
1 *small carrot*
½ *cup vegetable oil*
1½ *ounces bamboo shoots, sliced*
2 *ounces Napa cabbage, sliced*
1½ *ounces straw mushrooms, sliced*
1½ *ounces fresh bean sprouts*
1¾ *tablespoons tamari or light soy sauce*
1½ *cups chicken stock (pages 26-27)*
1 *tablespoon cornstarch*
1¼ *tablespoons oyster sauce*

Bring 2 quarts of lightly salted water to a boil. Add the noodles, return to a boil, and reduce the heat. Cook for 1½ minutes, then pour into a colander to drain.

Cut 2 scallions into 1½-inch pieces and mince the other; set aside. Cut the squid into squares, cut scallops in half horizontally, and cut the fish into small strips. Place all of the seafood in a dish and pour on the ginger wine. Set aside for 15 minutes. Cut the celery and carrot diagonally into thin slices.

Heat 1½ tablespoons of the oil in a wok or large skillet over high heat. Stir-fry the seafood for about 1¼ minutes until barely done; remove and set aside. Stir-fry the carrot and celery for 1 minute, add the bamboo shoots, cabbage, mushrooms, and bean sprouts and stir-fry for 2 minutes, then remove.

Add the remaining oil and heat until smoky. Add the noodles and cook for about 2 minutes, then turn and cook the other side. Add the large scallion pieces and stir-fry briefly.

Return the cooked ingredients to the pan and sizzle the soy sauce on. Combine the stock and cornstarch, pour over the noodles, and cook, stirring, until the sauce glazes the noodles. Lift onto a large plate and garnish with the minced scallion. Pour on the oyster sauce in thin lines. Serve.

Mee rebus *is a big, one-plate meal. The noodles and bean sprouts are spread on a large platter, the curry sauce poured over, and the various garnishes then arranged over the top. It's a great party dish for those who like it spicy.*

Spicy Malaysian Noodles

(MEE REBUS)

Serves 4, or 6 to 8 sharing several dishes

1 pound round or skirt beef
½ teaspoon black pepper
1½ pounds fresh Hokkien mee (thick yellow noodles)
½ pound fresh bean sprouts

SAUCE:
1 ounce dried shrimp
½ cup roasted peanuts
5 dried chilies, seeded and soaked in hot water for 20 minutes
10 whole scallions, trimmed and roughly chopped
3 thick slices fresh ginger
3 thick slices galangal (kha/Thai ginger)
5 kemiri nuts (candlenuts) or macadamias
3 large cloves garlic, peeled
2 teaspoons blacan (shrimp paste)
6 tablespoons vegetable oil
1½ tablespoons mild curry powder
2 tablespoons taucheo (salted yellow bean sauce)
1 tablespoon white sugar
Salt and pepper to taste

ACCOMPANIMENTS:
2 cakes firm tofu (bean curd)
2 limes, cut into wedges
½ cup sliced whole scallion
¾ cup sliced long (snake) or green beans, boiled for 3 minutes
¾ cup thinly sliced cucumber
¼ cup (or less) sliced fresh chili
2 eggs, hard-boiled and cut into wedges
½ cup fried onion flakes (see sidebar, page 89)

Slice the beef very thin and cut into strips, sprinkle with pepper, and set aside.

To make the sauce, grind the dried shrimp to a light and fluffy floss in a blender, mortar, or food processor fitted with a metal blade. Remove. Grind the peanuts to a powder and remove. Next grind the chilies, scallions, ginger, *galangal*, candlenuts, garlic, and shrimp paste to a thick paste.

Heat half the oil and fry the seasoning paste over medium heat for 5 minutes, stirring to prevent it from sticking. Add the curry powder, mashed yellow beans, sugar, shrimp floss, and peanuts. Cook for 1 minute, stirring. Add the beef with water to cover. Cook for about 20 minutes, until the sauce is thick and very fragrant. It should be the consistency of cream; add more water if needed. Check the seasonings, adding salt and pepper to taste.

Next prepare the accompaniments. Slice the tofu thin and fry it in the remaining oil over high heat until the edges are crisp, about 2 minutes. Drain well. Set aside with the other accompaniments.

Bring 2 quarts of water to a boil, add the noodles, and return to a boil. Reduce the heat slightly and cook for 2 minutes, then drain and set aside. Blanch the bean sprouts in boiling water for 30 seconds, drain, refresh under running cold water, and drain again.

Spread the noodles on a platter, evenly scattering the bean sprouts over them. Pour on the curry sauce and arrange the accompaniments attractively around the platter and over the noodles. Serve.

Do-ahead note: The curry sauce and garnishes can both be prepared in advance and refrigerated under plastic wrap. Reheat the curry sauce in a microwave for about 5 minutes on high, stirring several times.

thailand

In a land where the rice is as fragrant as jasmine, it's little wonder the Thais have few noodle dishes in their cuisine. But when they do use noodles, Thai cooks prepare them with distinction, mingling spices with herbs for freshness and a spontaneity of taste that's utterly irresistible. *Mee krob* is a culinary feat—a bold blending of crisp noodles and a sweet-tart sauce. Too much sauce, or too long in the pan, and the feathery rice noodles are reduced to toffied strings; too little, and the dish is dry and without accent. It's one of only a few noodle dishes that are served at the start of a Thai meal, and done right it's a sensation.

Like the Vietnamese, Thai cooks prefer rice noodles to those made from wheat flour. True, you can find typical southern Chinese stir-fried noodles in many restaurants and snack houses in Thailand, but most classic Thai noodle dishes use flat rice sticks or extruded thin rice vermicelli. The exception are fresh, plump egg noodles of the *Hokkien mee* style, which Thais usually cook with a sweet-and-salty brown gravy (I have included a recipe in the vegetarian chapter, on page 205).

Salads are appropriate to the perennial warmth of the Thai climate, and Thai cooks bathe them in tangy dressings that combine their favorite seasonings—fresh lime juice and salt-pungent *nam pla* (fish sauce)—with a hint of sugar and chili. Indigenous leafy vegetables and herbs, cooked meats and seafoods, and crisp fresh vegetables are tangled with softened bean threads or rice vermicelli, or as in nearby Burma, with thick egg noodles. They stimulate the appetite and prepare the palate for other exciting flavors to come.

Crispy Thai Noodles
(MEE KROB)
Serves 4, or 6 to 8 sharing several dishes

4 ounces skinless, boneless chicken breast
1 tablespoon nam pla (Thai fish sauce)
1 cup peanut oil
3 ounces fresh firm tofu (bean curd), diced
4 ounces small shrimp, shelled and deveined
2 whole scallions, trimmed and chopped
2 cloves garlic, minced
2 large eggs, lightly beaten
3 to 4 cups oil for deep frying
7 ounces fine rice vermicelli
3 ounces fresh bean sprouts
6 to 8 garlic chives, cut into 2-inch lengths

SAUCE:
1/2 cup white sugar
2 tablespoons fresh lime juice
1 tablespoon distilled white vinegar
2 tablespoons nam pla (Thai fish sauce)
2 tablespoons ketchup
2 tablespoons water
1 teaspoon mild chili powder

Combine the sauce ingredients in a small saucepan and bring to a boil. Reduce the heat and simmer for 2 minutes, then remove and leave to cool. Marinate the chicken in the fish sauce for 10 minutes.

Heat 1 cup of the oil in a large wok or skillet over high heat until a haze of smoke appears over the pan. Carefully add the diced tofu and fry, stirring occasionally, until golden brown on the surface. Remove with a wire skimmer and set aside on absorbent paper to drain.

Fry the chicken until it changes color and is lightly cooked, about 1 minute. Remove and set aside. Carefully pour off all but 2 tablespoons of the oil into a heatproof container and reserve. Reheat the oil and sauté the shrimp, scallions, and garlic until the shrimp turn pink, then remove and set aside with the chicken.

Rinse the wok or skillet and rub the inside with a paper towel dipped in oil, leaving a light film of oil on the inner surface. Reheat the pan over medium-high heat, pour in the eggs, and swirl the pan to spread the eggs in a reasonably thin layer. Cook lightly, turn, and cook the other side until golden. Break the omelette into small pieces with a spatula, remove from the pan, and set aside.

Rinse the wok or skillet again and dry thoroughly. Pour in the remaining oil and reheat over high heat to about 375°F. Place the rice vermicelli in a plastic or paper bag and bat with a rolling pin to break into short lengths. Pour half into the oil to cook for just a few seconds, turning the mass over with a wire skimmer as soon as it expands and turns snowy white. Remove before it begins to color. Cook the remaining vermicelli in the same way.

Carefully pour off the deep oil and wipe out the pan. Pour 2 tablespoons of the oil reserved from cooking the bean curd and chicken into the pan and reheat over high heat until smoky. Add half the noodles and half the sauce. Quickly turn the noodles in the sauce until each strand is coated and the sauce absorbed, then remove to a plate.

Cook the remaining noodles and sauce in the same way, then return the first batch of *mee krob* to the pan, adding the other cooked ingredients. Briskly mix together until the ingredients are thoroughly blended. To serve, mound into a cone shape on a serving plate. Surround with the bean sprouts and garlic chives and serve while it is still hot and crisp.

Being frugal cooks, and also aware that flavor often comes from unexpected ingredients, Thais use not just the leaves but also the firm green stems and the fleshy cream-colored roots of the cilantro plant as an herb. So next time you buy cilantro, select only whole plants, and if you don't need the roots and stems for your recipe, freeze them for use in a curry paste.

Spicy Pork Rolls Wrapped in Noodles
(SARONGS)
Makes 18

4 large dried black mushrooms, soaked in cold water for 25 minutes
6 ounces fine egg noodles
3 teaspoons minced garlic
1 teaspoon minced fresh ginger
1 tablespoon minced scallion, white part only
1 tablespoon chopped cilantro (Chinese parsley) leaves
3 teaspoons minced cilantro stems and cream-colored roots
2 teaspoons minced lemon grass (see sidebar, page 128)
½ pound ground lean pork
2 tablespoons finely diced pork fat (optional)
1 tablespoon nam pla (Thai fish sauce)
½ teaspoon white sugar
1 egg white, lightly beaten
Salt and white pepper
1 tablespoon cornstarch
1 quart oil for deep-frying

Drain the mushrooms and remove stems. Squeeze out excess water and mince the caps fine. Cook the noodles in boiling water for 2 minutes or until *al dente*. Drain and set aside.

Combine all of the ingredients except noodles and oil, mixing thoroughly. For ease, place in a heavy-duty food processor fitted with a metal blade and process to a smooth consistency. Use wet hands to form the mixture into small patties about the size of a sea scallop. Wrap a single layer of noodle strands around each *sarong* and set aside.

Heat the oil to 360°F over high heat. Fry the patties, six at a time, until golden brown and cooked through, about 3½ minutes. Drain on absorbent paper.

Arrange on a platter strewn with finely shredded Boston lettuce and serve with bottled sweet Thai chili sauce or tamarind sauce for dipping.

Chicken Noodles in Coconut Soup

Serves 4 to 6

½ pound boneless, skinless chicken breast, cut in ½-inch cubes

2 teaspoons **nam pla** *(Thai fish sauce)*

1 teaspoon rice wine or dry sherry

6 thin slices fresh ginger, cut into fine shreds

1½ cups coconut milk

3 fresh or frozen Kaffir lime leaves, or use 4 dried leaves reconstituted in boiling water

1 lemon grass stem, halved lengthwise

1 teaspoon salt

⅓ teaspoon white pepper

1 quart chicken stock (pages 26-27)

1 large tomato, cut into wedges

4 ounces fine rice vermicelli

Extra **nam pla** *(Thai fish sauce)*

Wedges of fresh lime

Place the chicken in a dish with the fish sauce, rice wine, and ginger and mix well. Cover with plastic wrap and set aside for 20 minutes.

Pour the coconut milk into a medium pan with a heavy base and bring almost to a boil over medium-high heat. Add the lime leaves, lemon grass, salt, and pepper. Reduce the heat and simmer for 25 minutes to reduce the liquid and intensify the flavor. Stir occassionally.

Add the chicken and cook gently for 5 minutes. Pour in the stock and tomato and bring barely to a boil. Add the vermicelli and cook until soft, 1 minute. Serve in deep bowls, offering extra fish sauce and lime wedges for your guests to add to their taste.

*F*resh lemon grass is readily available from good Chinese greengrocers or produce markets. When making your selection, choose plump, pale green stems with tightly packed leaves. They should be no more than 14 inches long. The deeper green leaves from the top can be brewed into a cooling and relaxing tea. Store lemon grass in the vegetable compartment of the refrigerator, for up to 2 weeks (also see sidebar, page 128).

If lemon grass is to be used sliced, it must be cut very fine or its hard, wooden texture will spoil the dish. Hold it firmly on a cutting board and with a cleaver or a very sharp paring knife cut across the stem into slices as thin as paper. It can be frozen in a small plastic freezer container for convenient use.

Shrimp in Coconut Soup with Rice Vermicelli

Serves 4, or 6 to 8 sharing several dishes

> 5 ounces dried rice vermicelli
> 1 pound medium shrimp, peeled, with tails left on
> 1 large yellow onion
> 2 tablespoons vegetable oil
> 3 teaspoons minced fresh ginger
> $\frac{1}{2}$ teaspoon minced garlic
> 1 lemon grass stem, thinly sliced
> 3 cups coconut milk
> 2 teaspoons ground coriander
> $\frac{1}{2}$ teaspoon kapi (fresh soft shrimp paste)
> $2\frac{1}{2}$ tablespoons nam pla (Thai fish sauce)
> 1 fresh red chili, seeded and chopped
> Salt and freshly ground black pepper
> $2\frac{1}{2}$ cups water
> 2 tablespoons chopped cilantro leaves (Chinese parsley); or 2 fresh Kaffir lime leaves, central ribs trimmed, and very finely shredded (see sidebar, page 97)

Soak the rice vermicelli in warm water for 3 minutes; drain well. Cut each shrimp along the center of its back to remove the dark intestinal vein. Rinse shrimp and dry with paper towels. Peel, halve, and slice the onion thin. Heat the oil over medium-high heat in a stewpan and sauté the onion until golden. Remove and reserve half of the onion, and continue cooking the remainder until very well browned, about 6 minutes.

Add the ginger, garlic, lemon grass, coconut milk, coriander, and shrimp paste to the pan. Cook over low heat for 20 to 25 minutes until the sauce is well reduced, with a film of oil floating on the surface. Remove half of the sauce to a bowl and set aside.

Add the reserved cooked onion, fish sauce, chili, salt, pepper, and the water to the sauce remaining in the stewpan and bring to a boil. Reduce the heat and simmer for 20 minutes. Add the shrimp and noodles and cook on medium heat until shrimp are tender, about 3 minutes.

To serve, pour a portion of the vermicelli and shrimp with its sauce into each bowl. Spoon the reserved reduced coconut sauce over, and garnish with cilantro or finely shredded Kaffir lime leaf. You may like to offer freshly squeezed lime juice, plus fish sauce, for your guests to add at the table to their taste.

Sweet-Sour Noodle Soup
(YEN TAH FAO)

Serves 4, or 6 to 8 sharing several dishes

- *½ pound lean, boneless pork*
- *1½ pounds fresh rice noodles or rice sheet dough, or 13 ounces dried thin rice sticks*
- *8 cloves garlic, peeled and thinly sliced*
- *½ cup vegetable oil*
- *6 ounces Napa cabbage or bok choy (Chinese white cabbage)*
- *6 ounces cleaned squid*
- *6 ounces freshly made or frozen fish balls*
- *6 ounces small shrimp, shelled and deveined*
- *1 tomato, peeled, seeded, and diced*
- *Salt and white pepper*
- *½ cup diced pineapple*
- *Extra nam pla (Thai fish sauce)*
- *Vinegar pickled chilies*

BROTH:
- *2½ tablespoons ketchup*
- *3 tablespoons nam pla (Thai fish sauce)*
- *1½ tablespoons distilled white vinegar*
- *2 green chilies, seeded and finely chopped*
- *4 slices fresh ginger, finely shredded*

In most good delicatessens and Asian stores you can purchase pickled chilies. If you want to make your own, slit fresh chilies and scrape out the seeds. Blanch in boiling water for 30 seconds and drain. Bring to a boil enough vinegar to cover the chilies, then add salt and sugar—usually 1 tablespoon sugar and 1 teaspoon salt to ¾ cup vinegar. Add chilies and boil for 3 minutes. Cool and store in a sterilized jar. Chop and add to soy sauce as a dip and condiment.

Place the pork in a saucepan with 2 quarts of water. Bring to a boil and simmer for about 45 minutes, until tender. Strain the pork cooking water into another saucepan and set aside. Place the pork on a plate to cool, then cut into thin slices.

Cover the fresh noodles with hot water for 3 minutes, then drain and set aside, or soften dried noodles in boiling water and drain.

Heat the oil in a small pan over medium-high heat and fry the garlic until well browned, taking care it does not burn and therefore turn bit-

ter. Remove to a paper towel to drain; reserve the oil for another recipe (it will add a wonderful nutty, garlicky taste).

Slice the cabbage fine, cut the squid into rings, and halve the fish balls. Bring the strained pork liquid to a boil, adding the broth ingredients. Simmer for 5 to 6 minutes, then season to taste with salt and pepper. Add the cabbage, seafood, and tomato and cook for about 5 minutes.

Drain the noodles and divide among soup bowls, adding pineapple and sliced pork to each. Or serve in a deep tureen. Pour on the hot broth. Scatter the fried garlic over each dish, adding some of the oil in which it cooked if you like a distinct garlic flavor.

Serve with extra fish sauce in a dispenser, and vinegar-pickled chilies (see sidebar, page 129).

Shrimp and Bean-Thread Salad

Serves 4, or 6 to 8 sharing several dishes

5 ounces bean-thread vermicelli
12 medium shrimp, in their shells
2 teaspoons nam pla (Thai fish sauce)
2 teaspoons fresh lime juice
1 teaspoon palm or dark brown sugar
¼ cup chopped whole scallions
¼ cup finely sliced straw mushrooms
⅓ cup sliced water chestnuts
1 cup fresh bean sprouts, roots and seed pods removed
1 small red bell pepper, seeded and julienned
1 red onion, peeled and finely sliced
¼ cup loosely packed cilantro (Chinese parsley) leaves
¼ cup loosely packed basil leaves
¼ cup loosely packed mint leaves
2 teaspoons vegetable oil

SALAD DRESSING:
1½ tablespoons nam pla (Thai fish sauce)
1 tablespoon fresh lime juice
1 teaspoon palm or dark brown sugar

This is a great picnic dish, cool and refreshing on a hot day outdoors! Pack it in an insulated container and pop into a chiller with the drinks. It's excellent with a barbecue.

1½ tablespoons corn oil or other flavorless vegetable oil
2 teaspoons Thai sweet chili sauce
1 teaspoon minced garlic (optional)

Soak the vermicelli in boiling water for 1½ minutes. It will be semi-transparent and crisp-tender. Drain in a colander and cool under running cold water. Use kitchen shears to cut into 3-inch lengths. Transfer to a mixing bowl.

Combine the dressing ingredients. Pour half over the vermicelli, mix well, and set aside.

Shell the shrimp, leaving the last segment of the shell and the tail in place (reserve heads and shells for stock or bisque; they can be frozen until needed). Make a deep cut down the center of each shrimp's back and pull away the dark vein. Press the shrimp open. Place in a dish and season with the fish sauce, lime juice, and sugar. Set aside.

Prepare the remaining ingredients, except the oil, and add to the vermicelli in the bowl. Mix in evenly.

Heat the oil in a small pan over high heat and stir-fry the shrimp until they turn pink. Remove and add to the salad, along with the reserved dressing. Toss for a few moments to thoroughly combine the ingredients and moisten evenly with the dressing. Pile onto a platter and serve.

Do-ahead note: The salad can be made ahead, covered with plastic wrap, and refrigerated for several hours before serving.

Rice Vermicelli and Roast Pork Salad

This is quite a treat served tsarn choy bow style as an appetizer. Use only half of the dressing on the salad. Serve with small lettuce cups for wrapping the salad into delicious crisp bundles to eat with the fingers. Dip into the remaining dressing before eating.

Serves 4, or 6 to 8 sharing several dishes

> *10 ounces cha siu (Chinese roast pork)*
> *4 ounces fresh bean sprouts*
> *3 ounces fine rice vermicelli*
> *4 ounces small shrimp, shelled, deveined, and cooked*
> *4 ounces cooked crabmeat, flaked*
> *1 rib of celery, julienned*
> *1 medium carrot, julienned*
> *1 red onion, finely sliced*
> *1/3 cup sliced scallions*
> *1/2 cup loosely packed fresh herbs (basil, mint, dill, parsley, cilantro)*
> *1 fresh red chili, seeded and finely sliced*
> *4 to 5 romaine lettuce leaves*
> *1/4 cup peanuts, salted, roasted, and chopped*

> SALAD DRESSING:
> *6 tablespoons nam pla (Thai fish sauce)*
> *6 tablespoons fresh lime juice*
> *2 1/3 teaspoons sugar*

Slice the roast pork thin, then cut into fine shreds. Blanch the bean sprouts in boiling water for 5 seconds, then drain and refresh in cold water. Drain again and set aside.

Soften the vermicelli in boiling water for 4 to 6 minutes, then drain. Cool under running cold water, drain again, and cut into 3-inch lengths.

Combine the salad ingredients, except the lettuce and peanuts, in a bowl. Whisk the dressing ingredients together, pour over the salad, and toss to moisten evenly. Cover with plastic wrap and chill for at least 1 hour.

Wash and carefully dry the lettuce and arrange in a cartwheel formation on a platter. Mound the salad on top and scatter on the peanuts.

Onion and Noodle Salad from Burma

Serves 4 to 6

1½ pounds fresh thick egg noodles, or 9 ounces spaghetti
1 large yellow onion
½ cup flavorless vegetable oil
3 to 5 garlic cloves, peeled and thinly sliced
1 tablespoon dried shrimp, chopped
½ teaspoon ground turmeric
3 tablespoons ground dried chickpeas or besan (chickpea) flour
4 to 5 Boston lettuce leaves
3 tablespoons chopped scallion
3 tablespoons chopped red onion or shallots
1½ tablespoons roasted peanuts, chopped
Cilantro (Chinese parsley) sprigs
Shreds of red chili
Wedges of fresh lime

SALAD DRESSING:
2 tablespoons nam pla (Thai fish sauce)
2 tablespoons fresh lime juice
Salt and freshly ground black pepper

Bring 2 quarts of lightly salted water to a boil. Add the noodles and cook for 2 to 3 minutes, until *al dente*. Pour into a colander to drain and set aside. (If using spaghetti, cook in salted water for about 12 minutes, drain, then rinse with cold water and set aside.)

Peel the onion and cut into narrow wedges (see sidebar, page 68). Heat the oil in a wok or skillet over medium heat. Fry the onion until softened and transparent, taking care it does not burn. Add the garlic and dried shrimp and cook until the onions are deep brown. Remove with a slotted spoon and spread on absorbent paper to drain.

Sprinkle the turmeric and ground chickpeas or chickpea flour into the pan and cook over medium heat until golden. Return the cooked onions and mix well. Pour over the noodles and mix in. Leave to cool. Combine the salad dressing ingredients, seasoning generously with salt and pepper. Pour over the noodles, add the chopped scallions and onion or shallots and stir well.

Spread the lettuce on a serving plate. Pile the noodle salad in the center and scatter on the peanuts, cilantro, and chili. Arrange lime wedges around the salad and serve.

Ground chickpeas give a characteristic nutty taste and add texture to the dish. I have tried using coarsely ground raw cashews, macadamia nuts, and roasted peanuts with equal success. Experiment and enjoy!

Concentrated tamarind liquid is easier to use than tamarind seeds or pulp, but if the latter is all that is available, measure about 2½ times the recipe requirement into a bowl, cover with boiling water, and mash with the back of a spoon to release the tamarind. Pour through a nylon strainer to remove excess fiber and seeds. You will have more liquid than the recipe calls for, but the intensity of the tamarind should be about the same. If necessary boil down in a small pan. Lemon juice can be used in place of tamarind.

Fried Noodles with Chicken
(GAI PAD THAI)
Serves 2 to 4, or up to 8 sharing several dishes

10 ounces dried rice-stick noodles
4 ounces firm tofu (bean curd)
4 tablespoons peanut or vegetable oil
3 eggs, lightly beaten
½ pound skinless, boneless chicken breast
3 shallots, sliced
1 teaspoon minced garlic
1 tablespoon dried shrimp, finely chopped
⅓ cup unsalted roasted peanuts, coarsely chopped
4 ounces fresh bean sprouts
3 whole scallions, cut into 1-inch pieces
Salt and white pepper

SAUCE:
1½ cups water
1 tablespoon tamarind concentrate
⅓ cup palm or dark brown sugar
2½ tablespoons nam pla (Thai fish sauce)

ACCOMPANIMENTS:
Seeded and sliced fresh red chilies
Lime wedges
Granulated white sugar
Garlic chives, cut into 2-inch lengths
Roasted chili powder (see sidebar, page 88)
Extra nam pla (Thai fish sauce)

Cover the noodles with hot water and set aside to soften, about 15 minutes (time may vary among different brands of noodles).

Combine the sauce ingredients in a small saucepan and bring to a boil. Simmer until reduced to approximately ¾ cup, then set aside. Drain the noodles in a colander.

Cut the tofu into small dice. Heat the oil in a wok or large pan over high heat, fry the tofu until the surface is golden, remove, and set aside. Pour the oil into a heatproof container and reserve. Strain half the beaten egg into the hot pan and cook swirling it around so that it spreads into a thin crepe. Cook briefly, then flip and lightly cook the

other side. Remove and leave to cool. Cook the remaining egg in the same way and set aside to cool, then cut all the egg into fine shreds.

Cut chicken into ½-inch cubes. Return half the reserved oil to the pan and sauté the chicken until it changes color. Add the shallots, garlic, and dried shrimp and sauté for about 1½ minutes. Remove.

Add the remaining oil to the pan and reheat over high heat until the oil is smoking. Drain the noodles, transfer to the pan, and sauté briefly. Return the sautéed ingredients to the pan and add the shredded egg, peanuts, bean sprouts, and scallions, plus salt and pepper to taste. Sauté for 1½ minutes, then pour in the sauce. Cook, stirring continuously, until the ingredients are well mixed and the sauce has been absorbed.

Transfer the noodles to a large plate and surround with the prepared accompaniments, or serve them separately in small dishes.

Spicy Thai Chicken and Bean Curd on Rice Sticks

Serves 3 to 4, or 4 to 6 sharing several dishes

> **10 ounces boneless, skinless chicken breast**
> **1 tablespoon nam pla (Thai fish sauce)**
> **5 ounces rice-stick noodles**
> **4 whole scallions**
> **4 long (snake) beans, or 12 young green beans**
> **2 teaspoons Thai red curry paste**
> **1 cup thick coconut milk (coconut cream)**
> **One 4-inch piece lemon grass (the pale green shoot end)**
> **2 thin slices fresh ginger**
> **⅓ cup peanut or flavorless vegetable oil**
> **Salt and white pepper**
> **2 ounces fried tofu (bean curd) cubes**

Cut the chicken into ½-inch cubes and marinate with the fish sauce for 10 minutes. Bring 1½ quarts lightly salted water to a boil. Add the noodles and cook for about 5 minutes until tender, drain, and cover with cold water. Set aside.

Trim the scallions. Cut the white parts into 1-inch pieces; slice the green tops thin and reserve for garnishing. Cut the beans into 1-

Fried tofu cubes are readily available in packs of 6 or 12 at Chinese grocers. Store in the refrigerator until ready to use; any unused portion should be tightly wrapped in plastic and returned to the refrigerator. If you need to make your own, purchase firm, fresh bean curd, cut into 1-inch cubes, and slowly fry in deep oil over high heat until the surface is a deep golden brown.

inch pieces, cook in boiling water for 2 minutes, and drain.

Combine the curry paste and coconut milk in a saucepan. Bruise the lemon grass stalk to release the flavor and add to the pan along with the ginger. Bring to a boil, then reduce the heat and simmer for 15 minutes to thicken the sauce and intensify its flavors.

Heat half the oil in a medium saucepan, sauté the tofu cubes for 2 minutes, then remove and set aside. Reheat the pan, add the chicken, and stir-fry until barely cooked, 1½ minutes. Return the tofu, add the sauce along with ½ cup water, and bring almost to a boil. Reduce heat and simmer for 7 to 8 minutes. Check the seasonings, adding salt and pepper to taste.

In the meantime, heat the remaining oil in a wok or large skillet over high heat until a haze of smoke appears over the pan. Stir-fry the scallions and beans briefly, then remove. Reheat the pan, add the well-drained noodles, and stir-fry for 2 minutes. Return the beans and scallions and mix in. Spread on a serving platter or shallow dish. Pour on the sauce, garnish with the reserved scallion greens, and serve.

Garlic chives are deep green, slender members of the onion family which look like flattened scallion greens. They have a pronounced garlic taste and a slighty more coarse texture than scallions. They keep for 3 to 4 days in the vegetable compartment of the refrigerator, loosely packed in plastic, preferably with aeration holes.

Rice-Stick Noodles with Ginger and Garlic Chives

(THAI GWAYTEOW)
Serves 2 to 3, or 4 to 6 sharing several dishes

10 ounces skinless, boneless chicken breast
1 tablespoon nam pla (Thai fish sauce)
1 teaspoon rice wine or dry sherry
1 teaspoon cornstarch
8 ounces dried rice-stick noodles, or 1¼ pounds fresh rice sheets or rice noodles
3 tablespoons peanut or vegetable oil
1 teaspoon minced fresh ginger
¾ teaspoon minced garlic
2 ounces fresh bean sprouts
1 ounce sliced bamboo shoots
18 garlic chives, cut into 1½-inch pieces
Salt and white pepper
1 fresh red chili, seeded and finely shredded

1 tablespoon chopped cilantro (Chinese parsley)
1 tablespoon crushed unsalted roasted peanuts
¼ teaspoon roasted chili flakes (see sidebar, page 000)
Lime wedges
Nam pla *(Thai fish sauce)*

SAUCE:
⅓ cup chicken stock (pages 26-27)
2 tablespoons **nam pla** *(Thai fish sauce)*
1 teaspoon cornstarch
¼ teaspoon black pepper
1 teaspoon sugar

Slice the chicken thin and cut into fine shreds. Combine the fish sauce, rice wine, and cornstarch in a bowl, add the chicken, and mix well. Set aside to marinate for 20 minutes.

Combine the sauce ingredients in a bowl and set aside. If using fresh noodle dough, cut into ¼-inch strips, cover with warm water for 20 seconds, and drain. Cook dried noodles in boiling water for 1½ minutes and drain well. They should be barely tender.

Heat half the oil in a wok or large skillet over high heat until a haze of smoke appears over the pan. Stir-fry the chicken with ginger and garlic for 2 minutes. Push to the side of the pan. Stir-fry the bean sprouts, bamboo shoots, and garlic chives for 30 seconds. Mix the ingredients together, then remove from the pan.

Heat the remaining oil. Stir-fry the noodles on high heat for 1 minute, add the cooked ingredients, and continue to stir-fry until thoroughly combined. Add the sauce and cook until absorbed. Season to taste with salt and pepper.

Transfer to a platter or a shallow bowl. Scatter the shredded chili, cilantro, peanuts, and chili flakes evenly over the noodles and serve lime wedges and fish sauce separately.

Basil leaves bring a fresh aroma and wonderful nuances of taste to Thai dishes. You may be able to add dried basil to an Italian pasta sauce, but it does not work the same way in a curry sauce. If fresh basil leaves are unavailable, you would do better to simply omit, or use cilantro instead.

Spicy Ground Beef on Rice Noodles
(RADNA NUE)

Serves 4, or 6 to 8 sharing several dishes

9 ounces narrow rice sticks
10 ounces coarsely ground lean beef
2 teaspoons minced garlic
1 teaspoon freshly ground black pepper
2 tablespoons nam pla (Thai fish sauce)
1 teaspoon plus 1½ teaspoons dark soy sauce
3 tablespoons flavorless vegetable oil
1 medium yellow onion, finely sliced
1 tablespoon chopped basil leaves

SAUCE:
2 cups beef stock (pages 25-26) or chicken stock (pages 26-27)
2 teaspoons Thai red curry paste
2 teaspoons kecap manis (sweet soy sauce)
1 tablespoon cornstarch or tapioca/arrowroot starch

Soak the noodles in warm water for 25 minutes, then drain well and sprinkle on a little oil to prevent them from sticking together.

Combine the ground beef with the garlic, pepper, fish sauce, and 1 teaspoon soy sauce and set aside for 15 minutes. Mix the sauce ingredients in a bowl and set aside. Heat half the oil in a wok or large skillet over medium-high heat. Stir-fry the onion until softened and lightly golden. Add the beef and stir-fry over high heat until lightly cooked. Pour in the sauce and cook on medium to low heat, stirring frequently, until very aromatic, about 6 minutes.

In another pan heat the remaining oil and stir-fry the drained noodles with the remaining soy sauce until each strand is glazed and brown. Transfer to a plate. Pour on the sauce and garnish with basil. Serve roasted chili powder (see sidebar, page 88) or fresh chili sauce (see sidebar, page 139) on the side.

Hot Thai Noodles

(PAD THAI PRIK)

Serves 3 to 4, or 4 to 6 sharing several dishes

11 ounces dried rice-stick noodles (Vietnamese banh pho or Thai sen mie)

3 teaspoons sugar

¼ cup nam pla (Thai fish sauce)

1 tablespoon ketchup

3 teaspoons sriracha chili sauce

1¼ tablespoons chopped garlic

4 tablespoons vegetable oil

10 ounces small shrimp, peeled and cooked

7 ounces fresh bean sprouts

GARNISH:

3 teaspoons dried shrimp

3 tablespoons chopped scallion

2 tablespoons chopped roasted peanuts

1 tablespoon granulated white sugar

3 to 4 garlic chives, cut into 1½ inch pieces

Cilantro (Chinese parsley) sprigs

Lime wedges

Soak the noodles in hot water for at least 12 minutes to soften, then drain well. Combine the sugar, fish sauce, ketchup, and chili sauce in a small bowl.

Prepare the garnish ingredients. Place the dried shrimp in a blender or spice grinder and grind until finely shredded. Arrange the garnishes on a plate to serve with the noodles.

Fry the garlic in the oil over medium heat until very aromatic, about 1 minute. Add the shrimp and fry for 40 seconds. Pour in the sauce mixture and cook briefly, then add the noodles and toss until thoroughly coated with the sauce. Add half the bean sprouts and cook, continuously tossing and stirring, until the bean sprouts have softened.

Transfer to a platter, scattering the remaining bean sprouts over the top. Serve with the platter of garnishes, allowing guests to add what they want, to taste.

Sriracha is a bright red, moderately hot Thai chili sauce which is now readily available. If you want to make your own, slice open fresh chilies and scrape out the seeds and membranes. Puree in a food processor, with a splash of vinegar and large pinches of salt and sugar, until smooth. Store in the refrigerator.

Bean Sauce Rice Noodles
(RADNA MOU)

Serves 4, or 6 to 8 sharing several dishes

14 ounces narrow rice sticks
10 ounces lean pork
1 tablespoon plus 3 tablespoons nam pla (Thai fish sauce)
1 teaspoon minced garlic
½ teaspoon black pepper
6 ounces gai larn or choy sum (Chinese greens)
3 teaspoons dark soy sauce
2 tablespoons hoisin sauce (sweet bean paste)
2 cups pork stock (page 26)
2 tablespoons cornstarch or tapioca/arrowroot starch
2½ tablespoons flavorless vegetable oil
2 tablespoons chopped scallion greens
Cilantro (Chinese parsley) sprigs
Red chili shreds or slices
Marinated chilies or fresh chili sauce

Soak the noodles in hot water for 5 minutes. Slice the pork thin, then stack the slices together and cut across them into narrow strips. Place in a dish with 1 tablespoon fish sauce, garlic, and pepper; mix and set aside for 15 minutes.

Rinse the Chinese greens and shake off excess water. Cut the stems into thin diagonal slices. Bring a small pan of water to a boil and blanch the stems for 1½ minutes, then drain. Cut the leaves into 1-inch strips and set aside.

Combine the remaining fish sauce, soy sauce, and bean paste in a dish and the pork stock and starch in another. Set aside. Heat the oil in a wok or skillet over high heat. Stir-fry the pork until it changes color. Add the Chinese cabbage stems and stir-fry for 20 seconds. Push to the side of the pan.

Add the noodles and stir-fry until coated with the oil. Add the mixed fish and soy sauces and stir in the cabbage stems and pork. Cook, stirring energetically, over a high flame for 1 minute.

Stir the stock and starch and pour into the pan. Cook, stirring occasionally, until the sauce thickens and glazes the noodles.

Add the green leaves and scallions and cook briefly. Transfer to a plate garnished with cilantro and chili shreds. Offer sliced red or green chilies marinated in vinegar, or fresh chili sauce (see sidebar, page 139), to add to taste.

Curried Noodles for the New Year
(NAM YA)

Serves 6, or up to 10 sharing several dishes

> *10 ounces skinless, boneless chicken, diced*
> *1 tablespoon nam pla (Thai fish sauce)*
> *½ teaspoon fine sugar*
> *½ pound small shrimp, shelled and deveined*
> *1 teaspoon grated fresh ginger*
> *1¼ pounds dried fine rice vermicelli*
> *1 red chili, seeded and sliced*
> *1 green chili, seeded and sliced*
> *4 ounces fresh bean sprouts, blanched and drained*
> *Extra nam pla (Thai fish sauce)*
> *Roasted chili powder (see sidebar, page 88)*

> CURRY SAUCE:
> *3 cups coconut milk*
> *2 teaspoons minced garlic*
> *½ cup chopped scallions (white and green parts, reserving some green*
>   *for garnish)*
> *1 lemon grass stem (the pale green shoot end), cut in half lengthwise*
>   *and bruised to release flavor*
> *5 thick slices galangal (Thai ginger)*
> *4 thin slices fresh ginger, cut into fine shreds*
> *2 ounces dried salt fish, soaked for 20 minutes in warm water*
> *1 tablespoon mam ruoc (Thai shrimp paste)*
> *1 cup thick coconut milk*
> *Salt and white pepper*

Combine the chicken with the fish sauce and sugar and set aside for 15 minutes. In another small dish marinate the shrimp with the grated ginger for 10 minutes. Soak the rice sticks in warm water for 20 minutes, then drain in a colander.

To prepare the sauce, pour the 3 cups coconut milk into a saucepan and add the garlic, scallions, lemon grass, *galangal*, ginger, and drained salt fish. Bring to a boil, stirring slowly, then reduce heat and simmer for about 20 minutes, until a film of oil floats on the surface.

In the meantime, roast the shrimp paste (see sidebar) and scrape into the sauce. Cook a further 5 minutes. Add the thick coconut milk,

Shrimp paste adds a surprising depth of flavor to a curry sauce and enhances it even more when roasted first. Place a block of compressed shrimp paste (blacan) or a measured quantity of the moister mam ruoc in the center of a square of aluminum foil. Fold into a small, loose parcel and place over a gas flame, in a moderately hot oven, or in a wok over a medium to high flame. Cook for about 6 minutes. Unwrap and mash into the sauce.

plus salt and pepper to taste. Then add the chicken and shrimp. Simmer for 5 minutes.

Add the noodles, chilies, and bean sprouts and heat through. Serve in deep bowls with the fish sauce and roasted chili powder on the side.

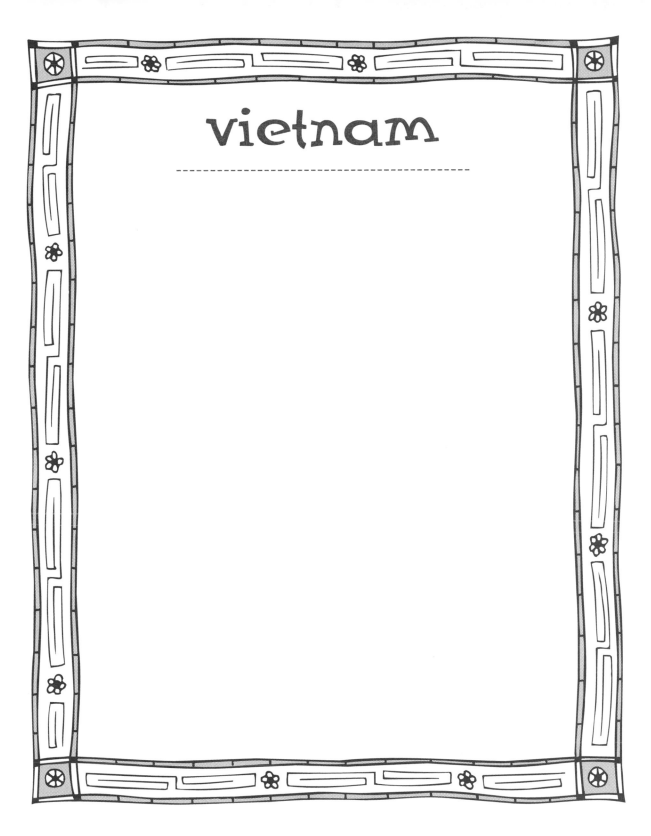

vietnam

Perhaps nowhere else in Asia are noodles as important as they are in Vietnam. Soup noodles occupy much of the Vietnamese diner's attention and appetite. The choice of noodle is *banh pho* or *bun*—narrow, flat ribbons of rice dough, sometimes reinforced by the firmer starch of tapioca or the flour of a type of starchy pea. The Vietnamese float them in clear meat broths bobbing with meatballs or chunks of tender meat and aromatic with lemon grass or star anise, or in powerfully spiced soups pungent with *nuoc mam* (fish sauce) and *mam ruoc* (shrimp paste). They combine them with the salt-chewiness of dried bamboo shoots or the subtle sweetness of *cha siu* (roast pork) in broths of delicate flavor and subtle seasoning.

Softened rice vermicelli is ubiquitous on the Vietnamese table. Snowy mounds of cold *banh hoi* (fine rice vermicelli) have a natural place on the vegetable platter that accompanies many meals. This salad of native minty herbs, pickled carrot, fresh bean sprouts, and lettuce or indigenous salad greens can accompany soup-noodles to nibble beside, or dunk into the broth. Rice vermicelli is also obligatory with grilled meats and snacks, finding its way, cold and cut in short lengths, into finger-sized snacks that are hand-rolled at the table in *banh trang* rice paper wrappers.

Rice sheets, soft crepes of rice dough bought fresh from the market, can be cut into noodles, but Vietnamese cooks also use them to wrap broiled meats, vegetarian fillings, or fresh shelled shrimp to steam and serve as a delicious alternative to a noodle dish.

Because they eat them so often, the Vietnamese are particular about the noodles they buy. They will remain loyal to a brand or noodle maker for years if the product is right. When they select bean-thread vermicelli for a dish, they look for the one that promises elasticity, recognizing it in the pack for its translucence rather than its whiteness. It is enjoyably *al dente* and is ideal for stuffing into a whole fish or bulking up a clay-pot braised dish.

Noodle Salad Platter

This two-way dish can be served as a salad or wrapped in *banh trang*
rice papers to eat from the fingers.
Serves 4 to 6

> *4 ounces rice vermicelli*
> *¹⁄₂ pound* **cha siu (Chinese roast pork)**
> *¹⁄₂ pound cooked chicken*
> *¹⁄₂ pound shelled, cooked shrimp*
> *2 small Japanese or Kirby cucumbers*
> *1 red Italian onion*
> *1 cup fresh herb leaves (mint, basil, cilantro)*
> *Mixed lettuce leaves*
> *2 tablespoons chopped roasted peanuts*
> *1¹⁄₂ tablespoons pickled garlic, finely sliced*
> *3 to 4 tablespoons scallion oil (see sidebar)*

> *IF YOU WANT TO WRAP:*
> *8 to 12* **banh trang** *rice paper sheets*
> *¹⁄₃ cup Vietnamese sauce* (nuoc cham *[page 150]*) *for dipping*

Soak the vermicelli in hot water for 7 minutes, drain, and cut into 2-
inch lengths. Cut the roast pork and chicken into thin slices, then stack
the slices together and cut across them into narrow strips. Cut the
shrimp in half lengthwise.

Cut the cucumbers in half lengthwise, then into thin slices. Peel the
onion, cut in half, and slice fine. Combine the meats, shrimp, cucumber, onion, and half the herbs.

Arrange the lettuce and vermicelli on a platter. Pile the combined
salad ingredients on top and scatter on the peanuts and pickled garlic.
If it is to be served as a salad, garnish with the remaining herbs and
pour on the scallion oil just before taking to the table.

If you plan to have your guests wrap it in rice paper sheets, drizzle
fried scallions (see sidebar) and some of their oil evenly over the salad
at this point, to moisten the ingredients. Soften the rice paper sheets
by dipping in cold water until they are barely pliable, then spread on a
kitchen towel. A generous portion of salad should be placed in the center of each sheet—have your guests do this themselves at the table—
and rolled up, egg-roll fashion. Dip into the *nuoc cham* and eat.

Chilled Noodles with Crabmeat and Abalone

Serves 4

$\frac{1}{2}$ *tomato*
2 tablespoons fresh or frozen green peas or beans
1 rib of celery
3 ounces cooked crabmeat
1 piece canned or cooked abalone
$5\frac{1}{2}$ ounces thin egg noodles
3 to 4 lettuce leaves

DRESSING:
1 tablespoon sesame oil
$\frac{1}{2}$ cup chicken stock (pages 26-27)
$\frac{1}{2}$ teaspoon salt
$\frac{1}{2}$ teaspoons tahini (sesame paste/butter)
$\frac{1}{2}$ teaspoon chili oil
$\frac{1}{2}$ teaspoon tamari or light soy sauce
$\frac{1}{2}$ teaspoon Chinese red vinegar

To peel the tomato, place it in a pan of boiling water for 12 seconds. Remove and let cool slightly, then lift the skin and carefully peel away. Cut open and squeeze to remove seeds. Cut the tomato into small dice. Parboil peas or sliced beans until barely tender. Dice celery, parboil for 1 minute, and drain.

Separate the crab into small pieces. Cut the abalone into small dice. Bring $1\frac{1}{2}$ quarts of water to a boil and salt sparingly. Add the noodles, cook for about 4 minutes until *al dente*, and drain. Combine the dressing ingredients, pour over the noodles, and set aside for 5 to 6 minutes.

Add the prepared ingredients, toss to combine, and arrange over the lettuce on a serving plate.

Use any leftover abalone as a luxurious Chinese side dish, gently poached in stock with lettuce leaves, then dressed with oyster sauce. Large abalone will have a gill around the center. Trim this off with a sharp knife. Hold the abalone firmly on a cutting board and cut in thin horizontal slices before cooking.

griddle-cooked beef with vermicelli salad

Serves 4

1 pound rump or sirloin steak
3 teaspoons mashed garlic
1½ tablespoons minced scallion, white part only
1 tablespoon finely minced lemon grass
2½ tablespoons nuoc mam *(Vietnamese fish sauce)*
2 teaspoons fine white sugar
1 tablespoon sesame oil
1½ tablespoons vegetable oil
3 ounces rice vermicelli
12 banh trang *rice paper wrappers*
12 small Boston lettuce leaves
1 cup loosely packed mint leaves
1 cup pickled carrot (see sidebar, page 156)

DIPPING SAUCE:
2 tablespoons rice vinegar
3 tablespoons thick coconut milk
1 tablespoon sugar
1 tablespoon crushed roasted peanuts
Nuoc mam *(Vietnamese fish sauce)*
Salt and black pepper

In their dried state, which is usually how they are sold, banh trang *rice paper wrappers* look like disks of semitransparent hard plastic. These edible wrappers must be dipped into cold water to soften them for eating. Hold in the water just long enough for the wrappers to become quite pliant, then place on a tray to partially dry. They are eaten raw in traditional fashion, lined with lettuce, filled with the ingredients of the dish and a few sprigs of fresh herbs, and then rolled into a cylinder with the ends tucked in.

Cut the beef into paper-thin slices across the grain. Set aside. In a dish large enough to hold the beef, combine the garlic, scallion, lemon grass, fish sauce, sugar, sesame oil, and vegetable oil and whisk until emulsified. Add the beef and mix with the fingers until each slice is coated with the marinade. Set aside for 2 hours.

Bring 3 cups of water to a boil. Place the vermicelli in a bowl and cover with very hot water. Let sit for 1 minute, then drain and cut into 3-inch lengths with kitchen shears.

In another bowl dip the rice papers into cold water to soften. Spread on a cloth, and cover to keep them damp and pliable. Arrange the vermicelli, lettuce, mint, and pickled carrot on a platter, place the rice papers over them, and take to the table.

Combine the sauce ingredients in a bowl, mixing well. Rub an iron hot plate or griddle with a paper towel dipped in vegetable oil. Heat over very high heat. Quickly cook the beef on the griddle to no more than medium-rare; overcooking will toughen it and spoil the dish. Use a spatula to lift the beef onto a warmed serving plate. Take to the table with the sauce.

To assemble, diners should place a piece of lettuce in the center of a piece of rice paper, add several pieces of meat, then some of the vermicelli, mint, and carrot. Roll up, tucking the sides in. Dip into the sauce before eating.

Little Shrimp and Noodle Parcels
(Cuon Deep)
Serves 4 to 6

> *4 ounces* bun *(thin rice sticks)*
> *6 ounces boiled or roasted pork*
> *6 ounces cooked, shelled shrimp*
> *4 whole scallions, trimmed and chopped*
> *⅓ cup cilantro (Chinese parsley) leaves*
> *⅓ cup assorted mint leaves (spearmint, garden mint, Vietnamese, etc.)(see sidebar)*
> *⅓ cup shredded carrot*
> *12 Boston lettuce leaves*
> *Extra scallion greens for tying the parcels (optional)*
> **Nuoc cham** *sauce (page 150)*

Soak the noodles in boiling water to soften; drain well. Cut the pork into julienne strips and the shrimp in half lengthwise.

Present all the ingredients attractively on a platter for your guests to roll their own parcels, wrapping a little of each ingredient in a piece of lettuce leaf. Or serve "prepackaged" parcels by rolling a portion of each of the ingredients in a leaf, trimming the edges neatly, and tying the center with a strip of scallion green.

Serve *nuoc cham*, the classic Vietnamese sauce, as a dip (recipe follows).

The fabulous fresh flavor of mint is much appreciated by the Vietnamese, who add sprigs of it to all sorts of dishes. It's easy to grow. Plant a large pot of assorted mints, including the pungent Vietnamese mint with its long, narrow leaves, so you have plenty on hand.

Vietnamese Sauce
(NUOC CHAM)
Makes ⅓ cup

> 1 red chili
> 2 cloves garlic, peeled
> 3 teaspoons sugar
> Juice of ½ small lime
> 2¾ tablespoons nuoc mam *(Vietnamese fish sauce)*
> 2 to 3 tablespoons water

Cut open the chili and scrape out the seeds and the inner membranes (these provide most of the heat, so the chili you use will be less challenging). Cut half of it into fine shreds and set aside, the remainder into pieces to place in a mortar with the peeled garlic and sugar. Grind to a paste, then squeeze on the lime juice, scraping in the pulp as well. Scoop the mixture out of the mortar and transfer to a bowl. Whisk in the fish sauce and water, then add the chili shreds. Fine shreds of carrot make an attractive addition to this sauce.

You would never see a Vietnamese table without a bowl of nuoc cham *sauce for dipping into, splashing over, and adding its bright, fresh flavors to just about any dish. It is based on* nuoc mam, *the pungent fermented fish sauce, highlighted with lime juice, sweetened with sugar, and fired up with chili and garlic. Prepare it fresh for a full flavor burst.*

Rice Noodles and Meatballs in Soup

Serves 4, or 6 sharing several dishes

> MEATBALLS:
> 12 ounces round or flank of beef
> 1 tablespoon grated fresh ginger
> 1 teaspoon Chinese five-spice powder
> 1 teaspoon salt
> 3 tablespoons cornstarch
> 2 egg whites
> 5 ounces banh pho *(rice-stick noodles)*
> 5 cups aromatic beef stock *(page 25)*
> 12 spinach leaves or small lettuce leaves
> Salt and freshly ground black pepper
> 2 tablespoons chopped scallion greens
> 1 tablespoon shredded bamboo shoots
> 1 tablespoon chopped cilantro (Chinese parsley) leaves

I'll often make a batch of these meatballs when there is a little spare beef in my kitchen. They can be poached and then frozen for easy use when I need a quick meal. Grill them to serve in rice papers, with salad and cold rice vermicelli, or pop into a noodle soup.

Cut the beef into small cubes and place in a food processor with the ginger, five-spice powder, salt, cornstarch, and egg whites. Process the mixture to a smooth paste, then add 3 tablespoons of cold water to make a voluminous, smooth mass.

Bring a 2-quart pan of salted water to a boil. Drop spoonfuls of the beef mixture into the bubbling water and cook until they rise to the surface, about 2½ minutes. Cook another 1 minute, then remove with slotted spoon and set aside.

In the same pan of water, cook the noodles for about 3 minutes, until tender. Using a wire ladle, transfer the noodles directly to soup bowls. Discard the cooking water and rinse the pan.

Bring the stock to a boil. Add spinach and check seasonings, adding salt and pepper to taste. Pour over the noodles, divide the meatballs among the bowls, and garnish with the scallion, bamboo shoots, and cilantro. Have fish and chili sauces on the table for your guests to add to their bowls, as desired.

Chicken Noodle Soup with Bamboo Shoots

(BUN MANG)

Serves 6

½ **pound** bun *(dried thin rice sticks)*
2¼ *quarts chicken broth (pages 26-27)*
2 *chicken legs or thighs*
4 *ounces boneless, skinless chicken breast*
1½ *cups sliced bamboo shoots*
1½ *tablespoons* nuoc mam *(Vietnamese fish sauce)*
2 *tablespoons minced scallion*
Salt and white pepper
Chopped cilantro (Chinese parsley) leaves

Bring 1½ quarts of water to a boil, add the rice sticks, cook for about 3½ minutes, and drain.

In another pan bring the chicken broth to a boil, add the chicken legs or thighs, cover and cook gently for 15 minutes, then add the breast meat and cook a further 15 minutes until tender. Remove the chicken from the broth. Skin and debone the legs or thighs and tear or

If you discover a bag of dried and salted bamboo shoots at your Asian grocery, take them home to use in a soup like this. Soak them in several changes of cold water to decrease their saltiness, then simmer in the broth for a few minutes to soften them and bring out their full flavor. They are quite different from fresh bamboo, and very appealing.

cut the meat into small pieces. Slice the chicken breast very thin. Reheat the noodles by immersing in a pan of boiling water, then remove and divide among six bowls. Strain the broth and return it to the pan. Return the chicken to the broth and add the remaining ingredients. Heat briefly and check seasonings, adding more salt and fish sauce as needed, then pour over the noodles and serve.

Reheating noodles

Noodle Soup with Seafood Balls

Serves 4

*1 package (6 to 7 ounces) shrimp, crab, or squid balls,
or see recipe on page 81*
½ pound **ban pho** *(rice-stick noodles) or* **bun** *(rice sticks)
or rice vermicelli*
5½ cups fish stock (page 27)
1 tablespoon **nuoc mam** *(Vietnamese fish sauce)*
Salt and black pepper
1 tablespoon chopped cilantro (Chinese parsley) leaves
1 tablespoon finely sliced whole scallion

Cut the seafood balls in half. Bring 1½ quarts of water to a boil, add the noodles, and cook 3½ minutes for rice sticks or about 1½ minutes for rice vermicelli, until tender. Drain well. Divide among four bowls.

Bring the fish stock to a boil, add the seafood balls and fish sauce, heat to boiling, then reduce heat and simmer for 2 minutes. Check the seasonings, adding salt and pepper, plus extra fish sauce if needed.

Pour over the noodles, dividing the seafood balls evenly among the bowls. Garnish with the cilantro and scallion and serve.

Beef and Lettuce Soup

Serves 6

BEEF BROTH:
1½ **pounds flank or shin beef**
4 **pounds beef rib bones**
1 **teaspoon black peppercorns**
8 **thick slices fresh ginger**
3 **scallions**

TO FINISH:
1 **pound fresh banh pho** *(rice-stick noodles)*
3 **to 4 cups roughly sliced Boston or Chinese lettuce leaves**
Vegetable or sesame oil
Nuoc mam *(Vietnamese fish sauce)*
Salt and white pepper
Fresh chili sauce *(see sidebar, page 156)*

Cut the beef into chunks and place in a stockpot with the ribs, 3 quarts water, the peppercorns, ginger, and the white parts of the scallions, reserving the green tops for another recipe.

Bring to a boil, skim the surface, reduce heat so the liquid is barely bubbling, and cook, covered, for about 2½ hours. Skim occasionally during cooking.

Remove the bones with a wire skimmer and discard. Retrieve the meat and tear into shreds with the fingers. Set aside in a dish covered with a little of the broth to keep it moist.

Bring a kettle of water to a boil. Pour over the noodles and drain immediately. Divide noodles among six deep soup bowls and add a portion of lettuce to each with a teaspoon of vegetable oil or ½ teaspoon of sesame oil—this helps prevent the lettuce from turning brown when heated by the broth.

Strain the broth and return it to the pan with the meat. Reheat and season to taste with fish sauce, salt, and pepper. Pour over the noodles and take to the table with a small bowl of fresh chili sauce.

Lettuce is enjoyed as a cooked vegetable in Chinese households. Bring a pan of water to a boil and add a tablespoon of oil and a sprinkle of sesame oil. Add the lettuce and heat just long enough to wilt. Transfer to a plate and pour thin streams of oyster sauce over it. Serve and eat at once.

Aromatic Beef Broth Noodles
(BUN PHO)
Serves 6

1 recipe aromatic beef stock (page 25)
3 tablespoons nuoc mam *(Vietnamese fish sauce)*
12 ounces rice vermicelli
2 tablespoons flavorless vegetable oil
1 pound beef tenderloin, very thinly sliced
1 medium-sized yellow onion, very thinly sliced
2 cups fresh bean sprouts

ACCOMPANIMENTS:
¾ cup finely sliced scallion
¼ cup chopped cilantro (Chinese parsley) leaves
¼ cup small mint leaves
3 tablespoons Hoisin sauce
Freshly ground black pepper
1 to 2 red chilies, seeded and sliced

Bring the stock to a boil and flavor to taste with fish sauce. Place the rice vermicelli in a bowl and pour boiling water over to generously cover. Let stand for 3 minutes, then drain. Divide the noodles among six deep soup bowls.

Heat a wok or skillet over very high heat and add the oil. Stir-fry the beef for no more than about 45 seconds, then remove. Add the onion and stir-fry until golden brown. Place some of the meat and some of the onion in each bowl of noodles.

Blanch the bean sprouts in boiling water for 20 seconds and divide among the bowls. Pour the broth over the noodles. Take the bowls to the table along with a tray containing the scallions, cilantro, mint, Hoisin sauce, a pepper mill, and a small dish of sliced chilies.

"Hue" Soup Noodles

Serves 6

- **2 pounds gravy beef (flank, round, etc.)**
- **2 lemon grass stems**
- **Salt and freshly ground black pepper**
- **12 ounces banh pho rice-stick noodles**
- **2 tablespoons vegetable or peanut oil**
- **1 tablespoon tomato paste**
- **1 to 2 teaspoons chili flakes**
- **1 teaspoon mam ruoc (fresh shrimp paste)**
- **1 medium chayote, julienned**
- **1 small onion, halved and thinly sliced**
- **1 cup coarsely shredded Boston or Chinese lettuce**
- **1 cup shredded spinach leaves**
- **1 tablespoon chopped cilantro (Chinese parsley) leaves**
- **2 to 3 tablespoons finely sliced scallion greens**
- **Nuoc cham (Vietnamese sauce)**

Most Vietnamese dishes are subtle, almost bland in flavor. "Hue" Soup Noodles is the exception. It is a classic that will become an all-time favorite with those who like powerful flavors.

Cut the beef into 1½-inch cubes and place in a stockpot with 2½ quarts cold water. Cut the lemon grass in half lengthwise and bruise by batting with the side of a Chinese cleaver or a rolling pin. Add to the stock and bring to a boil. Skim the surface, reduce heat to very low, and simmer, covered, for 3 hours with the water just occasionally bubbling. Skim from time to time. Add salt and pepper to taste.

Strain the broth and set aside, keeping warm. You should have at least 7 cups of broth. Discard lemon grass. Use two forks to break at least half of the beef into shreds, then set aside in a bowl, covered with a little of the broth to prevent it from drying out. Unused beef can be set aside to shred into Vietnamese or Thai salads.

In another pan cook the noodles in 2 quarts boiling water until barely tender, about 3 minutes, and drain well.

Heat a wok or sauté pan over medium heat and fry the tomato paste, chili flakes, and shrimp paste in the vegetable oil for about 1½ minutes, stirring constantly, until very fragrant. Pour on a little of the stock and bring to a boil, stirring to mix well. Add this mixture to the stockpot and bring it back to a boil.

Add the chayote and onion to the stockpot and simmer for 3 to 4 minutes. Add the lettuce and spinach and return the beef and its liquid to the pot. Simmer until well heated, without allowing it to boil. Check

the seasonings again, and add cilantro and scallions to taste.

Divide the noodles among six large bowls and pour on the soup. Serve at once with the *nuoc cham*.

Saigon Soup

Serves 6

¹⁄₂ **pound** banh pho *(rice-stick noodles)*
6 ounces boneless, skinless chicken breast
6 ounces lean pork
2 teaspoons plus 2 ¹⁄₂ tablespoons nuoc mam *(Vietnamese fish sauce)*
6 large shrimp, shelled and deveined
¹⁄₂ **teaspoon chopped garlic**
3 tablespoons thinly sliced French shallots
2 tablespoons vegetable oil
¹⁄₂ **rib of celery, finely sliced diagonally**
7 cups chicken stock (pages 26-27)
12 water spinach leaves, washed and torn in half
¹⁄₂ **cup finely sliced whole scallions**
¹⁄₄ **cup roasted peanuts, chopped**
Nuoc cham *(Vietnamese sauce) (page 150)*
Pickled carrot *(see sidebar)*

Bring at least 2 quarts of water to a boil, add the noodles, and cook for 3 to 3¹⁄₂ minutes until barely tender, then drain. Slice the chicken and pork wafer thin and season with 2 teaspoons of the fish sauce. Cut the shrimp in half lengthwise.

Brown the garlic and shallots in oil over medium heat without allowing them to burn, about 8 minutes. Drain well and set aside.

Sauté the celery briefly in the same oil, then remove. Add the chicken and pork to the pan and stir-fry over very high heat for about 1¹⁄₂ minutes, then add the shrimp and sauté until they change color.

Heat the stock in another pan and add the remaining fish sauce. Add the noodles and warm through, then add the cooked chicken, pork, shrimp, and celery, and the water spinach and the scallions. Heat briefly. Ladle into deep bowls and scatter the roasted peanuts, garlic, and fried shallots over the top.

Serve with small dishes of *nuoc cham* and shredded pickled carrot.

Pickled carrot is featured frequently in Vietnamese dishes as a tangy flavor accent with grilled meatballs, salads, and chicken. To make your own, peel 2 medium-sized carrots and cut in half lengthwise, then slice fine. Place in a dish and add distilled white vinegar to barely cover. Add 1¹⁄₂ teaspoons salt and 1 tablespoon sugar. Set aside for at least 1 hour.

It's also easy to make up fresh chili sauce, but unfortunately this dynamite sauce doesn't keep for long, though you can freeze it. Slit open 6 fresh red chilies and use a small, sharp knife to trim away the inner membranes and scrape out the seeds. Chop them roughly and place in a spice grinder, blender, or mortar. Add 1 teaspoon sugar and 2 teaspoons salt with 3 teaspoons water. Grind to a paste. Wear latex gloves while you work with chilies—or pay the price!

Shrimp Ball and Roast Pork Soup Noodles

(BANH CANH BOT LOC)
Serves 4 to 6

½ pound dried rice-stick noodles
7 cups chicken stock (pages 26-27)
Salt and freshly ground black pepper
1 to 2 tablespoons nuoc mam (Vietnamese fish sauce)
3 scallions, diagonally sliced, with white parts and green tops separated
6 straw mushrooms, thinly sliced
2 ounces fresh bean sprouts
7 ounces cha siu (Chinese roast pork; see sidebar, page 86)

SHRIMP BALLS:
5 ounces shrimp, shelled
3 ounces fatty pork or fresh bacon, diced
1 tablespoon minced scallion whites
2 teaspoons minced cilantro (Chinese parsley) leaves
2 teaspoons nuoc mam (Vietnamese fish sauce)
Salt and white pepper

Make a substantial snack by serving a platter of salad ingredients with a Vietnamese noodle soup. Scraps of Boston lettuce, mint leaves, shredded cucumber, carrot, and fresh bean sprouts are the usual combination.

Bring 1½ quarts of water to a boil. Place the rice sticks in a bowl, pour on the water, and let sit for about 6 minutes to soften. Drain well.

To make the shrimp balls, place the shrimp and pork in a food processor fitted with a metal blade and grind to a smooth paste. Add the minced scallion whites, cilantro, fish sauce, salt, and pepper. Process again to a smooth paste.

Bring the stock to a boil and check the seasoning, adding salt, pepper, and fish sauce to taste. Drop teaspoonfuls of the shrimp batter into the stock to poach. When they float to the surface cook for 1 minute, then remove with a wire skimmer.

Add the drained noodles to the stock, along with the sliced scallion whites and the mushrooms, and heat for 2 minutes.

Divide the shrimp balls, bean sprouts, and sliced pork among large soup bowls. Pour on the hot broth. Sprinkle on the sliced scallion greens and serve.

Combination Rice-Stick Noodles

Serves 2 to 3

> **1 chicken thigh and leg (about ½ pound)**
> **2 ounces lean pork**
> **6 large shrimp, peeled and deveined**
> **2 large scallions**
> **1 small carrot**
> **2 to 3 baby bok choy (Chinese white cabbage)**
> **6 small broccoli or cauliflower florets**
> **12 ounces fresh banh pho (rice-stick noodles) or rice sheet dough**
> **4 tablespoons flavorless vegetable oil**
> **½ teaspoon minced garlic**
> **1½ ounces sliced bamboo shoots**
> **½ cup chicken stock (pages 26-27)**
> **1½ teaspoons cornstarch**
> **Salt and white pepper**
> **2 to 3 teaspoons oyster sauce**

Skin the chicken and cut the meat into small cubes. Slice the pork thin, then cut into ¾-inch strips. Cut the shrimp in half lengthwise. Cut the white parts of the scallions into 1-inch pieces. Cut the green tops into fine diagonal slices and reserve for garnish.

Peel and slice the carrot thin, cutting on the diagonal. Cut the bok choy in half lengthwise. Bring 3 cups of lightly salted water to a boil, blanch the bok choy for 1½ minutes, and remove. Blanch the broccoli or cauliflower and the carrot for 1 minute and drain. Set aside.

Pour hot water over the noodles and drain immediately. If using rice sheet dough, cut into narrow noodles, about ⅓ inch wide, soak briefly in hot water, and drain.

Heat 2 tablespoons of the oil in a wok or large skillet over very high heat. Fry the garlic briefly, add the noodles, and stir-fry for 1 minute until well-coated with the oil. Remove to a plate and set aside.

Add a little more oil to the pan if needed, and stir-fry the chicken and pork for 1½ minutes. Add the shrimp, stir-fry until it changes color, and remove.

Add the remaining oil. Stir-fry the white parts of scallion, the broccoli or cauliflower, carrot, bok choy, and bamboo shoots for 2 minutes over high heat, stirring and tossing the ingredients continuously.

Combine the stock and cornstarch. Return the meat and noodles to the pan, pour in the stock, and cook on the highest heat possible for about 2 minutes. Season to taste with salt and white pepper, and add the oyster sauce. If the dish needs extra flavor, sprinkle on fish sauce.

Transfer to warmed plates and scatter on the scallion tops. Serve at once.

Steamed Fish with Bean Threads

Serves 4, or 6 to 8 sharing several dishes

1 1/4 pounds white fish fillets, cut into 1-inch pieces
2 1/2 tablespoons nuoc mam (Vietnamese fish sauce)
3 ounces bean thread vermicelli
6 dried black mushrooms, soaked for 25 minutes in warm water
1 to 2 teaspoons vegetable oil
1 small carrot, peeled and julienned
2 ounces sliced bamboo shoots, julienned
2 ounces peeled and seeded cucumber, julienned
1/2 rib of celery, julienned
3 slices fresh ginger, finely shredded
2 large whole scallions, trimmed, cut into 2-inch lengths, and shredded lengthwise
1/3 teaspoon black pepper
4 tablespoons thick coconut milk
4 to 6 sprigs cilantro (Chinese parsley) leaves

Sprinkle the fish with 1 tablespoon of the fish sauce and set aside. Bring a kettle of water to a boil. Place the noodles in a dish, pour on the water, and soak for 30 seconds. Then drain and cut into 2-inch lengths with kitchen shears.

Drain the mushrooms, squeeze out excess water, and trim off the stems. Shred the mushroom caps fine. Brush the bottom of a heatproof dish with oil. Mix the noodles with prepared vegetables and arrange half in the dish. Place the fish on top in a single layer, sprinkle on the pepper, and cover with the remaining vegetables and noodles, using only half the scallion. Pour the remaining fish sauce evenly over the dish.

Select a steamer or pan large enough to accommodate the dish. Pour in 2 inches of hot water and position a rack in the pan to hold the dish. Set dish on the rack. Place over medium-high heat. Cover and steam for 10 minutes. Pour on the coconut milk and steam a further 6 to 7 minutes. Garnish with cilantro and the reserved scallion and serve in the dish.

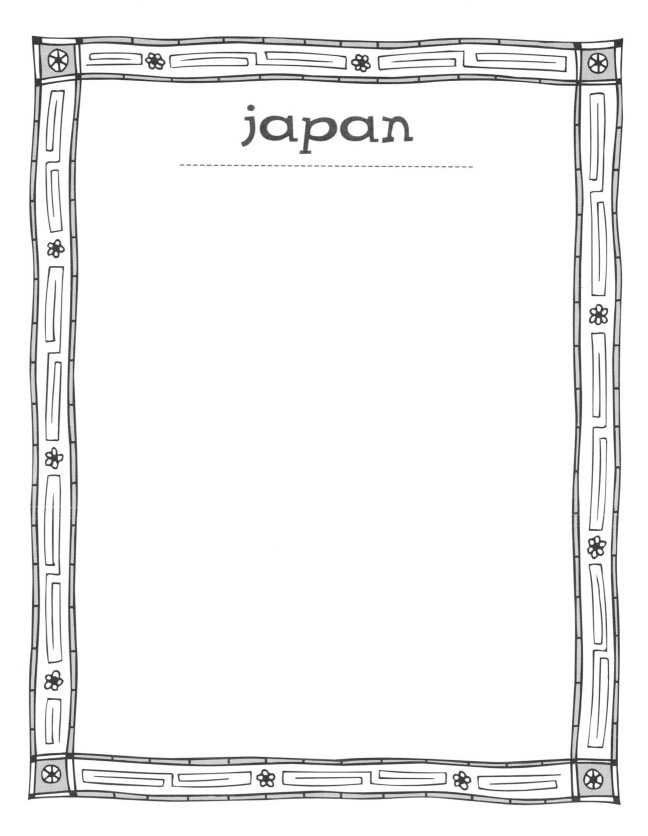

japan

Every Japanese worth his sushi probably eats a bowl of noodles at least once a day. Now immigrant Japanese and Japanese-food enthusiasts can enjoy real Japanese noodles right in the heart of Manhattan at restaurants like Omen, Honmura-an, and Manchanko-tei, where the noodles are handmade according to generations-old family recipes. In San Francisco there's Dojima An and Katana Ya Ramen, and the list goes on. The people who run these restaurants are mainly "from the trade," modelling their American establishments after the family restaurant at home in Kyoto, Kyushu, or Tokyo, and the noodles are every bit as good as the ones back home.

Although *ramen* and *saimin* have been prominent in Hawaii for several decades, the noodle-shop craze has hit American cities with the force of an eastern typhoon. Thousands of steaming bowls of Japanese *ramen* and *udon* are passed across glazed-wood counters every day to noisily slurping pastophiles. And those even more in the know request attractive baskets of iced noodles, which caress the palate and help to cool summer's stifling heat.

Gray-beige *soba* noodles made from buckwheat flour vie for popularity with plump white wheat-starch *udon* noodles, although the finer *somen* and the Chinese-style *ramen* are also strong contenders. Most are served in *dashi* broth, based on that famous duo of *kombu*, a type of kelp, and *katsuobushi*, feathery flakes of dried bonito fish. It may be made thick and salty with a last-minute addition of *miso*, a fermented soybean paste, or sweetened with *mirin* (sweet Japanese rice wine) and sugar.

The Japanese also enjoy noodles cooked absolutely plain, served cold over ice or hot in a wooden bowl of boiling water. These they will submerge into an accompanying citrus-soy dip with a dab of fiery *wasabi* horseradish.

Shiratake translates as "white waterfall," an apt description for the translucent noodles Japanese cooks use in *sukiyaki* and hot pots. They may look similar to bean-thread vermicelli, which of course you could substitute, but are made from *konnyaku*, an indigenous root vegetable.

Miso Soba

The Japanese feel just as strongly about the texture of their noodles as the Italians do about that of their pasta. *Al dente* is the rule.
Serves 4

> *12 ounces soba (dried buckwheat noodles)*
> *4 ounces* **kamaboko** *(Japanese fish cake) (see sidebar)*
> *4 medium shrimp, peeled and deveined*
> *¼ ounce dried* **wakame** *(curly seaweed), soaked in cold water for 25 minutes*
> *7 cups Dashi Stock No. 2 (page 24)*
> *1¼ tablespoons white* **miso** *(soybean paste concentrate)*
> *3 tablespoons finely sliced scallion, rinsed (see sidebar, page 165)*
> *4 slivers of lemon peel*

Bring 2 quarts of water to a boil, add the noodles, and bring the water back to a boil. Add 1 cup of cold water, bring again to a boil, then add ½ cup cold water. When it has boiled again, add another ½ cup of cold water, then cook the noodles until barely tender. Drain, rinse with cold water, then transfer to a wire strainer and set aside.

Cut the fish cake into 8 slices. Butterfly the shrimp and make an incision through the center. Push the tail into the incision and pull through to the other side. Bring a small pan of water to a boil, add the shrimp, and cook until they turn pink, about 1 minute. Remove with a slotted spoon.

Drain the seaweed and cut into small strips. Pour the stock into a pot, add the seaweed, and bring to a boil. Remove from heat and stir in the *miso*. Do not boil again.

Plunge the strainer filled with the noodles into a pan of boiling water, or pour a kettle of boiling water over the noodles to reheat. Divide among four bowls.

Pour on the stock. Add 1 shrimp and 2 pieces of fish cake to each bowl, plus some of the *wakame*, a sprinkle of scallion, and a sliver of lemon peel. Serve.

chicken on Soba Noodles

Yield: 4 servings

> **14 ounces dried soba (buckwheat noodles)**
> **½ pound skinless, boneless chicken breast**
> **1 tablespoon very finely minced fresh ginger**
> **½ cup minced white and green scallion**
> **1 sheet nori (dried, compressed seaweed sheet)**
> **1 tablespoon white sesame seeds**
> **2½ cups Dashi Stock No. 1 (page 23)**
> **¼ cup tamari or light soy sauce**
> **1 tablespoon mirin (Japanese sweet rice wine)**
> **2 tablespoons flavorless vegetable oil**
> **1 to 3 teaspoons shichimi (Japanese pepper condiment) or chili flakes**

Bring 1 quart of lightly salted water to a boil, add the noodles, and return the water to a boil. Add ½ cup of cold water, bring back to a boil again, and add another ½ cup of cold water. When the water again returns to a boil, cook the noodles for 3 minutes, then test. They should be *al dente*. Transfer to a strainer and rinse under running hot water. Set aside.

Cut the chicken into bite-sized cubes. Place the minced ginger on a small piece of clean cloth, gather the cloth around it, and squeeze the contents to extract the ginger juice, sprinkling it evenly over the chicken. Set aside for 5 minutes.

Rinse the cloth, discarding the ginger. Place the minced scallion on the cloth, enclose it, then rinse it under running cold water and squeeze dry (see sidebar). Cut the seaweed into fine shreds (see sidebar, page 176). Toast the sesame seeds in a dry pan over medium heat until they begin to pop.

Bring 2 quarts of unsalted water to a boil. Reheat the noodles in the boiling water, then remove and drain well. In another small saucepan heat the stock with soy sauce and *mirin* until it reaches a boil.

Heat the oil in a skillet and sauté the chicken until it changes color. Remove from the pan.

Divide the noodles and chicken among four bowls. Add the scallion. Pour on the hot broth and garnish with the shredded seaweed, sesame seeds, and a pinch of the *shichimi* or chili flakes.

Japanese cooks add sliced scallions to many dishes, for flavor or as a garnish. But they do not appreciate an excessively oniony taste. To eliminate this the scallions—both white and green parts, finely sliced—are placed in a piece of clean cloth and rinsed thoroughly in cold or hot water (depending on the amount of onion flavor the cook wishes to eliminate). Then the cloth is squeezed until all excess liquid has been removed. This leaves a very mild onion flavor.

"Gazing at the Moon" Soba

Serves 4

> *You may prefer to poach the spinach in the broth. Place it in a small saucepan and pour on broth to barely cover, cook gently for about 4 minutes, strain the broth back into the pot, and bundle the spinach as described in the recipe. Spinach cooked in this way can be served in a shallow pool of broth, and with a sprinkle of crushed toasted sesame seeds over the top, as a side dish or appetizer with a Japanese meal.*

> 4 large shiitake mushrooms (if dried, soak for 15 minutes in cold water)
> 14 ounces dried soba (buckwheat noodles)
> 6 ounces fresh young spinach leaves
> 2 thin scallions (green and white parts)
> 4 eggs

> BROTH:
> 4 cups Dashi Stock No. 1 (page 23)
> 1½ tablespoons mirin (Japanese sweet rice wine)
> 1 tablespoon sake (Japanese rice wine)
> ¼ cup tamari or light soy sauce
> Sugar and salt to taste

Drain the mushrooms, place in a small bowl, pour on ½ cup boiling water, and set aside for 15 minutes. Strain, reserving the liquid. Remove the stems and slice each mushroom separately into fine shreds.

Bring 5 cups of water to a boil. Add the noodles and return the water to a boil. Add 1 cup of cold water and bring back to a boil, then add ½ cup of cold water and bring back to a boil again. Repeat the process one more time, then reduce the heat slightly and simmer with the water lightly bubbling, until the noodles are tender. Test frequently so you stop the cooking at the exact moment they are done, *al dente* and no more. Drain and rinse under cold water, then drain again and set aside.

Rinse the spinach in several lots of cold water, drain, and place in a small saucepan with only the water that still clings to the leaves. Cover and cook on low heat for 6 minutes, shaking the pan occasionally. Wrap several leaves together around a pair of chopsticks to make small bundles, one for each serving.

Trim the scallions and cut diagonally into 1½-inch pieces. Bring 2 quarts of water to a boil. Reheat the noodles in boiling water, drain, and divide among four bowls. In another pan heat the broth ingredients to boiling, adding the reserved mushroom soaking liquid.

Pour the broth over the noodles. In each bowl, arrange 1 sliced mushroom, a bundle of spinach, and several pieces of scallion, placing them to the side to allow room for the egg. Make a shallow depression in the top of the noodles and break 1 egg into each bowl. Serve immediately. The egg will partially cook in the hot broth.

Tempura Soba

Serves 4

> 1 pound dried **soba** *or* cha-soba *(buckwheat noodles)*
> 8 large shrimp
> ½ *cup all-purpose flour*
> 3 *cups vegetable oil for deep-frying*
> 2 *tablespoons sesame oil*
> 6 *cups noodle broth (page 24)*
> 2 *ounces thinly sliced bamboo shoots*
> 2 *tablespoons finely sliced scallion, rinsed (see sidebar, page 165)*
> ⅓ *sheet* **nori** *(compressed seaweed), shredded*
> 1½ *teaspoons* **shichimi** *(Japanese pepper condiment) or toasted white sesame seeds*
> 4 *slivers lemon peel (optional)*
>
> *BATTER:*
> 1 *egg yolk*
> 1 *cup ice water*
> 1 *cup all-purpose flour, sifted*

Bring 2 quarts of water to a boil, add the noodles, and bring back to a boil. Pour in ½ cup of cold water, return to a boil, add another ½ cup of cold water, return again to a boil, then add another ½ cup of cold water and cook until the noodles are tender. Drain.

Shell the shrimp and cut deeply along the center of their backs. Pull away the dark vein. Coat the shrimp lightly and evenly with ½ cup flour, shaking off excess.

Heat the deep-frying oil to 375°F. Add the sesame oil. Heat the broth to boiling, then lower the heat and keep warm.

To prepare the batter, beat the egg into the ice water. Measure 1 cup flour into a bowl. Pour in the egg-water and mix with just a few stirs of the chopsticks (overmixing ruins tempura batter). Dip in the shrimp, one by one, coating generously.

Deep-fry the shrimp in the hot oil until the batter is crisp and golden and the shrimp are barely cooked through, about 1¼ minutes. Lift out, drain on paper towels, and set aside.

Divide the noodles among four deep bowls. Pour on the broth, add the bamboo shoots and scallion, sprinkle on the *shichimi* (or sesame seeds) and *nori*, and add a strip of lemon peel, if desired. Place 2 shrimp on top of each bowl of noodles and serve at once.

Tenzaru *is another appetizing way to combine* soba *noodles and crisp, battered shrimp. In lacquered boxes serve cold* soba *noodles mounded to one side, with the other side occupied by 4 or 5 large, crisply fried tempura shrimp. Serve a bowl of slightly tangy dipping sauce, such as the one on page 180, as an accompaniment.*

Haikara soba *combines little crunchy balls of fried tempura batter, sliced scallions, and shreds of egg crepe (see sidebar, page 100) in broth with* soba *noodles.*

Shichimi *is the Japanese seven-spice condiment, a snappy, aromatic collection of seasonings sold in a convenient shaker bottle. At the top of the list of ingredients is* togarashi *(red chili flakes), and there are fragments of* nori, *white and black sesame seeds, hemp seeds,* sansho *(Chinese brown peppercorns), and tiny bits of dried mandarin orange peel.*

It is sprinkled over noodles to add a bit of pep and is also used to enhance the flavor of broth. Chili flakes on their own are an alternative, if you like it hot!

Teriyaki Soba

Serves 4

> **12 ounces soba** *(buckwheat noodles)*
> **1½ teaspoons sesame oil**
> **10 ounces turkey** *(or chicken)* **breast**
> **12 small whole scallions**
> **2 tablespoons vegetable oil**
> **1 cup teriyaki sauce, homemade** *(recipe follows)* **or bottled**
> **shichimi** *(Japanese pepper condiment) (see sidebar)*

TERIYAKI SAUCE:
> **⅓ cup sake** *(Japanese rice wine)*
> **½ cup tamari or light soy sauce**
> **1 tablespoon mirin** *(Japanese sweet rice wine)*
> **2 tablespoons fine sugar**

If you are preparing the teriyaki sauce, combine the sauce ingredients in a small bowl.

Bring 1 quart of water to a boil, add the noodles, and return the water to a boil. Add 1 cup of cold water, then again return the water to a boil, reduce heat slightly, and simmer until the noodles are barely tender. Test them frequently after 2½ minutes. Pour into a colander to drain, sprinkle with sesame oil, and set aside.

Cut the turkey or chicken into thin slices and then into shreds. Trim the scallions and cut into 2-inch pieces. Heat the oil in a skillet over high heat. Fry the chicken shreds until done, 1½ minutes. Remove.

Fry the scallions for 1 minute. Add the teriyaki sauce and cook until the scallions are glazed and tender. Add the chicken and glaze with the sauce.

Bring a large kettle of water to a boil. Pour over the noodles in a strainer to reheat. Divide the noodles among four appetizer plates or small lacquered wooden trays. Arrange the chicken and scallions over the noodles and sprinkle sparingly with *shichimi*. Serve.

Ramen with Corn and Crab

Serves 4

> 12 ounces **ramen** *(Chinese-style noodles)*
> 4 ounces *boiled or roasted* **pork tenderloin**
> ½ pound **corn kernels** *(fresh, frozen, or canned)*
> 4 blue swimmer **crab claws** or four 4-inch pieces of Alaskan crab claw,
>   *boiled in lightly salted water for 6 minutes*
> 1½ tablespoons sliced **scallion greens**, *rinsed (see sidebar, page 165)*

> **BROTH:**
> 2 quarts **Dashi Stock No. 2** *(see page 24)*
> ½ ounce dried **wakame** *(curly seaweed), soaked for 25 minutes in*
>   *warm water*
> 1½ to 2 tablespoons white **miso** paste *(soybean paste concentrate)*
> 2 teaspoons fine **sugar** *(optional)*

Bring 2 quarts of water to a boil and add the noodles. Cook at a simmer for about 3½ minutes until tender, then drain. Slice the pork thin and set aside.

To make the broth, bring the *dashi* to a boil with the *wakame* and simmer for 5 minutes. Retrieve the *wakame* with a slotted spoon and cut into shreds. Remove the broth from the heat and stir in the *miso* and sugar, if desired.

Divide the noodles among four deep bowls. To each bowl add a portion of corn, some *wakame*, several slices of pork, a crab claw, and a sprinkle of scallion greens. Pour on the broth and serve at once.

The Japanese love ramen, which is actually a Chinese noodle, but you can use just about any sort of noodle instead in ramen dishes in general. I actually favor plump udon that I've made myself above all others when cooked with Japanese flavors. I would probably then use the stronger-tasting red miso instead of the white.

When choosing dried shiitake or dried black Chinese mushrooms, select those that are a cream color underneath, with a thick, gray-brown cap. They should smell intoxicatingly aromatic; if they do not, they are of inferior quality or have been incorrectly stored and have begun to mold.

Always store them in an airtight container, with a little sachet of silica gel to absorb moisture. After soaking them 15 minutes in boiling water (25 minutes in warm, or about 30 in cold) to reconstitute, use a small, sharp knife to cut away the woody stem. Mushroom soaking water can be strained into soups and braised dishes as it retains quite a bit of the mushroom flavor.

Fresh shiitake mushrooms should be wiped and their stems trimmed before using.

Wakame Ramen

Serves 4

> *12 ounces **ramen** (Chinese-style noodles)*
> *4 **shiitake** mushrooms (if dried, soak in cold water for 30 minutes)*
> *1½ ounces dried **wakame** (curly seaweed), soaked for 25 minutes in cold water*
> *2 to 3 tablespoons finely sliced and rinsed scallion greens*
> *1½ ounces **kamaboko** (fish cake) or **cha siu** (Chinese roast pork)*
> *2 teaspoons toasted white sesame seeds, lightly crushed*

BROTH:
> *5 cups Dashi Stock No. 1 (page 23)*
> *1 tablespoon **sake** (Japanese rice wine)*
> *2 tablespoons **mirin** (Japanese sweet rice wine)*
> *3 tablespoons tamari or light soy sauce*
> *2 tablespoons dark soy sauce*
> *½ to 1 tablespoon fine white sugar*

Add the noodles to 2 quarts of boiling water and cook for about 3 minutes, until firm-tender. Drain.

Drain the mushrooms, squeeze out excess water, and trim the stems close to the caps. Cut a cross in the top of each mushroom cap by cutting away two narrow wedges (see sidebar, page 182). Drain and shred the *wakame*. Bring 1½ quarts of water to a boil. Pour over the noodles in a strainer to reheat, then drain and divide among four deep soup bowls.

Bring the broth ingredients to a boil and add the mushrooms and *wakame*. Heat for 2 minutes. Pour the broth over the noodles, placing a mushroom, a few fragments of *wakame*, and a sprinkle of scallion in each bowl. Cut the fish cake (or roast pork) into thin slices. Arrange on the noodles, scatter on sesame seeds, and serve immediately.

Miso Ramen with Cha Siu

Serves 4

> *14 ounces **ramen** (Chinese-style noodles)*
> *6 ounces **cha siu** (Chinese roast pork; see sidebar)*
> *2 ounces **kamaboko** (fish cake), thinly sliced*

12 small spinach leaves, well rinsed
2½ tablespoons finely sliced scallion, rinsed (see sidebar, page 165)

BROTH:
9 cups Dashi Stock No. 1 (page 23)
1 tablespoon mirin (Japanese sweet rice wine)
1 tablespoon fine sugar
2 tablespoons tamari or light soy sauce
2½ tablespoons white miso (soybean paste concentrate)

Bring 1½ quarts of water to a boil, add the *ramen*, and cook for about 3½ minutes, until tender. Drain. Divide among four large lacquer soup bowls.

Bring the broth ingredients, except the *miso*, to a boil. Remove from the heat and stir in the *miso*.

Slice the *cha siu* thin. Place portions of pork, fish cake, spinach, and scallion in each bowl and pour on the broth. Serve at once.

Although you might not find it in Japan, cha siu, or Chinese sweet roast pork tenderloin, became a popular ramen ingredient in Hawaii and is now in general use. Buy a strip next time you pass a Chinese barbecue shop, or try the simple recipe on page 171.

Tonkatsu Ramen

Serves 4

14 ounces ramen (Chinese-style noodles)
1 quart noodle broth (page 24)
1 tablespoon finely sliced scallion greens

TONKATSU:
4 1½-ounce slices pork loin
Salt and freshly ground black pepper
½ cup all-purpose flour
2 eggs, lightly beaten
1½ cups fine, dry breadcrumbs
1 quart oil for deep-frying
1 tablespoon sesame oil
Tonkatsu sauce (see Vegetarian Yaki Soba, page 194)

To prepare the *tonkatsu*, bat the pork slices with the side of a cleaver or a meat mallet to flatten to ¼-inch thickness. Season with salt and pepper and coat lightly with flour, shaking off excess. Dip into beaten egg and coat with breadcrumbs.

There are all sorts of bits and pieces you can pop into a bowl of ramen to make a delicious and filling snack at any time: steamed or deep-fried siu mai (Chinese dumplings), "pot sticker" dumplings, gyoza (Japanese dumplings), shredded chicken or turkey, slivers of roast beef, Chinese seafood balls, meatballs, grilled chicken livers, fried fish, or chicken tenderloin. Or you might like them plain, with a splash of soy sauce or a generous sprinkle of sea salt.

Bring a large pan of water to a boil and add the noodles. Reduce the heat slightly and simmer for about 4 minutes, until tender. Drain and set aside. Heat the noodle broth in another pan.

Heat the oils to 375°F in a pan suitable for deep-frying. Carefully lower the pork into the oil and cook until the coating is crunchy and golden brown, about 5 minutes. Remove and drain on absorbent paper, then cut crosswise into ½-inch slices.

Divide the noodles among four large bowls. Pour on the broth, making sure it does not cover the noodles, or the crumbs on the pork will become waterlogged and unpalatable. Add a sprinkle of the scallion greens. Arrange a portion of pork on top of each bowl and drizzle on some of the sauce in thin streams. Serve at once.

Niku Udon

Serves 4 generously

> *1 pound dried* **udon** *(thick wheat noodles) or 1½ pounds fresh* **udon** *(page 18)*
> *4 ounces tip end of beef filet (or pork tenderloin)*
> *2 teaspoons vegetable oil*
> *2 ounces or 4 to 8 dried shiitake mushrooms (if using dried shiitakes, soak for 25 minutes in cold water)*
> *½ cup tamari or light soy sauce*
> *½ cup Dashi Stock No. 1 (see page 23)*
> *Large pinch of sugar*
> *1 medium yellow onion, halved and finely sliced*
> *8 cups noodle broth (page 24)*
> *3 tablespoons sliced whole scallion*
> *1½ teaspoons* **shichimi** *(Japanese pepper condiment) or toasted white sesame seeds, lightly crushed*

Bring 2 quarts of water to a boil. Add the noodles and cook for 1 minute, add 1 cup of water, cook until the noodles are tender, and drain. Fresh *udon* take only about 3 minutes to cook; dried take about 6 minutes.

Rub the beef with the oil. Heat a hot plate or skillet over medium heat. Grill the filet, rolling it constantly over the surface of the pan, until the meat is cooked rare inside with a well-seared surface, about 3 minutes. Set aside.

Enokitake are tiny golden mushrooms on elegant, long, slender stems. They grow in bunches and are packed that way—either in cans or, if you're lucky, fresh from your greengrocer. What they lack in flavor—though there is a subdued mushroomy taste to them—they make up in visual appeal. They're stunning as a garnish!

If using shiitake mushrooms, they should be simmered for 3 to 4 minutes in the soy sauce, *dashi* stock, and sugar.

Bring 1 cup of water to a boil, add the onion, blanch for 20 seconds, then remove and rinse in cold water. Drain well. Heat the noodle broth to boiling. Divide the noodles among four deep bowls. Place a serving of onion, mushrooms, and scallion in each bowl. Pour on the hot broth.

Cut the beef into thin slices, place on top of the noodles, scatter on sesame seeds or *shichimi*, and serve at once.

Note: Fresh *enokitake* mushrooms can be used instead of shiitake, and will not require simmering in soy and dashi.

Kama Age Udon

Serves 4

> 1¼ *pounds dried* udon *(wheat noodles), or* 1¾ *pounds fresh* udon
> ¾ *cup minced whole scallion*
> 1¼ *tablespoons* wasabi *paste or powder*
>
> DIPPING SAUCE:
> 1¾ *cups water*
> ½ *teaspoon instant* dashi *stock granules or powder*
> ⅔ *cup tamari or light soy sauce*
> ¼ *cup freshly squeezed lemon juice*
> 1 *tablespoon sugar*

Bring 2 quarts of water to a boil, add the noodles, and bring the water back to a boil. Add 1 cup of cold water, return to a boil, and add another cup of cold water. Return again to a boil, then cook until the noodles are tender, testing frequently after 2½ minutes to ensure they are done just right; they should be just slightly chewy. Drain and divide among four large bowls (preferably large lacqered Japanese bowls). Place each of these on its own tray.

Beside each bowl place a small dish containing some of the minced scallion and a knob of *wasabi* paste. (If using *wasabi* powder, mix to a paste with a little *sake* or water).

Combine the sauce ingredients in a small saucepan and heat almost to boiling. Remove from the heat. Bring a large kettle of water to a

Treat wasabi *with the respect its fiery nature demands. What clings to the tips of your chopsticks should be enough to give any mouthful of noodles a kick you'll notice. Buy it ready-made in a plastic squeeze tube for convenience, or mix the powder to a paste with a splash of* sake *or water.*

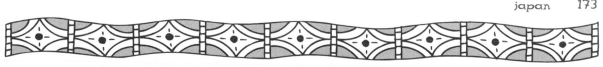

boil. Pour about 1½ cups of boiling water into each of the bowls of noodles. Pour the warm sauce into four other bowls, place on the serving trays, and take immediately to the table.

To eat, sprinkle scallion onto the sauce, add *wasabi* paste to taste, and stir with chopsticks to dissolve. Lift the noodles from the hot water, hold them over the bowl a few seconds to drain, dip into the sauce, and eat with the noisy, splattering splurp of a noodle professional.

Sansai Udon

Sansai is a fernlike indigenous vegetable the Japanese like to call "mountain vegetable." Cooked, it has a slightly bitter flavor and pleasing tender texture. Young radish or beet greens make a good substitute.
Serves 4

> *1 pound dried* udon *(thick wheat noodles), or 1½ pounds fresh* udon *(page 18)*
> *4 ounces* sansai *(Japanese mountain vegetable)*
> *¼ ounce dried black fungus (cloud ear or wood ear), soaked for 30 minutes in warm water (see sidebar)*
> *7 cups noodle broth (page 24)*
> *2 ounces* nameko *mushrooms*
> *1 ounce carrot (about 1 small carrot), cut in long, thin shreds*
> *1 ounce* daikon *(icicle radish), cut in long, thin shreds*
> *2 ounces* kamaboko *(fish cake), thinly sliced in half-moons*

Bring 1½ quarts of water to a boil. Add the noodles and cook for 1 minute. Add 1 cup of cold water, bring back to a boil, and cook another 1 minute. Add another cup of cold water, bring back to a boil, and cook until *al dente*. Drain.

Blanch the *sansai* in simmering water for 30 seconds and drain. Drain the black fungus and cut into small shreds.

Bring the broth to a boil. Divide the noodles among four deep bowls. Add a portion of each of the cooked and raw vegetables and the fish cake to each bowl, pour on the broth, and serve at once.

We call the gray-black edible dried fungus "cloud ear" or "wood ear" for its appearance. Its texture, if you can compare it from personal experience, has the crunchy chewiness of a pig's ear—a favorite Chinese snack. There the resemblance ends. Dried fungus, small and twisted when dried, expands to four times its volume on soaking. Bundle it up when softened, cut into fine shreds, then treat like any other mushroom.

Kitsune

These noodles are named *kitsune*, or "fox noodles," because foxes are said to have quite a fancy for tofu and would steal a quick meal of it if they had the chance. The thin slices of tofu are simmered in a sweet soy sauce before being added to the soup.

Serves 3 to 4

> **14 ounces dried udon *(thick wheat noodles)***
> **12 spinach leaves**
> **Eight 2-inch squares aburage *(deep-fried tofu/bean curd)***
> **¾ cup sliced whole scallions**

> BROTH:
> **5 cups Dashi Stock No. 2 (page 24)**
> **1 tablespoon sake *(Japanese rice wine)***
> **3 tablespoons tamari or light soy sauce**
> **½ teaspoon salt**
> **3 to 4 teaspoons sugar**

> SAUCE FOR BEAN CURD:
> **1 cup Dashi Stock No. 2**
> **2½ tablespoons tamari or light soy sauce**
> **1¾ teaspoons sugar**

Bring 2 quarts of water to a boil. Add the noodles and cook until it returns to a boil. Add ½ cup of cold water, bring back to a boil, add another ½ cup of cold water, and bring back to a boil again. Cook until barely tender. Drain.

Rinse the spinach leaves thoroughly and cut off their stems. To prepare the broth, bring the stock to a boil, add the *sake* and the spinach, and boil 1 minute. Season with soy sauce, salt, and sugar and cook another minute. Retrieve the spinach with a wire skimmer and set aside to cool.

Place the tofu in a dish and cover with boiling water, steep for 5 to 6 minutes, then drain and squeeze out as much water as possible. This removes excess oil. Place tofu in a saucepan with the sauce ingredients, simmer for 10 minutes over medium heat, and drain.

Bring 1½ quarts of water to a boil and add the noodles to reheat them. Drain and divide among three or four bowls. Stack the spinach leaves and roll into a tight cylinder. Cut across into 3 to 4 pieces. Place one in each bowl with 2 pieces of simmered tofu and pour on the broth. Add the scallions and serve at once.

Make your own aburage *by slicing fresh, semifirm (cotton) tofu into slices 2 inches square and ⅙ inch thick. Heat a 1-inch layer of vegetable oil in a flat pan, add 2 tablespoons of sesame oil, and fry the bean curd for about 6 minutes, until the surface is a deep golden brown, bubbly, and partially crisped. Remove and drain on absorbent paper.*

ori is the thin seaweed

Nori is the thin seaweed sheet used to wrap rolled sushi. The Japanese like to sprinkle shreds of it over noodles and soups as a garnish. Nori should be toasted before use to bring out its full flavor and improve its texture. Hold a sheet several inches over a high gas flame, or over the heating element of an electric cooker. It is ready when it develops a toasty fragrance and the edges begin to singe and curl up; this takes no more than about 20 seconds. Use a very sharp knife or kitchen shears to cut a sheet into ¼-inch strips, then cut across the strips into shreds. Store in an airtight container.

Seaweed and Fried Tofu on Udon

Serves 4

> 1½ *pounds fresh* **udon** *(wheat-flour noodles, page 18)*
> ½ *ounce dried* **wakame** *(curly seaweed), soaked for 25 minutes in warm water*
> 2 *quarts* **noodle broth** *(page 24)*
> 4 *pieces* **aburage** *(fried tofu/bean curd; see sidebar, page 175)*
> 2 *to 3 ounces canned* **nameko** *mushrooms, drained, or* ⅔ *cup finely grated* **tororo** *(mountain yam); omit if unavailable*
> ½ *cup sliced* **scallion greens**
> 2 *tablespoons shredded* **nori** *(compressed seaweed; see sidebar)*
> **Shichimi** *(Japanese pepper condiment) to taste*

Bring 2 quarts of water to a boil, add the noodles, cook for about 2½ to 3 minutes, until tender, and drain. Drain the seaweed and cut into small pieces, about 1 inch x ½ inch. Heat the noodle broth and add the seaweed. Simmer for 5 minutes.

Bring 1½ cups of water to a boil. Place the tofu in a dish and pour on the boiling water, soak for a few minutes, then drain and squeeze out excess water. Dry between pieces of paper towel. Cut the bean curd into thin slices. It may be simmered in a sweet soy sauce to intensify its flavor, as in the previous recipe.

Divide the noodles among four deep bowls. Pour on the broth and seaweed, add the bean curd, the mushrooms or *tororo*, and the scallions. Scatter on *nori* shreds and add *shichimi* to taste.

Classic Cold Soba

These delicious chilled noodles are served on flat cane baskets or lacquered trays, with sauce in a bowl at the side. Diners add ginger, scallions, and *wasabi* to the sauce to suit their own taste.

Serves 4

> 1 pound dried **soba** *or* **cha-soba** *noodles (see sidebar)*
> 2 teaspoons **sesame oil**
> ½ sheet **nori** *(compressed seaweed)*
> ¾ cup chopped whole **scallions**
> One 2-inch piece fresh **ginger**
> 1 tablespoon **wasabi** *powder or paste*
>
> DIPPING SAUCE:
> 1½ cups **water**
> ¾ cup lightly compacted **katsuobushi** *(bonito flakes)*
> ⅓ cup **tamari** *or light soy sauce*
> 3 tablespoons **mirin** *(Japanese sweet rice wine)*
> 2 teaspoons **fine sugar**

Bring 2 quarts of water to a boil, add the noodles, and bring the water back to a boil. Pour in 1 cup of cold water and return to a boil. Add another cup of cold water, return to a boil, and cook for about 3 minutes, until the noodles are barely tender. Drain, rinse under running cold water, and drain again. Transfer to a bowl and sprinkle on the sesame oil, then cover and chill.

Toast the *nori* over a flame until it turns bright green and feels crisp (see sidebar, page 176). Cut into fine shreds. Peel and grate the ginger very fine. If using *wasabi* powder, make a paste with cold water and a little *sake*.

Combine the sauce ingredients in a saucepan and bring to a boil. Reduce the heat and simmer for 3 minutes. Remove from the heat and leave to cool, then strain through a fine sieve and chill.

Serve the noodles in tangles on flat cane baskets, lacquered trays, or chilled plates. You may want to brush the plates with sesame oil to prevent the noodles from sticking.

Scatter the shredded *nori* on top and give each diner a small tray containing a little dish of scallions, a mound of ginger, a portion of *wasabi*, and a bowl of the dipping sauce.

This recipe is a good showcase for the unusual taste of cha-soba, *which are buckwheat noodles colored and flavored with finely ground, bright green Japanese tea leaves. Cha-soba are also good served simply in a* dashi *stock with one large, crisp-battered tempura shrimp.*

Mushroom Soba Salad

Serves 2 to 4

> *½ pound* soba *(buckwheat noodles)*
> *2 teaspoons sesame oil*
> *12 large dried* shiitake *mushrooms, soaked for 30 minutes*
> *2 cups Dashi Stock No. 1 (page 23)*
> *2 teaspoons fine sugar*
> *3 thin slices fresh ginger*
> *1 tablespoon tamari or light soy sauce*
> *12 spinach leaves*
> *4 ounces canned* enokitake *mushrooms, drained*

> **DRESSING:**
> *⅓ cup* mirin *(Japanese sweet rice wine)*
> *⅓ cup dark soy sauce*
> *2 tablespoons lightly compacted* katsuobushi *(shaved bonito; see sidebar)*
> *2 tablespoons preserved pink ginger, finely sliced*

Bring 1½ quarts of water to a boil, add the noodles, and cook until tender. Drain well, then sprinkle with the sesame oil and set aside.

Drain the *shiitake* mushrooms and trim the stems close to the caps. Place these mushrooms in a small saucepan with the *dashi*, sugar, ginger, and soy sauce. Bring to a boil and reduce the heat to medium. Partially cover the pan and cook the mushrooms for 20 minutes. Remove the mushrooms with a skimmer. Cut into fine strips and set aside.

Strain the mushroom stock through a fine nylon strainer and discard the ginger. Thoroughly rinse the spinach. Reheat the stock, add the spinach leaves, poach for 1 minute, and remove with a strainer. Strain the stock again if necessary. There should be 1 cup of liquid.

To make the dressing, boil the *mirin* in a small saucepan until reduced by half. Add the mushroom stock and remaining sauce ingredients, simmer for 5 minutes, and strain. Pour into four dipping bowls.

Arrange the noodles in bundles on chilled plates. Scatter the sliced *shiitake* mushrooms and the *enoki* mushrooms over the top. Stack the spinach leaves together and roll into a sausage shape. Cut into four even-sized pieces and place one beside each serving of noodles with a little mound of preserved ginger. Serve the dressing separately, for dipping.

Japanese cooks use katsuobushi, feathery flakes of dried bonito, as the base ingredient for their dashi stock. Its companion is the wide, salted, tangle kelp, kombu. Together they give the taste that makes Japanese food unique. After you buy katsuobushi, it must be stored in an airtight container, accompanied by a sachet of silica gel to keep it dry. When used to make up a stock, the first infusion in hot water has the best flavor. Subsequent infusions can be made, but each at a loss of taste and aroma.

Chilled Noodles with Chicken and Vegetable Shreds

Serves 6

1 pound dried **somen** (*fine wheat-starch noodles*)

1 pound skinless, boneless chicken breast

1½ tablespoons **mirin** (*Japanese sweet rice wine*)

Few drops chili powder or chili oil

3 small Japanese cucumbers (*or acid-free cucumbers about 3 inches long*), *cut into matchstick-sized pieces*

1 small **daikon** (*icicle radish*), *about 5 inches long (or a 5-inch part of a larger one), cut into matchstick-sized pieces*

1 medium carrot, *cut into matchstick-sized pieces*

½ cup finely sliced scallion greens

DRESSING:

⅓ cup white sesame seeds

1 cup Dashi Stock No. 1 (*page 23*), *or 1 to 1¼ teaspoons instant* **dashi** *granules in 1 cup of warm water*

¼ cup **mirin** (*Japanese sweet rice wine*)

2 teaspoons fine white sugar

⅓ cup **tamari** or light soy sauce

On a hot day, I serve this over ice, by filling a wide, shallow dish with cracked ice and arranging the salad over it. Think of this dish the next time you're preparing a picnic lunch. It's easy enough to pack and transport and is deliciously refreshing.

Bring a pan of water to a boil, add the noodles, and cook until *al dente*. Drain, rinse with cold water, drain again, and set aside.

Cut the chicken into ½-inch slices, arrange on a heatproof plate, and sprinkle with 1½ tablespoons *mirin* and chili powder or oil. Set on a rack in a steamer to cook for 15 minutes. Remove and allow to cool.

Arrange the chicken, cucumber, radish, and carrot around the edge of a large platter and mound the noodles in the center. Scatter on the scallions, then cover and chill.

To prepare the dressing, cook the sesame seeds in a dry skillet over medium heat until they smell fabulously toasty. Grind in a mortar or a spice grinder. Bring the remaining sauce ingredients to a slow boil, reduce the heat, and simmer for 3 minutes. Remove from the heat and cool over ice. Stir in the ground sesame seeds. Serve the sauce in individual dipping bowls, with the platter in the center of the table.

Tororo is one of several types of edible yam enjoyed in Japan. This particular one has white flesh which, when grated, becomes rather sticky and viscous, with a texture not unlike un-cooked egg white. It is said to be an excellent digestive.

Yamakake Noodles

Serves 4

14 ounces soba *or* udon
½ cup chopped whole scallions, rinsed (see sidebar, page 165)
½ cup shredded nori (compressed seaweed; see sidebar, page 176)
3 ounces kamaboko (fish cake), thinly sliced
¾ cup finely grated tororo (mountain yam); omit if unavailable
3 cups Dashi Stock No. 2 (page 24)

DIPPING SAUCE:
¼ cup tamari or light soy sauce
2 tablespoons mirin (Japanese sweet rice wine)
1 tablespoon sugar

Bring 2 quarts of water to a boil, add the noodles, and cook until they are barely tender, testing frequently after 2½ minutes of cooking. Drain well and divide among four bowls.

Add scallion, *nori*, and *kamaboko* to each bowl and place a spoonful of the grated yam on top, if using. Combine the sauce ingredients, bring to a boil, and simmer for 3 to 4 minutes. Pour into a jug to cool.

Heat the *dashi* to boiling and pour over the noodles. Pour a little of the dipping sauce into a small dish for each guest. Serve the noodles hot, or allow to cool to room temperature.

This tangy, salty dip can be served with plain noodles of any kind, warm or cold, as a quick snack: Combine ¼ cup mirin (sweet rice wine) with ½ cup broth made by adding ½ teaspoon pow-dered or granulated instant dashi to 2 tablespoons light soy sauce and 2½ teaspoons freshly squeezed lemon or lime juice. Add a tea-spoon of sugar. Heat together for 1 minute, then cool.

Iced Hiyashi Somen

Serves 2 to 4

6 ounces somen (fine wheat-flour noodles)
4 large shrimp
4 shiitake mushrooms (if dried, soak in warm water for 30 minutes)
2½ tablespoons light or tamari soy sauce
2 teaspoons sugar
2 tablespoons mirin (Japanese sweet rice wine)
2 to 4 sprigs mitsuba (Japanese parsley) or watercress

DIPPING SAUCE:
1 cup Dashi Stock No. 2 (page 24)

⅓ cup mirin (Japanese sweet rice wine)
⅓ cup dark soy sauce
1 teaspoon fine sugar

Bring 1½ quarts of lightly salted water to a boil and add the noodles. Return to a boil, add 1 cup of cold water, and when it comes to a boil again allow the noodles to cook for about 1½ minutes before testing. They should be barely tender. Drain, rinse in cold water, and set aside to drain again.

Shell the shrimp, leaving the tails on, and devein. Poach in a small pan of lightly salted water until tender, about 2½ minutes. Drain and cool by plunging into cold water. Set aside.

Trim off the woody mushroom stems, place the mushroom caps in a small pan, and add the soy sauce, sugar, and *mirin*. Add ⅓ cup water. If using dried mushrooms, cover and cook very gently for 10 minutes; if using fresh, cook for 2 minutes. Drain. Cut the caps into narrow shreds.

Combine the sauce ingredients and heat for 1 minute, pour into small dip dishes, and allow to cool. Assemble the noodles in a tangled bundle over a bed of cracked ice on a small tray, or place equal portions in lacquered bowls and cover with ice water. Place a shrimp and a little mound of mushroom shreds beside them, and decorate with the parsley or watercress. Serve immediately with the dipping sauce.

When preparing mushrooms to use whole in a dish, Japanese cooks cut a cross in the cap as a traditional decorative touch. Drain the mushrooms, then use a small, sharp knife to cut out one shallow wedge from just inside one edge to the other. Turn the mushroom 180 degrees and cut another wedge of the same depth and length. See also notes on mushroom preparation, page 170.

Udon Hot Pot
(NABEYAKI UDON)

Serves 4

1 pound dried **udon** *(wheat-flour noodles)*
½ *pound boneless chicken breast, skin on*
4-ounce cake *"cotton"* tofu *(semifirm bean curd)*
2 ounces kamaboko *(Japanese fish cake)*
8 *small whole scallions*
4 shiitake mushrooms *(if dried, soak for 25 minutes in cold water)*
4 eggs
shichimi *(Japanese pepper condiment)*
4 tempura shrimp *(optional; see page 167 for procedure)*

BROTH:
5 cups Dashi Stock No. 2 *(page 24)*
¼ cup tamari or light soy sauce
2 teaspoons dark soy sauce
1½ tablespoons mirin *(Japanese sweet rice wine)*
1½ tablespoons sugar

Bring 1½ quarts of water to a boil, add the noodles, and bring the water back to a boil. Pour in 1 cup of cold water and again bring to a boil. Add another 1 cup of cold water and bring back to a boil. Cook for 2 minutes, then test. For this recipe the noodles should be still quite firm at this stage. Drain and cover with cold water.

Cut the chicken, tofu, and *kamaboko* into 4 even-sized pieces. Set aside. Cut the greens of 2 scallions into thin slices and set aside. Diagonally cut the remaining scallions into 3-inch pieces.

Heat the broth ingredients to boiling, then reduce the heat and keep warm. Divide the noodles evenly among 4 individual serving casseroles. Add the chicken, *kamaboko*, tofu, mushrooms, and scallion pieces to each casserole, add the broth, cover, and simmer for 6 to 7 minutes; they could also be cooked in the microwave on high for 2 minutes or placed in a hot oven (375°F) for 10 minutes.

Use chopsticks to make a depression in the center of the noodles. Break an egg over each portion of noodles. Place the tempura shrimp (if using) beside the egg. Cover the casseroles again and cook for another 2 to 3 minutes, without allowing the eggs to become too firm. Remove the covers, sprinkle on the reserved scallion greens, and take the casseroles straight to the table, placing them on heat-resistant mats. Serve *shichimi* on the side in its shaker dispenser.

In Japanese homes and restaurants sukiyaki is cooked in a flat, cast-iron pan with 1½-inch sides, rather like a skillet without a side handle but with a looped wire handle over the top. Sukiyaki can be cooked on a tabletop heating device of whatever kind you have available, such as a portable gas stove or electric skillet, but it must be capable of reasonable heat—a fondue spirit-burner would not provide sufficient heat.

Each guest cooks his own food in small quantities, beginning with the meat, then the vegetables and tofu, and finally the noodles. Meat is usually cooked rare. If your guests don't care for the taste or health risk of raw egg, reassure them they can forgo this step without offense.

Sukiyaki

Serves 6

> *1½ pounds sirloin or porterhouse steak*
> *9 ounces shiratake filaments (sukiyaki noodles)*
> *12 large dried shiitake mushrooms, soaked for 25 minutes in warm*
>   *water*
> *6 leeks*
> *6 large scallions*
> *14 ounces Napa cabbage*
> *12 ounces fresh soft tofu (bean curd)*
> *6 large eggs*
> *2-ounce piece fresh suet (or vegetable oil, if unavailable)*

> SAUCE:
> *1¼ cups Dashi Stock No. 2 (page 24)*
> *1 cup tamari or light soy sauce*
> *¼ cup dark soy sauce*
> *¾ cup mirin (Japanese sweet rice wine)*
> *3 tablespoons fine sugar*

Trim the steak of excess fat and any surface membrane. Cut across the grain into slices so thin you can almost see through them. Arrange them, overlapped, on a platter.

Soften *shiratake* filaments in hot water, drain well.

Drain the mushrooms and use a small, sharp knife to trim the stems close to the cap. Trim the leeks at the root end and remove most of the green leaves, leaving only the pale green, tightly packed stem section. Cut this into 1¼-inch lengths, then cut across each of these at a sharp angle; this will produce pieces that will each have a flat base and one sharply sloping side. Stand these on the platter and arrange the mushrooms near them.

Trim the scallions and cut into 1¼-inch pieces, discarding at least half of the green tops. Cut the Napa cabbage into 1¼-inch slices. Cut the tofu into 1-inch cubes. Arrange scallions, cabbage, and tofu on the platter with the other ingredients.

Combine sauce ingredients in a small saucepan, bring to a boil, then reduce the heat slightly. Simmer for 1 minute, then strain into a jug and take to the table.

If using eggs, break an egg into each of six bowls and place at each table setting.

Assemble a tabletop cooking pan (see sidebar, page 184) and heat it. Rub the suet over the surface of the pan until it is well greased (or moisten with vegetable oil). Add a portion of the sauce; when it begins to bubble, the cooking can begin.

Using wooden chopsticks or fondue forks, everyone cooks his or her own meal. The ingredients should not swim in the sauce but be glazed by them. Add a little water to the pan from time to time during the meal, as the sauce will become more concentrated as it cooks.

Dip each mouthful of cooked food into the beaten egg before eating; the heat of the ingredients will partially cook the egg, turning it into a creamy coating (see sidebar).

vegetarian dishes

Noodles are a useful and beneficial ingredient in the vegetarian diet. They offer a satisfying chewability and provide essential fiber and energizing carbohydrates. They can be adapted to many cooking styles and combined with all kinds of ingredients to make nourishing and delicious meals.

Soba, the buff-colored Japanese buckwheat noodles, are a particular favorite among vegetarian cooks, their special nutty taste suited to hot dishes, soups, and salads. Imitation "egg" noodles, made without egg, are a boon for the vegan, while rice noodles are an excellent and easily digested substitute for rice or other carbohydrates in many menu applications.

Chinese noodle makers also manufacture a limited range of wheat-starch noodles or imitation egg noodles flavored and colored with vegetable extracts. They look wonderful on the plate and have subtle and appealing flavor undertones.

I have selected recipes from all over Asia for this collection of vegetarian noodle dishes, all of which could accept the addition of sliced or shredded meat or seafood for nonvegetarian cooking. They encapsulate a full range of Asian flavors and include several deliciously refreshing salads, which could be served as first courses or as part of a wider menu of main courses in the Asian style.

Soba in Broth with Leeks

Serves 4

> 13 ounces **soba** *(dried buckwheat noodles)*
> 1 tablespoon **white sesame seeds**
> 3 small, tender **leeks** *(or 4 large whole scallions)*
>
> BROTH:
> 5 cups **Dashi Stock No. 1** *(page 23)*
> 3½ tablespoons **dark soy sauce**
> 2 tablespoons **sugar**
> 2 tablespoons **mirin** *(Japanese sweet rice wine)*
> **Salt**

Bring 1 quart of water to a boil. Add the noodles, and when the water boils again, add 1 cup of cold water. When it boils again, add a final cup of water. Cook the noodles until al dente, about 3 minutes.

Japanese dashi contains extracts of bonito fish. If this cannot be used in your diet plan, substitute a combination of two broths, one made by infusing kombu (kelp), the other by simmering dried shiitake mushrooms.

Toast the sesame seeds in a hot oven or in a dry nonstick pan over medium heat until they are aromatic, golden, and beginning to pop. Remove. Trim the leeks or scallions and cut into 3-inch pieces. Cut in half lengthwise, then into very fine shreds.

Combine the broth ingredients in a saucepan and bring to a boil. Reduce the heat and keep warm.

Bring a large pan of water to a boil. Transfer the noodles to a strainer and immerse in the boiling water to reheat. Drain well. Divide among four warmed bowls, pour on the broth, and garnish each bowl with leeks and sesame seeds.

Vegetarian Soup Noodles

This is a good "catch-all" dish. Any bits of vegetable and any type of noodle could be used to make a filling bowl of soup noodles. I like to add "egg threads," beaten egg added to the hot soup in a thin stream so it forms fine threads, and I pep up the flavor with a dash of Chinese red vinegar.

Serves 6

2 ounces rice-stick noodles
1 ounce bean-thread vermicelli
4 scallions
1 piece **gai larn** (Chinese cabbage)
1 cup small cauliflower florets
2 cups vegetable stock (pages 27-28) or water
1 medium carrot, peeled and sliced
1 1/2 tablespoons vegetable oil
1/2 cup sliced bamboo shoots
1/4 cup sliced straw or oyster mushrooms
1 ounce fresh bean sprouts
1/2 cup cubed soft tofu (bean curd)

BROTH:
5 cups vegetable stock or water
3 teaspoons dark soy sauce
1 1/2 tablespoons tamari or light soy sauce
Salt and freshly ground black pepper

Bring 3 cups of water to a boil, add the rice sticks, and boil until tender. Drain, rinse under running cold water, and set aside. Soak the bean-thread vermicelli in hot water for 7 minutes to soften. Trim the scallions, cut the white ends into 1-inch pieces, and shred some of the green tops for garnish.

Cut the *gai larn* stem into 1-inch lengths and chop the leaves coarsely. Blanch the stems and cauliflower for 2 minutes in 2 cups vegetable stock and remove, reserving the stock.

Heat the oil in a wok over high heat. Stir-fry the carrot slices for 1 minute and remove. Add the drained *gai larn*, cauliflower, and scallions and stir-fry for 1 minute. Add the bamboo shoots and straw mushrooms and stir-fry another minute.

Pour the broth ingredients, plus the stock used for cooking the *gai larn*, into a pot and bring to a boil. Add the blanched vegetables and simmer until tender. Check the seasonings, then add the rice sticks, vermicelli, *gai larn* leaves, bean sprouts, and bean curd. Warm through and serve.

Thai Jumbo Spring Rolls

Makes 8 large rolls; serves 8 as an appetizer or 4 as a main course

3 ounces bean-thread vermicelli
6 dried black mushrooms, soaked in cold water for 25 minutes
4 ounces firm tofu (bean curd)
1 cup finely shredded bamboo shoots
½ cup finely shredded carrot
½ cup finely shredded jicama or celery
¾ cup fresh bean sprouts, pods and roots removed
¼ cup loosely packed cilantro (Chinese parsley) leaves
⅓ cup shredded scallion
8 large spring roll wrappers
2 quarts oil for deep-frying
3 tablespoons nam pla (Thai fish sauce)
⅓ teaspoon white pepper
1 tablespoon minced garlic

FOR DIPPING:
Sweet-and-sour sauce
Hoisin sauce
Sweet or hot chili sauce
Nam pla (Thai fish sauce)

These make an elegant appetizer. Cut in half diagonally, place in the center of a plate, and surround with diced tomato and cucumber and individual cilantro leaves. Drizzle sweet-and-sour sauce in lines over the rolls, or serve two sauces in separate pools on the plate.

Soak the vermicelli in hot water for 15 minutes. Pour into a fine strainer to drain. Drain the mushrooms, squeeze out excess water, remove the stems, and cut the caps into fine shreds. Slice the tofu thin, then stack the slices and cut them into very fine shreds. Prepare the vegetables and combine in a mixing bowl, adding the cilantro and scallion.

Separate the spring roll wrappers and cover with a damp kitchen towel. Heat the oil to 360°F.

Cut the vermicelli into 1½-inch pieces and add to the vegetables along with the tofu, fish sauce, pepper, and garlic. Mix thoroughly.

Position the wrapper diagonally in front of you and place a portion of the filling on each wrapper, slightly above the center. Fold the top point over the filling and press to form a sausage shape. Fold in the two sides, then roll toward you. Moisten the remaining point of the wrapper with water and fold onto the roll, squeezing gently to make it adhere.

Fry the rolls, three or four at a time, for about 4 minutes, until golden brown and cooked through. Drain on absorbent paper before serving hot with the dipping sauces.

Unripe papaya and mango are common ingredients in Thai salads, giving them a pleasing hint of tartness. Japanese apples, firm and slightly underripe pears, or jicama are more accessible alternatives.

"glass noodle" salad
(YAM WUN SEN)
Serves 4 to 6

4 ounces fine bean-thread or sukiyaki noodles
3 cloves garlic, peeled and finely sliced
6 red or French shallots, peeled and finely sliced
3 ounces firm tofu (bean curd), cut into very small dice
⅓ cup flavorless vegetable oil
1 cup finely sliced Napa cabbage
1 cup finely sliced romaine lettuce
1 rib of celery, finely sliced diagonally
1 small carrot, finely sliced diagonally
1 cup coarsely grated or julienned unripe (green) papaya or mango
1 to 2 green chili peppers, seeded and very finely minced
1 red onion, finely sliced
¼ cup loosely packed cilantro (Chinese parsley) leaves

SALAD DRESSING:
¼ cup nam pla (Thai fish sauce) or tamari or light soy sauce

¼ cup fresh lime juice

1½ teaspoons palm or dark brown (Barbados) sugar

2 teaspoons toasted white sesame seeds or finely chopped roasted
   peanuts

Soak the noodles in warm water to soften, drain thoroughly, and cut into 3-inch lengths.

Fry the garlic, shallots, and tofu in the oil over high heat until crisp and golden brown. Spread on absorbent paper to drain. Reserve the oil to add to the dressing. Whisk the dressing ingredients together, adding oil to taste. Continue to whisk until emulsified. Set aside.

Prepare the remaining ingredients and combine in a large bowl. Add the noodles, the fried ingredients, and the dressing and toss thoroughly. Serve piled high on a serving platter.

Cold Buckwheat Noodle Salad

Serves 4

½ **pound dried** soba **(buckwheat noodles)**

2 to 3 teaspoons sesame oil

2 whole scallions

1 red bell pepper, cored, seeded, and cut into thin strips

1 small cucumber, seeded and thinly sliced into crescents

2½ teaspoons toasted white sesame seeds

DRESSING:

1 tablespoon tamari or light soy sauce

1 tablespoon Chinese brown (dark) rice vinegar

1 tablespoon freshly squeezed lemon juice

2 teaspoons sesame oil

1½ teaspoons mirin (Japanese sweet rice wine)

1 teaspoon sugar

Combine the dressing ingredients in a bowl, whisking to blend well.

Bring 1½ quarts of water to a boil, add the noodles, and bring the water back to a boil. Add ½ cup of cold water and bring back to a boil, then add another ½ cup of cold water, bring back to a boil again, and cook 2 to 3 minutes. Drain thoroughly. Stir in 2 to 3 teaspoons of sesame oil and set aside.

Cold noodles are great picnic fare. Store the noodles in a sealed container over ice, and pack the dressing separately.

Trim the scallions and cut both white and green parts into 1½-inch pieces. Cut in half lengthwise and then shred fine. Combine the noodles, scallions, bell pepper, and cucumber, toss with the dressing, and serve in attractive little mounds on lacquered platters, with sesame seeds scattered on top.

Vegetable Yaki Soba

Serves 4

> *3 dried shiitake mushrooms, soaked for 30 minutes in cold water*
> *8 ounces vegetable-flavored* somen *noodles*
> *3 tablespoons vegetable oil*
> *1½ cups finely shredded Napa (Chinese) cabbage*
> *8 spinach leaves, shredded*
> *1 medium carrot, peeled and julienned*
> *1 small* daikon *(icicle radish), peeled and julienned*
> *1 tablespoon very finely shredded fresh ginger*
> *6 ounces fresh bean sprouts*
> *1 whole scallion, very finely sliced*
> *¼ cup Japanese* tonkatsu *sauce (recipe follows)*

Drain the mushrooms and squeeze out excess water, then trim the stems and finely shred the caps.

Bring 1 quart of lightly salted water to a boil. Add the noodles and cook for about 3 minutes, until barely tender, and drain well.

Heat half the oil in a wok or large skillet over high heat and stir-fry the mushrooms, carrot, spinach, cabbage, and radish until barely tender, about 2 minutes. Set aside.

Heat remaining oil in another pan over high heat and sauté the noodles for 1½ minutes. Add ginger and sauté a further 45 seconds.

Add the cooked vegetables to the noodles along with the bean sprouts and scallions and cook for 1 minute on high heat, mixing thoroughly. Add the *tonkatsu* sauce, heat well, and stir to distribute the sauce evenly through the noodles. Serve.

Tonkatsu Sauce:

To make *tonkatsu* sauce, boil 2 tablespoons mirin (Japanese sweet rice wine) until reduced by half. Stir in 2 tablespoons ketchup, 1 tablespoon dark soy sauce, 1 tablespoon tamari or light soy sauce, 1 tablespoon Worcestershire sauce, 1 tablespoon mustard, and sugar to taste. Heat briefly, then allow to cool. Store in the refrigerator. Makes ⅔ cup.

Spicy Vegetarian Noodles from Singapore

Serves 4

> 10 ounces fine rice vermicelli
> 3 ounces firm tofu (bean curd)
> 2½ tablespoons peanut oil or mild-flavored vegetable oil
> 1 teaspoon sesame oil
> 1 large onion, halved and finely sliced
> 1 medium carrot, julienned
> 2 to 3 ribs of celery, julienned
> ½ green bell pepper, seeded and julienned
> ½ red bell pepper, seeded and julienned
> 1 teaspoon minced garlic
> 1½ teaspoons minced fresh ginger
> 1 tablespoon mild curry powder
> 2 teaspoons sugar
> 2 tablespoons tamari or light soy sauce
> 3 ounces fresh bean sprouts, blanched for 30 seconds in simmering
>   water and drained
> 1½ ounces garlic chives, cut into 2-inch pieces
> Salt and freshly ground black pepper
> 1½ teaspoons toasted sesame seeds

Soak the vermicelli in hot water until softened, about 8 minutes. Drain thoroughly and spread on a tray to partially dry.   Slice the tofu thin, then cut into narrow strips.

Heat both types of oil in a wok or skillet over high heat until a haze of smoke appears over the pan. Stir-fry the tofu for 2 minutes, until the surface is slightly crisp. Remove.

Toasted sesame seeds are a delicious, nutty additive to just about any noodle dish. Have a supply on hand; they will keep for weeks in a sealed spice jar. Heat a nonstick pan or wok, without oil, and pour in the sesame seeds. Cook over medium heat, shaking the pan to turn the seeds, until they are very aromatic and begin to pop, about 2½ minutes. Pour into a container and cool before sealing.

Add the onion and carrot and stir-fry over medium heat for about 3 minutes, until the onion is lightly browned and soft and the carrot is crisp-tender. Add the celery, peppers, garlic, and ginger, increase the heat to high, and stir-fry for about 2 minutes.

Add the noodles, curry powder, sugar, and soy sauce and stir-fry on high heat until the ingredients are thoroughly combined and the noodles are heated through. Add the bean sprouts, garlic chives, and salt and pepper to taste and stir-fry another 1 minute. Transfer to a warm serving plate and sprinkle with toasted sesame seeds.

If you are fortunate enough to have access to freshly extracted coconut milk, use it whenever you can. Canned coconut milk varies enormously from brand to brand. When making your selection, shake the can and listen to the slosh of the contents. A thinner coconut milk will splash more noisily than a thicker extraction, which is usually a better value as it can be thinned with water if necessary. Coconut milk does not keep well, so decant any unused portion into a small container and freeze. It can be added, without thawing, to your next dish.

Indonesian-Style Vermicelli in Coconut Sauce

Generous one-bowl meal.
Serves 4 to 6

> **6 ounces rice vermicelli**
> **2 large potatoes, peeled and sliced**
> **½ pound green beans, cut into 2-inch lengths**
> **2 small carrots, peeled and sliced**
> **1½ tablespoons peanut or vegetable oil**
> **4 ounces firm tofu (bean curd), sliced**
> **1 pound Napa cabbage, sliced**
> **3 ounces fresh bean sprouts**
> **4 whole scallions, cut into 1½-inch pieces**
> **2 tablespoons chopped cilantro (Chinese parsley) leaves**
> **1 tablespoon chopped basil leaves**
> **Freshly squeezed lime juice**
> **Salt and freshly ground black pepper**
> **Fish and soy sauce to taste**

> COCONUT SAUCE:
> **2 tablespoons peanut or vegetable oil**
> **1 cup finely chopped yellow onion**
> **4 cloves garlic, minced**
> **1 fresh red chili, seeded and minced**
> **2 lemon grass stems, trimmed and halved lengthwise**
> **2 teaspoons minced fresh ginger**

1 tablespoon ground coriander

1 teaspoon ground cumin

1 teaspoon ground laos (galangal)

½ teaspoon freshly ground black pepper

¾ teaspoon blacan/trassi (shrimp paste), or 2 to 3 teaspoons yellow
    bean sauce

1 teaspoon soft brown or palm sugar

3 curry leaves (optional)

3 cups coconut milk

3 cups vegetable stock (pages 27-28)

Soak the vermicelli in warm water for 8 minutes.

To make the sauce, heat the 2 tablespoons of peanut oil in a wok or
large skillet over medium heat and stir-fry the onion until softened and
and golden brown, about 4 minutes. Add the garlic, chili, lemon grass,
and ginger and sauté briefly, then add the spices and stir. Mash the
shrimp paste or yellow bean sauce against the side of the pan and stir
in. Add the sugar, curry leaves, and coconut milk and bring to a boil.
Simmer for about 12 minutes, until the coconut milk has thickened
and separated—a film of oil will float on the surface.

Add the stock, potatoes, beans, and carrots and cook until vegetables
are barely tender, about 10 minutes.

In the meantime, drain the vermicelli thoroughly. Heat the 1½ tablespoons of peanut oil in a small pan and fry the tofu until golden.
Use a slotted spoon to transfer it to the sauce along with the noodles,
cabbage, bean sprouts, scallions, and half the cilantro. Cook for 3 to 4
minutes, then add the basil leaves. Check the seasonings, adding salt,
black pepper, lime juice, and fish sauce or soy sauce to taste. Serve in
deep dishes, garnishing with the reserved cilantro.

When I have the minutes to spare, and it only takes a few, I fry my own tofu to achieve a fresher flavor. Cut soft but firm fresh (cotton) tofu (bean curd) into 1½-inch cubes and slide carefully into hot oil in a wok. Fry until the surface is golden brown and slightly bubbly, about 6 minutes. The interior of each cube will be partially cooked away.

Vegetable Combination on Browned Noodles

Serves 2, or 4 sharing several dishes

> **6 ounces thin egg noodles**
> **4 ounces firm tofu (bean curd)**
> **4 2-inch pieces fried tofu (bean curd; see sidebar, page 200)**
> **1 medium onion**
> **1½ cups vegetable oil**
> **½ rib of celery, thinly sliced**
> **¼ cup diced red bell pepper**
> **¼ cup sliced straw mushrooms**
> **¼ cup sliced bamboo shoots**
> **6 snow peas**
> **6 spinach leaves**
> **1 tablespoon tamari or light soy sauce**
>
> SAUCE:
> **¾ cup vegetable stock (pages 27-28) or water**
> **2 teaspoons dark soy sauce**
> **1 teaspoon sugar**
> **2 teaspons cornstarch**

Bring 2 quarts of water to a boil, add the noodles, and boil until barely tender. Pour into a colander and set aside to drain. Slice the raw tofu thin and cut into strips. Cut the fried tofu into quarters. Peel the onion and cut into thin wedges, separating the layers (see sidebar, page 68).

Heat the oil in a wok or skillet over high heat until a haze of smoke floats over the pan. Place the noodles in the pan in a thick layer and cook without disturbing for 2 minutes, or until well browned underneath. Turn and cook the other side, then lift onto a serving plate and keep warm.

Pour off all but 2 tablespoons of the oil. Stir-fry the onion until softened and golden brown, 2½ to 3 minutes. Add the tofu and stir-fry 1 minute. Add the celery and peppers and stir-fry for 1 minute, then add the remaining vegetables and heat through. Add the soy sauce, sizzling it against the side of the pan.

Combine the sauce ingredients and pour into the pan. Cook, stirring, until thickened. Pour over the noodles and serve.

Singaporean Vegetarian Chow Mein

Serves 3 to 4

7 ounces thin Chinese noodles

3 dried black mushrooms, soaked for 20 minutes in warm water

8 small broccoli florets

3 tablespoons vegetable oil

1 small carrot, peeled and thinly sliced diagonally

1 rib of celery, thinly sliced diagonally

8 snow or sugar snap peas, stemmed

1 ounce sliced bamboo shoots, rinsed and drained

2 ounces fresh bean sprouts

4 ounces firm tofu (bean curd), thinly sliced

1 teaspoon minced fresh ginger

$\frac{1}{2}$ teaspoon minced fresh garlic

2 tablespoons minced whole scallion

Cilantro (Chinese parsley) leaves

SAUCE:

1$\frac{1}{2}$ tablespoons tamari or light soy sauce

$\frac{1}{3}$ teaspoon chili oil

$\frac{1}{2}$ teaspoon sugar

Salt and freshly ground pepper

$\frac{3}{4}$ cup water or vegetable stock (pages 27-28)

3 teaspoons cornstarch

When I need a meal in minutes for a hungry family or friends, I begin by opening my refrigerator. Whatever bits and pieces of vegetables (or meat) I find are diced and tossed into a hot wok for a huge stir-fry. It's quick and satisfying, and it tidies up the fridge!

Bring 2$\frac{1}{2}$ quarts of salted water to a boil. Add the noodles, bring back to a boil, and stir to untangle the noodle bundles. Reduce heat and cook with the water barely bubbling for 3 to 3$\frac{1}{2}$ minutes, until cooked to firm-tender. Drain, rinse with cold water, and drain again. Set aside.

Drain the mushrooms, squeeze out excess water, and trim the stems. Cut the mushroom caps into narrow strips. Blanch the broccoli in boiling water for 1 minute, drain, refresh under running cold water, and drain again.

Mix the sauce ingredients in a bowl and set aside.

Heat the oil in a wok or large skillet. Add the vegetables, except the bean sprouts, stir-fry for 2 minutes, and remove. In the same pan, stir-fry the tofu on medium-high heat for 2 minutes, and remove. Next, stir-fry the noodles over maximum heat for 1$\frac{1}{2}$ minutes, until well coated with the oil. Add a little extra oil if needed. Remove to a serving plate.

Add the ginger, garlic, and scallion to the pan and cook until aromatic, about 45 seconds. Stir the sauce, pour into the pan, and cook until it begins to thicken. Return the vegetables to the pan and add the bean sprouts and tofu.

Heat thoroughly, stirring until the ingredients are well mixed. Serve over the noodles and garnish with the cilantro.

great gravy noodles

Serves 4

> **6 ounces thin Chinese noodles**
> **5 dried black mushrooms, soaked for 25 minutes in warm water**
> **One 2-inch piece Chinese dried black fungus, soaked for 25 minutes in warm water**
> **4 ounces firm tofu (bean curd)**
> **1½ ounces dried bean curd skin, soaked for 25 minutes in warm water**
> **2 tablespoons dried shrimp (optional), soaked for 25 minutes**
> **1 rib of celery, julienned**
> **4 ounces sliced bamboo shoots, julienned**
> **3 ounces straw mushrooms or champignons, finely sliced**
> **2 to 3 eggs (optional)**
> **Salt and freshly ground black pepper to taste**
> **Sesame oil**
>
> GRAVY:
> **6 cups vegetable stock (pages 27-28)**
> **2½ tablespoons light or tamari soy sauce, or nam pla (Thai fish sauce)**
> **1 tablespoon rice wine or dry sherry**
> **1 teaspoon salt**
> **3½ tablespoons cornstarch**

Bring 1 quart of water to a boil and cook the noodles for about 3½ minutes, until tender. Drain and set aside.

Drain the black mushrooms, trim the stems close to the caps, and cut caps into fine shreds. Drain the fungus and cut into fine shreds. Slice the tofu thin, then stack the slices and cut them into narrow strips.

When bean curd is made, a smooth skin forms on the surface of the setting liquid. Lifted off and dried into a hard, cream-colored sheet, this becomes bean curd skin. Chinese cooks use it as a meat substitute in vegetarian cooking and as an edible wrapper for snacks. It can be boiled, steamed, or fried.

Drain the bean curd skin and cut into noodle-like strips. Drain the shrimp.

To prepare the gravy, bring the stock to a boil and add the soy sauce, rice wine, and salt. Add the fresh and dried mushrooms, the fungus, bean curd, bean curd skin, and shrimp, if using, and simmer on medium heat for 12 minutes.

Add the celery and bamboo shoots and simmer for 3 minutes. Moisten the cornstarch with a little cold water, stir into the gravy, and cook until the mixture thickens slightly.

If you are adding eggs, beat and strain them, then pour into the gravy in a thin stream and cook until set in threads. Check seasonings, adding salt, pepper, and extra soy or fish sauce to taste.

Add the noodles and heat them thoroughly, then pour into deep bowls and sprinkle on a few drops of sesame oil. Serve hot.

Vegetarian Pancit Canton

Serves 6

4 dried black mushrooms, soaked for 20 minutes
1 medium yellow onion, finely sliced
1 small carrot, finely sliced diagonally
½ rib of celery, finely sliced diagonally
1 cup cauliflower or broccoli florets, blanched
3 Napa cabbage leaves, sliced
10 ounces dried thin wheat-starch or somen noodles
3½ tablespoons vegetable oil
7 ounces firm tofu (bean curd), cubed
1½ tablespoons tamari or light soy sauce
1½ teaspoons rice wine or dry sherry
2 cups vegetable stock (pages 27-28)
2 tablespoons cornstarch
Salt and white pepper
1 tablespoon chopped cilantro (Chinese parsley) leaves

Drain the mushrooms, squeeze out excess water, and trim off the stems. Cut the caps into thin slices and set aside. Prepare the remaining vegetables.

Whole-wheat noodles can be used in many of these vegetarian recipes. Compare cooking times recommended on the package with those in the recipe and adjust accordingly.

Bring 1½ quarts of lightly salted water to a boil. Add the noodles and cook for about 4 minutes, to *al dente*. Drain.

Heat the oil in a wok or large, heavy skillet over high heat and stir-fry the tofu for about 1½ minutes. Remove with a slotted spoon and set aside.

Pour half the oil into a small dish, reserving it for later use. Reheat the wok and fry the noodles for 2 minutes over high heat, stirring and tossing to coat with oil. Remove to a serving plate.

Add the reserved oil if needed. Over high heat stir-fry the vegetables, except the cabbage, until cooked but still crunchy. Add the cabbage and cook until it wilts, then return the tofu to the pan. Sizzle the soy sauce and rice wine into the pan and stir.

Combine the stock and cornstarch and pour into the pan. Cook, stirring, over high heat until thickened. Season to taste. Pour over the noodles and garnish with the cilantro.

Eggless Chinese noodles can be used in this recipe. To convert it to a nonvegetarian meal, substitute diced chicken for the tofu.

Vegetarian Pad Thai

Serves 4

SAUCE:

1½ cups water
1 tablespoon tamarind concentrate
⅓ cup palm or dark brown (Barbados) sugar
1½ tablespoons nam pla (Thai fish sauce) or tamari or light soy sauce

NOODLES:

10 ounces dried rice-stick noodles, or 1½ pounds fresh rice-ribbon noodles
4 tablespoons peanut or vegetable oil
10 ounces firm tofu (bean curd), cubed
3 French shallots, finely sliced
¼ teaspoon minced garlic
1 tablespoon finely chopped dried shrimp (optional)
⅓ cup unsalted roasted peanuts
3 scallions, cut into 1-inch pieces
4 ounces fresh bean sprouts, blanched and drained

ACCOMPANIMENTS:

3 eggs, made into crepes (optional; see sidebar, page 100)
Seeded and sliced red chili
Lime wedges
Fine sugar
Garlic chives, cut into 1½-inch pieces
Roasted chili powder (see sidebar, page 88)
Nam pla *(Thai fish sauce), or tamari or light soy sauce*

Combine the sauce ingredients in a small saucepan and bring to a boil. Simmer until reduced to approximately ¾ cup, then set aside to cool.

If using dried noodles, boil for about 2 minutes to firm-tender, then drain. If using fresh, rinse in warm water and drain.

Heat the oil in a wok or large skillet over high heat until smoky. Add the tofu cubes and fry for about 2½ minutes, until the surface is golden brown, and remove. Discard half the oil. Pour off half the oil and reserve. Discard the other half. Add the shallots and stir-fry for 1½ minutes on high heat. Add the garlic, dried shrimp, peanuts, and scallions and stir-fry for 1½ minutes. Stir in the bean sprouts and cook briefly, then transfer to a plate and set aside.

Wipe out the pan and add the reserved oil. When it is very hot and smoky, add the noodles and stir-fry for 2 minutes, until each strand is coated with oil. Pour in the sauce and cook until partially absorbed, about 1½ minutes.

Return the stir-fried ingredients to the pan, stirring to mix them evenly into the noodles, and cook until thoroughly heated. Mound the noodles onto a plate and garnish with the egg crepes and other accompaniments, serving the chili powder and fish or soy sauce separately in small dishes.

Scarlet Noodles

Serves 2 to 3, or 4 to 6 sharing several dishes

> *on't be surprised by the sweetness of this dish. Thai cooks can be heavy-handed with the sugar bowl, but the flavors balance—and you can always use a little less if you're counting calories.*

10 ounces dried rice-stick noodles
5 tablespoons peanut or vegetable oil
10 ounces soft tofu (bean curd)
1 ½ teaspoons minced garlic
1 medium carrot, diced and parboiled
½ diced cucumber, blanched

SAUCE:
2 tablespoons nam pla *(Thai fish sauce)*, or tamari or light soy sauce
2 tablespoons ketchup, or 1 ½ teaspoons tomato paste
1 tablespoon palm or dark brown (Barbados) sugar
¼ cup vegetable stock or water

ACCOMPANIMENTS:
4 ounces fresh bean sprouts
3 scallions, trimmed and chopped
2 tablespoons chopped roasted peanuts
2 teaspoons minced red chili
½ cup cilantro (Chinese parsley) leaves
Nam pla *(Thai fish sauce)*, or tamari or light soy sauce
Freshly squeezed lime juice or lime wedges
Chili sauce (see sidebar, page 156)

Bring 1 ½ quarts of water to a boil, add the noodles, and cook for 1 ½ minutes, until barely softened. Pour into a colander to drain and cool under running cold water.

Mix the sauce ingredients in a small bowl and set aside.

Heat the oil in a wok or large skillet over high heat and fry the tofu until golden brown and crisp on the surface. Remove with a slotted spoon. Pour off most of the oil into a heatproof dish and set aside. Reheat the pan and stir-fry the garlic over high for 45 seconds. Add the carrot and cucumber and stir-fry until glazed with the oil. Remove.

Add the reserved oil and reheat. When smoky-hot, stir-fry the noodles to heat through. Add the sauce and cook until absorbed by the noodles, then return the tofu and vegetables to the pan and mix in evenly, cooking for 45 seconds.

Mound the noodles on a serving plate and surround with the accompaniments. Serve the fish or soy sauce, lime juice, and chili sauce in small dishes to be added to taste.

Plump Thai Noodles in Sweet Brown Sauce

(THAI PAD SYOUI)

Serves 2, or 4 to 6 sharing several dishes

1 ¼ pounds fresh thick Chinese noodles, or ½ pound dried spaghetti
1 ⅓ teaspoons salt
4 slices fresh ginger
5 ounces fresh bean sprouts
2 ounces kangkong *(water spinach) or spinach, thoroughly rinsed*
3 scallions
3 tablespoons peanut oil or flavorless vegetable oil
2 large eggs, lightly beaten (optional)
Cilantro (Chinese parsley) sprigs
Shredded red chili

SAUCE:
¾ cup vegetable stock (pages 27-28)
1 ½ tablespoons dark soy sauce
2 tablespoons tamari or light soy sauce
1 tablespoon palm or dark brown (Barbados) sugar
½ teaspoon mam ruoc *(Thai shrimp paste), or 1 ½ teaspoons soybean paste*

Bring 2 quarts of water to a boil and add the noodles and salt. If using fresh noodles, remove from the heat and let stand for 1 minute; if using dried spaghetti, boil for 12 minutes. Drain well.

Cut the ginger into fine shreds. Blanch the bean sprouts in boiling water for 30 seconds, drain immediately, and cool under running cold water. Cut the spinach into 2-inch pieces, blanch for 30 seconds in boiling water, drain and refresh in cold water, then drain again and set aside. Trim the scallions and cut the white parts into 1-inch pieces. Reserve the green tops for another recipe (or use instead of *kangkong*).

Mix sauce ingredients in a bowl.

If you are planning to add eggs, rub 2 teaspoons of the oil on the surface of a wok with a paper towel. Heat over medium heat, pour in the eggs, and cook until they begin to set. Break into small pieces with a spatula, cook until just firm, and remove.

Add the remaining oil and reheat the pan over very high heat. Stir-fry the noodles for 2 minutes and remove. Reduce the heat slightly, stir-fry the ginger, bean sprouts, spinach, and scallions for 1 minute, return the noodles, and mix well.

Add stir-fried shredded meat or diced seafood to convert any of these noodle dishes into a nonvegetarian meal. Also think of serving vegetarian noodles as a side dish with grilled meats.

Stir the sauce and pour it over the noodles. Cook until absorbed. Stir in the chopped egg, garnish with cilantro sprigs and chili shreds, and serve.

Tibetan Vegetable Vermicelli

Serves 2 to 3, or more sharing several dishes

¾ ounce dried black fungus (wood ears)
4 dried black mushrooms
½ pound dried bean-thread vermicelli
¼ cup vegetable or peanut oil
1 medium onion, finely sliced
2 cloves garlic, minced
2 teaspoons minced fresh ginger
1 tablespoon sesame oil
1 red chili pepper, seeded and shredded
2 to 3 cups shredded Napa cabbage
2 whole scallions, minced

Sauce:
2½ tablespoons tamari or light soy sauce
2 teaspoons dark soy sauce
1 to 2 teaspoons chili oil
1 teaspoon sugar
1 teaspoon Chinese brown (dark) vinegar
½ cup water

This recipe is a good one in which to use a variety of mushrooms. Include sliced straw mushrooms, wild mushrooms, fresh shiitakes, and oyster mushrooms, using with or instead of the fungus.

Soak the black fungus and mushrooms in hot water for 25 minutes. Drain. Finely shred the fungus; trim the mushroom stems and shred the caps fine. Soak the vermicelli for 15 minutes in warm water. Combine the sauce ingredients in a bowl.

Heat the vegetable oil in a wok or large skillet over medium-high heat and stir-fry the onion until it begins to soften. Add the garlic and ginger and stir-fry briefly, then add the fungus, mushrooms, sesame oil, chili pepper, and cabbage. Stir-fry for 1 to 2 minutes.

Add the noodles and sauce ingredients and stir together over moderately high heat for 2 to 3 minutes. Transfer to a plate, scatter on the scallions, and serve.

Bean-Thread Noodles with Cabbage

Serves 4, or 6 sharing several dishes

5 ounces bean-thread vermicelli
6 ounces firm tofu (bean curd)
2 tablespoons vegetable oil
1 tablespoon sesame oil
2 teaspoons minced garlic
1 rib of celery, finely sliced diagonally
1 medium carrot, finely sliced diagonally
2 eggs, lightly beaten (optional)
4 whole scallions, trimmed and cut into 1-inch pieces
3 cups finely sliced Napa cabbage
2 to 3 tablespoons nam pla *(Thai fish sauce)*
Salt and freshly ground black pepper

Soak the vermicelli in warm water for 15 minutes. Cut the bean curd into thin slices.

Heat the two types of oil in a wok or skillet over high heat. Stir-fry the tofu with the garlic for 2 minutes until tofu is crisp at the edges. Push to the side of the pan. Add the celery and carrot and stir-fry for 2 to 3 minutes, until they are crisp-tender. Remove all. If you plan to use the eggs, add them to the wok. Cook until they begin to firm up underneath, then turn over and break into small pieces with a wok spatula.

Add the noodles, scallions, and cabbage to the wok along with the cooked ingredients. Stir-fry on high heat until the cabbage is tender and all ingredients are well blended. Add the fish sauce, plus salt and pepper to taste.

Adding sesame oil to the vegetable oil when stir-frying is a trick I learned from one of my many Chinese cooking teachers, and which was reinforced when I took my first class on tempura cooking. The nutty aroma of the sesame oil adds a tantalizing dimension to an otherwise simple dish.

Dry-fried beans are a classic Sichuan dish, served with other appetizers at the beginning of most formal banquets or as a vegetable dish. Their usual accompaniment is garlic, and plenty of it. But I've also eaten them cooked with diced ham, chopped dried shrimp, or diced pickled vegetables.

Sichuan Dry-Fried Green Beans on Broadbean Noodles

Serves 2, or 4 to 5 sharing a menu of several dishes

6 **ounces dried broad-bean, arrowroot, or bean-thread noodles**
7 **ounces green (string) beans**
2 **tablespoons vegetable oil**
1 **teaspoon sesame oil**
1 **tablespoon minced garlic**
4 **ounces fried tofu (bean curd), very finely minced (see sidebar, page 46)**
1 **whole scallion, minced**
1 1/2 **tablespoons crushed roasted peanuts (optional)**

SAUCE:
1/2 **cup vegetable stock (see pages 27-28)**
1 **teaspoon dark soy sauce**
2 **teaspoons tamari or light soy sauce**
1 **teaspoon chili oil**
1 **teaspoon Sichuan sauce or chili bean paste (or** sambal ulek)
1 1/3 **teaspoons sugar**

Bring 1 1/2 quarts of water to a boil, add the noodles, and return to a boil. Reduce heat to medium and cook for about 3 minutes, until tender. Drain.

Trim the beans and cut into 1-inch lengths. Bring a small pan of lightly salted water to a boil. Add the beans, cook for 2 1/2 minutes, and drain well.

Heat the vegetable oil and sesame oil together in a wok. Stir-fry the beans for 2 1/2 to 3 minutes, until they begin to wrinkle. Add the garlic, tofu, and scallion and stir-fry for about 3 minutes, until the tofu is crisp and the beans are cooked.

Combine the sauce ingredients in a bowl and pour into the wok. Cook on high heat, stirring, for 1 1/2 minutes. Add the noodles and stir to mix well. Cook on medium heat until the noodles are heated through, stirring frequently. Transfer to a serving plate and scatter the peanuts over the top. Serve.

✔egetarian Casserole

Serves 4 to 6 as a one-pot meal

3 ounces bean thread vermicelli

½ ounce dried black fungus (wood ears)

½ ounce dried "golden needles" (see sidebar)

8 dried black mushrooms

½ piece dried tofu (bean curd) stick (page 31)

½ pound fried tofu (bean curd) cubes (see sidebar, page 198)

2 tablespoons vegetable oil

1 medium carrot, peeled and sliced

½ cup sliced bamboo shoots

½ cup straw mushrooms, halved

¼ cup champignons

4 whole scallions, trimmed and cut into 1-inch pieces

2½ cups Napa cabbage, coarsely chopped

BROTH:

2 quarts hot water

3 tablespoons tamari or light soy sauce

1 teaspoon salt

White pepper

Soak the vermicelli in warm water to soften. In separate dishes, soak the fungus, golden needles, black mushrooms, and tofu stick in warm water for 25 minutes. Cut the fried tofu cubes in half.

Heat the oil in a wok or skillet over medium-high heat. Fry the tofu cubes for 1½ minutes and remove from the wok. Stir-fry the vegetables for 2 minutes and transfer to a casserole or heavy pan along with the tofu cubes.

Drain the vermicelli and cut into 4-inch lengths. Drain the fungus and chop fine. Drain the golden needles. Drain the mushrooms, squeeze out excess water, remove the stems, and cut the caps in half. Drain the tofu stick and cut into small pieces. Add these ingredients to the casserole or pot.

Combine the broth ingredients and add to the casserole pot. Bring to a boil and reduce the heat to low. Simmer for 30 minutes and check the seasonings. Serve in the pot.

"*G*olden needles," the musky little dull-gold stamens from a type of day lily, are used in Chinese vegetarian cooking. You will find them in your Chinese store. Keep them in a tightly sealed spice jar away from light, heat, and moisture. They add a delicate nuance of flavor to dishes like this vegetarian casserole, but the dish won't suffer noticeably from their absence.

Bean Curd "Noodles"

Serves 2

2 large sheets dried tofu (bean curd) skin (see sidebar)
Six 1½-inch cubes fried tofu (bean curd) (see sidebar, page 198)
6 dried black mushrooms, soaked in boiling water 20 minutes
3 tablespoons vegetable or peanut oil
1½ teaspoons sesame oil
2 ounces sliced straw mushrooms
2 ounces sliced bamboo shoots
8 ounces fresh bean sprouts
2 tablespoons chopped whole scallions

SEASONINGS:
1 teaspoon salted black beans, finely chopped
1 tablespoon light soy sauce
1 teaspoon rice wine or dry sherry
1 teaspoon minced fresh ginger
⅓ teaspoon chili oil (optional)
Salt and freshly ground black pepper

Soak the tofu skins in cold water to soften, about 3 minutes, then lift out carefully onto a cloth to dry. Roll up and cut into narrow shreds that resemble noodles. Cut the fried tofu into strips by slicing thin, then cutting the slices into strips. Drain the soaked mushrooms, remove the stems, and cut the caps into narrow strips.

Heat the oils in a wok over very high heat. Stir-fry the fried bean curd for 2 minutes, until golden brown. Add the mushrooms, bamboo shoots, and bean sprouts and stir-fry for 1 minute. Remove and set aside.

Add the bean curd "noodles" to the pan and stir-fry for approximately 1 minute. Return the fried ingredients and add the seasoning ingredients. Stir them evenly into the dish over high heat, cooking for about 1 minute. Season to taste with salt and pepper and transfer to a serving plate. Garnish with the scallions.

noodles
my way

I have only touched on the versatility of noodles in this book. Over the years I must have eaten several thousand different dishes containing noodles, most of them done in classic Asian ways. But occasionally I've been served a noodle dish that doesn't fit the standard mold—and even noodles that have been cooked *in* a mold! It's fun to experiment, and particularly so when your base ingredient is inexpensive. If it doesn't work, at least it hasn't cost much.

I've married Mediterranean flavors with Asian, I've fried noodles into crisp baskets and nests to use as edible containers for appetizers or main courses. I've sliced wonton skins and fried them as noodles. I've discovered that egg noodles can be fried in cakes, to serve as a snack like a wedge of pizza or as an accompaniment to a main dish; and that rice vermicelli can be crumbled into batters and bread coatings.

Taking inspiration from Japan, China, and Thailand, I've learned that noodles can be superb as a salad ingredient. Slippery bean threads and buckwheat *soba* readily absorb salad dressings to develop full, deep flavors that complement their slightly chewy texture.

What is tender when boiled is pleasingly crisp when it emerges from a deep-fryer. Rice noodles expand into a snowy cloud of crackling crispness, *somen* and *soba* into brittle spines; egg noodles become crunchy and infinitely appetizing. They're an inspirational addition to a salad and an attractive garnish for fried foods.

I've tinted and flavored noodle dough with all kinds of ingredients— pureed red pepper or tomato, beet juice, spinach puree, squid ink, minced cilantro (Chinese parsley), chili and cracked peppercorns, and mashed seafood. Some have been successful experiments, prepared and eaten often. Others have been less effective, but it is always worth the effort to experiment, to push the established parameters a little farther. That is how new dishes are created.

Seafood Noodle Wraps

Makes about 20

> 6 ounces thin dried egg noodles
> 10 ounces raw seafood (shrimp, crab, scallops, clams)
> 2 whole scallions
> 4 thin slices fresh ginger
> 6 to 8 canned water chestnuts, drained
> 1 cup loosely packed cilantro (Chinese parsley) leaves
> ⅔ teaspoon salt
> ⅓ teaspoon white pepper
> Small pinch of chili powder
> 1 egg white, lightly beaten
> 2 cups vegetable oil, for frying
> 2 tablespoons sesame oil
> Sweet chili sauce

Bring 1 quart of lightly salted water to a boil, add the noodles, and cook for about 3½ minutes, until tender. Drain and set aside.

If using shrimp, devein. Slice the scallion greens finely on the diagonal and set aside for garnish. Cut the white parts roughly, place in a food processor fitted with a metal blade, and add the ginger, water chestnuts, and cilantro. Grind for a few seconds. Add the seafood and process to a smooth paste, adding the salt, pepper, chili powder, and egg white. Sprinkle on 2 tablespoons of ice water and process until the mixture is very smooth and voluminous, about 45 seconds.

Cut the well-drained noodles into 1-inch pieces. With wet hands, form the seafood paste into small balls and roll in the noodles, coating evenly.

Heat the vegetable oil to 375°F in a wok or large skillet. Add the sesame oil. Fry the seafood balls until they are golden brown and cooked through, about 3 minutes, turning occasionally. Retrieve with a wire skimmer and drain briefly on a double thickness of paper towel.

To serve, arrange the balls on a platter lined with a paper napkin or lettuce leaves and pierce each one with a cocktail pick. Scatter on the scallion greens and serve hot. The Thai sweet chili sauce labelled "chicken sauce" is the perfect dipping sauce for these tasty little appetizers.

Prickly Shrimp

Makes 18

> 18 medium-sized raw shrimp
> ¾ cup plus 3 tablespoons cornstarch
> 3 large egg whites
> 5 to 6 ounces fine rice vermicelli
> 5 cups vegetable oil, for deep-frying
> Sweet or hot chili sauce, or Chinese "roast duck" sauce

Shell the shrimp, leaving the last part of the shell and the tail in place. Make a deep cut along the back of each shrimp and remove the dark vein.

Coat the shrimp lightly with the ¾ cup cornstarch. Whip egg whites to soft peaks and fold in the 3 tablespoons cornstarch. Place the rice vermicelli in a strong plastic or paper bag and crush with a rolling pin into pieces about ¾ inch long. Pour onto a plate or tray.

Heat the oil in a wok or deep pan to 375°F, then reduce heat slightly. Dip each shrimp into the egg-white batter, covering thickly, and coat evenly with the crushed vermicelli.

Slide three shrimp into the oil and fry for about 2 minutes, until golden. Turn several times, using a wire skimmer and taking care not to break the vermicelli. Remove to absorbent paper to drain. Repeat with remaining shrimp.

If serving as a cocktail snack, arrange on a platter lined with a paper napkin or lettuce leaves and serve with a small bowl containing sweet or hot chili sauce, or the sweet bean sauce often served with roast duck. As a first course, present on wide plates, surrounded by mixed salad greens and herbs that have been sprinkled with a well-flavored, balsamic vinegar–based vinaigrette.

Scampi or small crayfish tails can be cooked in just the same way. Next time you shop for Japanese ingredients, look through the bottled sauces for some interesting dips such as pon zu, aji pon, *and* shiso.

You can cook lean pork in ex-actly the same way, or use lamb and add a dash of spice—ground coriander is best.

Crisp and Crunchy Chicken Bits

Makes about 24

>   12 ounces boneless, skinless chicken
>   1 tablespoon light soy sauce or Thai fish sauce
>   2 teaspoons rice wine or dry sherry
>   2 tablespoons minced scallion whites
>   1⅓ teaspoons minced fresh ginger
>   1¼ teaspoons sugar
>   ¾ teaspoon salt
>   2 egg whites, lightly beaten
>   2 tablespoons cornstarch
>   ½ pound rice vermicelli
>   5 cups vegetable oil, for deep-frying
>   Tamari soy sauce, spiked with chili oil
>   **Tonkatsu** *sauce (see page 195)*

Cut the chicken into cubes, place in a food processor with the soy sauce and wine, and grind to a smooth paste. Add the scallion and ginger and grind again. Season with the sugar and salt and add the egg whites and cornstarch. Work the mixture until it is very smooth. Remove from the food processor to a bowl. Knead the mixture for 3 to 4 minutes to thoroughly amalgamate the ingredients.

Break up the vermicelli and place in a heavy-duty plastic or paper bag. Use a rolling pin to crush it into pieces about ½ inch in length. Using wet hands, form the chicken mixture into small meatballs and, while they are still damp, roll them in the vermicelli, coating thickly.

In a wok or large skillet heat the oil to 375°F. Fry the meatballs, six or eight at a time, until golden and cooked through, about 2½ minutes. Retrieve with a wire skimmer and drain briefly on a double thickness of paper towel.

Arrange the meatballs on a platter lined with a paper napkin or finely shredded lettuce leaves, and pierce each one with a small cocktail pick. Serve at once, with a dip of light soy sauce spiked with a dash of chili oil, or with Japanese *tonkatsu* sauce.

Spicy Shrimp in a Tangle of Noodles

Serves 4 as an appetizer

- 5 ounces fine egg noodles
- 4 shiitake mushrooms (if dried, soak for 25 minutes in warm water)
- 1 medium carrot, peeled and julienned
- 4 large snow peas, julienned
- 1 leek or Japanese negi leek, trimmed, thoroughly rinsed, and julienned
- 12 medium-large shrimp, in their shells
- 1 tablespoon olive oil
- 3 tablespoons chopped whole scallions
- ¼ cup diced unripe mango (or substitute cucumber)
- ¼ cup seeded and diced tomato
- 2 tablespoons chopped cilantro (Chinese parsley) leaves

BEAN-SAUCE DRESSING:
- 1 teaspoon yellow bean sauce
- 1 teaspoon chili bean sauce
- ⅓ cup tamari or light soy sauce
- 2 teaspoons sugar
- 2 tablespoons rice vinegar
- ⅓ cup light olive oil
- Few drops chili oil or Tabasco

Bring 1 quart of water to a boil, salt lightly, and add the noodles. Cook to tender, drain, and cool under running cold water. Set aside to drain again. Drain the mushrooms, squeeze out excess water, remove stems, and shred the caps fine. Place the mushrooms, carrot, snow peas, and leeks on top of the noodles.

Shell the shrimp, leaving the tail on, and make a cut along the back of each to remove the dark vein. Combine the dressing ingredients in a bowl.

Heat the oil in a wok or sauté pan over high heat and sauté the shrimp until they change color. Add 1 tablespoon of the dressing and sauté until the shrimp are cooked and glazed with the sauce. Remove from the pan. Add the scallions, mango, and tomato to the pan and sauté briefly. Return the shrimp and mix. Keep warm.

Bring a large kettle of water to a boil. Pour over the noodles and vegetables to reheat; drain thoroughly. Transfer to a bowl, pour on the

dressing, and toss until well mixed. Arrange the noodles in mounds on each plate, with the shrimp fanned around them. Scatter on the cilantro and serve at once.

Seared Scallops Layered with Cilantro Pasta and Red Pepper Sauce

Serves 4

When a friend brought around a bag of plump, fresh scallops, they ended up on our plates in a similar recipe. I love fresh seafood that's so quickly seared in a red-hot skillet that the inside remains raw.

¹/₃ recipe cilantro noodle dough (pages 234-235)
32 scallops
3 tablespoons olive oil
2 leeks
8 small snow peas
2 small red chilies, finely sliced
2 tablespoons finely sliced scallion greens

RED PEPPER SAUCE:
2 red bell peppers
4 cloves garlic, peeled
¹/₂ teaspoon freshly ground black pepper
Salt
¹/₂ cup virgin olive oil
Chili oil

Plain noodle dough incorporating whole cilantro leaves looks spectacular. Pass the dough through a pasta machine, or roll it out, until it is as thin as possible. Arrange whole leaves evenly over half the top and fold the other side over to enclose them. Roll out again, or pass through the machine again, to join the layers. Cut into squares as required. This also makes a novel lasagne.

Make up the dough, allow it to rest for 1 hour, then roll out paper-thin with a pasta machine or by hand on a lightly floured worktop. Cut into 2¾-inch squares and dust with rice flour. Stack and set aside.

To make the sauce, roast the peppers and unpeeled garlic cloves over charcoal, under a broiler, or in a very hot oven until the garlic is soft and the skin of the peppers begins to peel and is flecked with black, about 15 minutes. Place the peppers in a paper bag for a few minutes, then remove the skin.

Cut the peppers open; scrape out and discard the inner membranes and seeds. Cut the pepper flesh roughly and place in a food processor fitted with a metal blade. Squeeze the garlic cloves from their skins into the processor. Add salt and pepper and process to a smooth paste.

With the machine running on its lowest speed, slowly add the olive oil in a fine stream until the sauce is thick and creamy. Add a sprinkle of chili oil and process briefly, then remove.

Brush the scallops with enough oil to moisten them and set aside. Trim the green leaves and roots from the leeks, slit open along their length, and rinse thoroughly. Shake out excess water. Cut into 2-inch pieces, then cut lengthwise into fine shreds. Bring a small pan of water to a boil, add the leeks, blanch for 20 seconds, and drain. Blanch the snow peas for 40 seconds and drain.

Bring 2 quarts of water to a boil, add 2 teaspoons oil and 1½ teaspoons salt. Boil the dough sheets for about 4½ minutes, until tender, then drain and sprinkle with enough oil to prevent them from sticking together.

In the meantime, heat a ribbed griddle and sear the scallops on both sides, for about 30 seconds. They should be just barely cooked. Heat 2 teaspoons oil in a wok over high heat and stir-fry the leeks and snow peas for a few seconds.

Assemble layers of pasta, leeks, snow peas, and scallops on each plate. Pour the red pepper sauce in thin lines across each dish and scatter chili and scallion around the rim of each plate. Serve at once.

Noodles are a great salad ingredient. Used soft, they add bulk and texture; fried, they impart the pleasing crunch of a crouton; marinated, they harbor wonderful flavors to release in the mouth; and cold, they soothe and refresh the palate. I love to scatter salad ingredients onto a snowy landscape of fried rice vermicelli.

Warm Chicken and Shrimp Salad on a Cloud

Serves 4

3 ounces rice vermicelli
1 whole boneless chicken breast (about 11 ounces)
8 medium-sized shrimp, in their shells
$\frac{1}{3}$ black bell pepper
$\frac{1}{3}$ green bell pepper
$\frac{1}{3}$ golden bell pepper
$\frac{1}{2}$ to 1 fresh red chili
1 medium-sized yellow onion
2 teaspoons white sesame seeds
3 tablespoons vegetable oil or light olive oil
2 teaspoons sesame oil
8 small sprigs cilantro (Chinese parsley)
8 small, decoratively cut carrot slices

SEASONING FOR CHICKEN:
$\frac{1}{4}$ cup tamari or light soy sauce
2 tablespoons sake (Japanese rice wine)
$1\frac{1}{2}$ tablespoons sugar
2 teaspoons sesame oil
Freshly ground black pepper

Soak the vermicelli in hot water for about 7 minutes, until tender. Drain, cover with cold water, and set aside.

Combine the seasoning ingredients in a small bowl. Place the chicken in another bowl and brush with the seasonings. Set aside to marinate for 30 minutes, brushing several times.

Prepare coals in a charcoal barbecue and ignite.

Shell the shrimp, leaving the last section of the shell and the tail in place. Make deep cuts along their backs to butterfly. Remove seeds from the peppers and chili and carefully trim away the inner membranes. Cut into fine julienne strips and set aside. Peel and halve the onion, and slice it fine. Toast the sesame seeds in a dry sauté pan over medium-high heat until they begin to pop. Remove and set aside to cool.

Drain the marinade from the chicken into a small saucepan and cook over medium heat until reduced by half. Grill the chicken over glowing coals until cooked, about 3 minutes on each side. Remove the skin, if preferred. Cut the chicken into thin slices. Set aside.

Brush the shrimp with enough vegetable oil to moisten them and grill until barely done, then remove from the barbecue. Heat half the vegetable oil with the sesame oil in a wok or sauté pan over high heat, stir-fry the peppers and chili in the oil until wilted, and remove. Add half the onion and stir-fry to a golden brown.

Combine the chicken, raw and cooked onion, peppers, and chili. Whisk the remaining oil into the reduced sauce and pour over the salad, tossing to coat each ingredient.

Bring 1 quart of water to a boil. Transfer the vermicelli to a strainer. Pour on the boiling water to reheat, then drain well. Divide among four entree plates. Arrange the salad ingredients over the vermicelli and scatter on the sesame seeds. Garnish with the carrot slices and cilantro and serve at once.

Rice Vermicelli and Turkey Salad with Lemon-grass Vinaigrette

Serves 4 to 6 as an appetizer

4 ounces rice vermicelli
12 ounces cooked, boneless turkey (or chicken) breast
1 large red Italian onion
3 ounces fresh bean sprouts
$\frac{1}{2}$ red bell pepper
2 ribs of celery
1 medium carrot
8 canned water chestnuts, drained
$\frac{1}{3}$ cup mixed mint, cilantro, opal basil leaves, the larger leaves torn into strips
Chopped chili
Nam pla *(Thai fish sauce)*
Shredded lettuce, or mustard greens, shredded and crisp fried

LEMON-GRASS VINAIGRETTE:
6 tablespoons vegetable oil
2 tablespoons white wine vinegar
1 tablespoon finely sliced lemon grass (see sidebar, page 128)
$\frac{1}{2}$ teaspoon salt
$\frac{1}{2}$ teaspoon minced fresh ginger
$\frac{1}{2}$ teaspoon minced garlic
Freshly ground black pepper

Bean-thread vermicelli, softened in boiling water, or boiled soba noodles can replace the rice vermicelli in this adaptable recipe, just as the turkey can be replaced by chicken.

Combine the vinaigrette ingredients in a jar; close the jar and shake to blend. Let stand overnight. Before using, add a little chopped chili if you like, and fish sauce to taste.

Cook the vermicelli for 1½ minutes in salted boiling water, drain, and rinse. Drain again. Cut or tear turkey or chicken into shreds. Peel the onion and slice fine. Blanch the bean sprouts in simmering water for 30 seconds and drain, cool under running cold water, drain again, and dry on paper towels. Trim the peppers, celery, and carrot and cut into narrow strips the size of matchsticks. Cut the water chestnuts horizontally into thin disks.

Combine the vermicelli, meat, vegetables, and herbs in a large bowl. Add the dressing, and toss to mix evenly. Serve over shredded lettuce or surround with crisp-fried mustard-green leaves.

grilled beef on soba salad

Serves 2

Two 4-ounce beef sirloin or filet steaks
1 teaspoon sesame oil
2 teaspoons tamari or light soy sauce
2 eggs
1 teaspoon vegetable oil or light olive oil
6 ounces soba *(dried buckwheat noodles)*
8 small romaine lettuce leaves, or 2 handfuls of mixed salad leaves including red sails, coral, oak, and chickory
1 medium carrot, finely sliced
¼ cup finely sliced whole scallions

SALAD DRESSING:
⅓ teaspoon Chinese brown peppercorns
2 teaspoons sesame oil
1 tablespoon tamari or light soy sauce
2 to 4 teaspoons freshly squeezed lime juice
Salt

You can substitute saimin or vegetable noodles for soba, cooking to al dente. I also enjoy a grilled pork or lamb chop, deboned and sliced, served with this salad.

Brush the steaks with the sesame oil and soy sauce and set aside for 15 minutes. Prepare coals in a charcoal barbecue or heat a broiler.

Beat the eggs and strain through a nylon sieve. Heat a wok or nonstick skillet over high heat and rub the surface with a paper towel dipped in the vegetable oil. When the pan is smoky-hot pour in half the egg to form a thin crepe. Cook until the underside is lightly golden, flip, and briefly cook the other side. Repeat with the remaining egg. Set aside to cool.

Bring 1½ quarts of water to a boil, add the noodles, and cook to *al dente*. Drain and cover with cold water to cool. Drain well.

Char-grill or broil the steaks until cooked to preference. Cut into ¼-inch slices.

For the dressing, pass the peppercorns through a pepper mill or grind semi-fine in a spice grinder or mortar. Combine with the remaining dressing ingredients, using lime juice and salt to taste, and whisk to emulsify.

Place the lettuce in two shallow bowls and divide the noodles between them. Arrange the sliced steak on the noodles and scatter on the carrot and scallion slices. Pour on the dressing.

Stack the two egg crepes together and roll into a cylinder. Cut across it into very narrow strips. Drape these over the salad and serve.

Cold Sesame Noodles on Char-Grilled Vegetables

Serves 2, or more as an appetizer

6 ounces fine wheat-starch noodles, flat egg noodles, soba, *or* **somen**
8 ounces cooked boneless chicken breast (see sidebar)
2 small Japanese or Kirby cucumbers, julienned
¹/₂ red bell pepper, seeded and julienned
6 sugar or snow peas, blanched in simmering water for 30 seconds
1 whole scallion, shredded
1 medium-sized slender eggplant, finely sliced
1 golden zucchini, finely sliced
1 green zucchini, finely sliced
Olive oil
Salt
Freshly ground black pepper

SESAME SAUCE:
2 tablespoons tahini (sesame paste) or smooth peanut butter
1¹/₂ tablespoons light olive oil or vegetable oil
1³/₄ teaspoons sesame oil
3¹/₂ teaspoons mirin (Japanese sweet rice wine)
1¹/₂ tablespoons minced whole scallion
¹/₂ teaspoon minced garlic

Cook the noodles in 1¹/₂ quarts lightly salted boiling water to *al dente*. Drain and cover with cold water to cool. Drain again.

Cut the chicken into narrow strips. Prepare the salad ingredients. Spread the eggplant and zucchini slices on a tray and sprinkle with salt. Set aside for 10 minutes to draw off bitter juices. Preheat a charcoal grill or broiler.

Combine the sauce ingredients in a bowl, adding cold water to dilute to a creamy consistency. Pour half the dressing over the drained noodles, mix with the handle of a wooden spoon to distribute evenly, and set aside.

Wipe the eggplant and zucchini with a dry cloth and brush with olive oil. Grill or broil until well cooked, with a smoky aroma, about 1 ¹/₂ minutes each side. Sprinkle with a little more olive oil and season with salt and a few twists from the pepper mill. Set aside.

Mix the chicken, cucumber, pepper, peas, and scallion with the noodles and serve in a tall mound in the center of each serving plate. Fan the grilled vegetables around the noodles and pour on the remaining sauce.

Chilled Noodles in a Curry Vinaigrette with Marinated Lamb

Serves 2, or more as an appetizer

5 ounces flat wheat-starch noodles
2½ tablespoons vegetable oil
8 ounces lean lamb
2 ounces raw cashew nuts
1 red Italian onion
Small assorted lettuce leaves
6 sprigs cilantro (Chinese parsley)

CURRY VINAIGRETTE:
3 tablespoons light olive oil or vegetable oil
3 teaspoons rice vinegar or freshly squeezed lime juice
1 teaspoon mild curry powder
⅓ teaspoon mashed garlic
Salt and freshly ground black pepper

MARINADE FOR LAMB:
2 teaspoons tamari or light soy sauce or fish sauce
1 teaspoon rice wine or dry sherry
⅓ teaspoon sugar
1 teaspoon ginger juice
¼ teaspoon Chinese brown pepper (optional)

Bring 1½ quarts of well-salted water to a boil and add 2 teaspoons of the vegetable oil. Add the noodles and cook until tender, drain, rinse with cold water, and drain again.

Slice the lamb thin and cut into narrow strips. Combine with the marinade and set aside for 20 minutes.

Heat the remaining vegetable oil in a wok over medium-high heat and fry the cashew nuts to golden brown, then remove and drain on paper towel. Peel the onion and slice it very fine.

Pour off all but 3 teaspoons of the oil used for the cashews, reheat the wok over very high heat, and stir-fry the lamb until crisp on the surface. Remove and set aside to cool.

Combine the curry vinaigrette ingredients in a jar, adding salt and pepper to taste. Close the jar and shake until thoroughly amalgamated. Pour two-thirds of the dressing over the drained noodles, adding the onion and cashew nuts. Mix.

In Australia, I tasted this dish made with kangaroo meat, which is very lean and supremely tender if cooked quickly in a very hot pan.

Place a handful of lettuce on each plate and top with a tangle of the noodles in the center of each serving plate with the lamb arranged on top. Pour the remaining sauce over the lamb in thin streams. Scatter on the cilantro and serve.

Jadeite Noodles

Serves 4 as an appetizer

> 3½ ounces flat, white wheat-starch noodles
> 3 ounces flat, green-colored vegetable noodles
> 1 tablespoon vegetable oil
> 8 fresh asparagus spears
> 2 tablespoons roasted pine nuts

JADEITE DRESSING:
> 1 teaspoon minced garlic
> 1½ teaspoons minced fresh ginger
> 3 teaspoons vegetable oil
> 1 teaspoon finely grated lime peel
> 3 tablespoons each finely chopped basil, cilantro (Chinese parsley),
>   and mint leaves, plus scallion greens
> 1½ tablespoons rice wine or dry sherry
> 1½ tablespoons sesame oil
> 1½ tablespoons nuoc mam (Vietnamese fish sauce)
> 2 teaspoons sugar
> ⅓ teaspoon chili oil

If you prefer a cold salad, chill the noodles in cold water, drain thoroughly, and do not sprinkle with oil. In the dressing, replace rice wine with rice vinegar and incorporate the vegetable oil not used on the noodles. Combine without heating and stir through the noodles, adding the asparagus along with halved cherry tomatoes for color.

You can also serve these noodles warm as a side dish with grilled, baked, or roasted meat. Think about these noodles, too, when planning a meal outdoors. They're ideal as an accompaniment to sliced cold cuts.

Bring 1½ quarts of generously salted water to a boil, add the noodles, and cook until tender, about 4 minutes (cooking time will depend on the type of noodles used). Pour into a colander to drain, sprinkle on the vegetable oil, and set aside.

Cut the hard ends off the asparagus and use a vegetable peeler to peel the lower end of each stem. Place in a steamer to steam for about 4 minutes, until crisp-tender. Cut into 1½-inch pieces and set aside.

Prepare the dressing: In a small saucepan cook the garlic and ginger in the vegetable oil for 2 minutes over medium heat, add the remaining dressing ingredients, and heat through.

Bring 2 quarts of water to a boil. Place the asparagus on the noodles,

pour on the hot water to reheat, drain well, and transfer to a mixing bowl. Pour on the dressing and toss until well mixed. Serve on warm plates and scatter on the pine nuts.

Peanut-Sauce Noodles

Egg noodles tossed with this tangy peanut sauce make an interesting accompaniment to barbecued or grilled meat.

Serves 4

> **6 ounces dried flat egg noodles**
> **¼ cup crunchy peanut butter**
> **2 tablespoons tamari or light soy sauce**
> **½ cup coconut milk**
> **2½ to 3 teaspoons fresh lime juice**
> **2 teaspoons ground coriander**
> **1 to 2 teaspoons Thai red curry paste**
> **1 teaspoon sugar**
> **⅓ teaspoon salt**

Bring 1½ quarts salted water to a boil and add the noodles. Bring back to a boil, reduce heat slightly, and simmer for 3½ to 4 minutes, until the noodles are tender. Drain.

Combine the remaining ingredients in a saucepan and cook on medium-low heat for 3 minutes, stirring continuously. Pour over the drained noodles and stir with a pair of chopsticks until the sauce coats each strand of noodle.

I was pleased with my experiment of cooking the noodles in coconut milk with a stem of lemon grass. I added 1 cup of coconut milk to 1 quart of salted water, plus a fresh lemon-grass stem cut in half lengthwise. I boiled the liquid for 12 minutes, to release the flavor of the lemon grass, before adding the noodles to cook for the usual 3½ to 4 minutes.

Two Dressings for Chilled Noodles

Toss one of these dressings, full of wonderful Asian flavors, over cold cooked noodles of any kind, to serve with all manner of meat dishes from simple grills to carpaccio-style prime beef, or to toss with salad greens and herbs.

HOISIN DRESSING:
1 tablespoon hoisin sauce
1 tablespoon dark soy sauce
1 tablespoon rice vinegar
2 tablespoons freshly squeezed lime juice
1 tablespoon white sugar

Combine the ingredients and pour over noodles. Toss well.

PESTO WITH AN ASIAN TWIST:
¼ cup raw cashew or macadamia nuts
4 garlic cloves, peeled
¾ cup each loosely packed basil, cilantro (Chinese parsley), and mint
  leaves, plus scallion greens
¾ cup mild olive oil
Salt and freshly ground black pepper
Freshly squeezed lime juice

Combine the nuts, garlic, and herbs in a food processor and grind with a metal blade until well pureed. With the motor running on its lowest setting, slowly add the olive oil in a thin stream until the dressing is as thick and creamy as mayonnaise and is a bright, pea-green color. Add salt and pepper to taste, plus a dash of lime juice to heighten the flavors. Process again very briefly. Pour over noodles and toss well.

ῃoodle ℘ancakes

I serve these crunchy egg-noodle-and-bacon pancakes as an entree. A dollop of sour cream and a pepped-up salsa go perfectly with them, or top with a fiery chili sauce. I also have a favorite recipe here for a mushroom sauté, which is a good accompaniment. These pancakes look good and taste great on the plate beside a grilled chicken thigh or rack of lamb and are a surprise accompaniment to a good spicy grilled sausage.
Makes 4

2 tablespoons finely chopped onion
2 tablespoons finely chopped bacon
2 to 3 tablespoons vegetable oil or olive oil

½ pound cooked egg noodles (page 15)
2 tablespoons chopped scallion greens and/or cilantro leaves
1½ tablespoons strong chicken stock made with a stock powder
2 teaspoons potato flour
Freshly ground black pepper

In a small pan over medium-high heat, sauté the onion and bacon together without oil until cooked. Remove.

Rinse out the pan and heat 2 teaspoons of the oil over high heat. When the pan is very hot, add one-quarter of the noodles and sprinkle on one-quarter of the bacon and onion. Press down with a spatula to compress into a cake. Cook until golden on the underside.

Stir the stock and potato flour together, adding pepper to taste. Sprinkle some of the scallion greens and/or cilantro over the noodle cake and pour on one-quarter of the stock. Cook briefly, then turn and cook the other side until firm. Turn again to cook the other side a second time, making the noodles very crisp on the surface and edges. Remove.

Cook the remaining noodles in the same way. Serve hot with a side dish with Mushroom Sauté (recipe follows). Or add a sauce or garnish of your choice.

MUSHROOM SAUTÉ:
12 large, fresh shiitake mushrooms
1 to 2 cloves garlic, finely chopped
1 tablespoon olive oil
1 tablespoon butter
1½ tablespoons chopped fresh herbs (try a mixture of basil, chives, and
  parsley)
1 teaspoon finely grated lime peel
1½ tablespoons cream
Salt and freshly ground black pepper

Wipe the mushrooms with a damp cloth, remove stems, and cut the caps into thin slices.

Heat oil and butter in a sauté pan and sauté the mushrooms and garlic over high heat, stirring continuously, until they release their liquid. Add the herbs, lime peel, and cream, season to taste, and heat thoroughly.

$picy Åhai Chicken on Crisp Åoodles

Serves 4 to 6 as an appetizer or 2 as a main course

> **2 skinless, boneless chicken breasts (about 14 ounces)**
> **1 tablespoon Thai red curry paste**
> **1 large yellow onion, finely sliced**
> **1½ tablespoons peanut oil**
> **¼ each red, green, gold, and yellow bell peppers, seeded and julienned**
> **½ cup coconut milk**
> **4 ounces fine rice vermicelli**
> **1½ quarts vegetable oil, for deep-frying**

Cut the chicken into ½-inch strips and place in a dish. Brush with the curry paste, reserving 1 teaspoon. Set aside for 40 minutes.

In a small skillet or sauté pan, sauté the onion in the peanut oil over medium-high heat, until golden. Add the peppers and cook for about 1½ minutes, to soften. Remove and set aside.

Reheat the pan and sauté the chicken strips for about 2½ minutes, until done. Remove from the pan.

Pour in the coconut milk and add the reserved curry paste. Simmer for 4 to 5 minutes on medium heat. Return the chicken, onion, and peppers and heat through. Keep warm on very low heat.

In a deep pan or wok, heat the vegetable oil to 385°F. Add the vermicelli in a bundle and flip it as soon as it has expanded and turned fluffy and white. Cook the other side only very briefly. When fully expanded, remove from the oil to drain on a double layer of paper towel.

Transfer the vermicelli to a serving plate and press with a wok spatula to partially crumble it; or crumble and serve on individual plates. Nestle the chicken and vegetables in the center. I like to sprinkle chopped roast peanuts over this dish for extra crunch and a real Thai taste (see sidebar).

Åoodle Åortilla

I serve wedges of this soft-crunchy noodle pancake with all sorts of meals. It takes the commonplace out of a barbecue, is interesting with a vegetable stir-fry, and gives texture to a casserole. My daughter and

her friends love it with a full-flavored Bolognese-style sauce for an after-school snack.

Serves 4 to 6

Simplify this attractive dish by serving over a bed of frothy white crisp-fried rice vermicelli.

> *10 ounces dried thin egg noodles*
> *1 medium-sized yellow onion*
> *2 to 3 tablespoons vegetable oil*
> *1 teaspoon sesame oil*
> *1 large clove garlic, minced*
> *3 lap cheong (Chinese sausages), very thinly sliced on the diagonal*
> *1 tablespoon dried shrimp, soaked for 20 minutes (optional)*
> *⅓ cup sliced straw mushrooms*
> *2 tablespoons chopped scallion greens*
> *1 tablespoon tamari or light soy sauce*

Bring 2 quarts of lightly salted water to a boil. Add the noodles and cook for 2¾ minutes, until firm-tender. Pour into a colander to drain, rinse under cold water, and set aside to drain again.

Peel the onion and slice it thin. Heat 2 teaspoons of the vegetable oil with the sesame oil in a wok or sauté pan over medium-high heat. Stir-fry the onion for 2½ minutes, until softened and lightly browned.

Drain and chop the dried shrimp. Add the garlic, sausage, and dried shrimp to the pan and stir-fry for 1½ minutes, then add mushrooms, scallions, and soy sauce and cook briefly.

Heat a heavy iron or nonstick skillet over very high heat and add 1 tablespoon oil. When the oil is very hot, reduce the heat to medium. Spread half the noodles in the pan and press them down firmly with a spatula. Spread the stir-fried ingredients evenly over the noodles and cover with the remaining noodles, pressing these down into a cake. Cook until the underside is golden brown. Place a plate directly on top of the noodles, then invert the pan to transfer the noodle tortilla to the plate. Pour the remaining oil into the pan and reheat over medium-high heat. Slide the tortilla back into the pan and cook for 1 minute, then reduce the heat and cook on medium until the underside is golden. Remove from the pan and cut into wedges to serve.

Note: For ease, you can prepare this recipe by assembling noodles and stir-fried ingredients in a well-oiled ovenproof dish; cover with aluminum foil and refrigerate until needed. Cook in a preheated, very hot oven for 10 minutes, then remove the foil and cook another 5 minutes or so, until the edges are crisp and the top is golden brown.

quail wearing pearls, served in noodle baskets

Serves 4

> 4 noodle baskets, made with 10 ounces cooked thin egg noodles (page 15)
>
> 4 quail
>
> 8 small pearl onions
>
> 1 golden zucchini
>
> 1 green zucchini
>
> ½ chayote
>
> 1 carrot
>
> ½ cup green peas
>
> 3 tablespoons vegetable oil
>
> 1 teaspoon minced fresh ginger
>
> ⅓ teaspoon minced garlic
>
> ½ cup roasted cashew nuts (optional)
>
> Salt and freshly ground black pepper
>
> Mixed small lettuce leaves
>
> Small sprigs or leaves of fresh herbs (cilantro, mint, basil)

> QUAIL MARINADE:
>
> 2 teaspoons tamari or light soy sauce
>
> 2 teaspoons hoisin sauce
>
> 1 teaspoon rice wine or dry sherry
>
> 1 teaspoon cornstarch

> SAUCE:
>
> ¾ cup chicken stock (pages 26-27)
>
> 3 teaspoons cornstarch
>
> 1 tablespoon hoisin sauce
>
> 1½ teaspoons chili bean paste
>
> 2 teaspoons rice wine or dry sherry
>
> Salt and freshly ground black pepper

Prepare the noodle nests in advance, following the directions on page 238, and place one on each dinner plate. Surround with mixed small lettuce leaves, cilantro, mint, and basil sprigs. Set aside.

Cut the quail into quarters. Combine the marinade ingredients in a flat dish and add the quail, brush with the marinade, and set aside for 30 minutes.

Peel the pearl onions and cut a cross in the base of each one to pre-

vent them from bursting during cooking. Peel the vegetables and use a small melon-ball scoop to shape the zucchini and chayote into balls approximately the size of the onions. Chop the carrot into similar-sized pieces. Bring 1 quart of water to a boil. Boil the onions, chayote, carrot, and peas for about 2 minutes, until almost tender. Add the zucchini and boil for 1 minute, then drain.

Combine the chicken stock and cornstarch in a bowl.

Heat the oil in a wok or large skillet over high heat and stir-fry the vegetables for 45 seconds, until glazed with the oil. Remove. Add the ginger and garlic with the marinated quail and stir-fry for about 3½ minutes, until cooked through.

Add the hoisin sauce, chili bean paste, and rice wine and stir over medium-high heat for 30 seconds. Return the vegetables to the pan. Stir the stock and pour into the pan. Cook, stirring, on high heat until the sauce thickens and forms a glaze on the quail and vegetables. Add the cashews, along with salt and pepper to taste. Serve in the noodle baskets and take to the table at once.

Orange Beef on Wonton Crisps

Serves 2 to 4

10 ounces beef sirloin or filet steaks
¼ cup chicken stock (pages 26-27)
1 teaspoon cornstarch
4 ounces fresh or frozen wonton skins
3 to 4 cups vegetable oil, for deep-frying
*2 pieces dried mandarin orange peel (1½ inches square), soaked and
   cut into strips*
½ to 1 dried red chili, seeded and sliced
½ teaspoon Chinese brown peppercorns
2 teaspoons tamari or light soy sauce
½ teaspoon sesame oil
Cilantro (Chinese parsley) sprigs

SEASONING FOR BEEF:
2½ teaspoons dark soy sauce
1½ teaspoons minced fresh ginger
1½ tablespoon minced whole scallion
1 teaspoon cornstarch

*C*hinese brown peppercorns, known also as Sichuan pepper, are strongly aromatic and peppery. If eaten to excess they have an astringent, almost anesthetic effect on the tongue and lips. They should be bought as whole berries and crushed or ground only as needed, to ensure their full flavor. Green peppercorns in brine can replace them in this recipe quite successfully.

Very thinly slice the beef (see sidebar, page 76) and cut into 1 ½-inch squares. Place in a dish with the seasoning ingredients and mix well. Set aside for 20 minutes.

Combine the chicken stock and cornstarch in a bowl. Cut the wonton skins into strips of about ⅓ inch. Heat the oil for deep frying in a wok or large skillet to 385°F.

Heat 3 tablespoons of the frying oil in a wok over high heat until a haze of smoke appears over the pan, then reduce heat to medium. Fry the orange peel, chili, and peppercorns for about 40 seconds, then remove. Add the beef and fry until very well cooked and crisp. Remove the meat with a slotted spoon and pour off excess oil. Return the beef to the pan with the orange peel and spices.

Sizzle the soy sauce and sesame oil onto the sides of the pan and stir into the meat as it runs down. Stir the stock and cornstarch and pour over the beef. Cook, stirring, on high heat until it coats the meat. Remove from the heat.

Slide the wonton-skin strips into the hot oil to cook for about 45 seconds, until crisp and puffy. Remove with a wire strainer and spread on a plate. Top with the beef, garnish with cilantro, and serve at once.

Cilantro Noodles

Makes 1½ pounds

> **3 cups bread flour**
> **1½ teaspoons salt**
> **3 large eggs**
> **1½ tablespoons light olive oil**
> **1½ tablespoons water**
> **½ cup very finely chopped cilantro (Chinese parsley) leaves**

Sift 2 cups of the flour and salt into a mound on a countertop. Beat the eggs, oil, and water together.

Make a depression in the center of the flour, pour in the egg mixture and the cilantro, then slowly incorporate it with your fingers until completely worked into the flour. Keep the remaining flour on hand to dust the board while kneading, and add additional flour to the dough as needed. It should be pliable enough to spring back when pressed with your thumb, but neither too firm nor too soft.

You can make original wonton wrappers with this dough, using them for the recipes on pages 52 and 233. Or try the recipe on page 17. One-third of the dough makes twelve 3-inch wonton skins.

234   the noodle shop cookbook

Lightly flour the countertop and knead for 7 to 8 minutes. Form into a ball, place in a dish, and cover with plastic wrap. Set aside for 1 hour.

Roll out thin on a lightly floured surface, or pass through a pasta machine to make thin, wide bands. Cut into noodles of the size you require.

Fresh noodles will cook in lightly salted boiling water—with a teaspoon or two of oil added to prevent them from sticking together—in about 3½ minutes. Drain and sprinkle with oil to prevent them from sticking. Reheat when needed by immersing in boiling water.

Three-Pepper Noodles

Makes 1½ pounds

> **3 cups bread flour**
> **2 teaspoons paprika**
> **1 teaspoon freshly ground black pepper**
> **1 teaspoon chili flakes**
> **3 large eggs**
> **2 tablespoons ice water**
> **1 tablespoon olive oil**

These orange-red noodles are especially good with veal or chicken, and interesting with fish.

Sift two cups of the flour with the spices into a mound on a countertop. Make a depression in the center.

Beat the eggs, water, and oil together and pour into the depression. Cover with flour, then slowly work the liquid into the flour to make a dough. Add additional flour, as needed, to make a firm, resilient dough.

Lightly flour the countertop and knead the dough for 7 to 8 minutes, then place in a dish and cover with plastic wrap or a cloth. Set aside for 1 hour.

Roll out thin on a lightly floured surface, or pass through a pasta machine, and cut into noodles as required. Cook in well-salted water, with 2 teaspoons of oil added, for about 3½ minutes, until barely tender. Drain, rinse, and drain again. Reheat when needed by immersing in boiling water.

Noodle Pyramids

These are fun to serve beside lamb cutlets or a grilled steak.

Fine egg noodles
Vegetable oil for deep-frying

Cook the egg noodles in boiling water until tender. Drain but do not rinse. Heat deep oil to 375°F. Dip a conical sieve into the oil. Loosely pack 2 ounces of noodles into the point and lower into the oil. Cook until golden, then turn out onto a rack over a double layer of paper towel to drain.

Noodle Tangles

Serve these crisp and crunchy bundles as a side dish.

Fine or flat egg noodles
Vegetable oil for deep-frying

Cook the egg noodles in boiling water until tender. Drain but do not rinse. Heat deep oil to 375°F. Place a handful of the noodles into the oil. They will bubble and fly apart. Gather together with a pair of chopsticks, forcing them into a loose bundle. Hold the bundle in the oil until golden and crisp. Lift out and drain on absorbent paper.

Vegetable Noodle Bundles

Brightly colored, vegetable-based noodles make an interesting garnish when served with a sauce, or when fried into tangles as in the previous recipe.

Noodle Brushes

This is a traditional garnish on tempura, but it can also be used to give an impressive touch of the exotic to other dishes.

Tempura batter (page 167)
Somen *or fine wheat-starch noodles*
Vegetable oil for deep frying

Prepare the tempura batter. Bundle several strands of noodles together. Dip one end in the batter. Use chopsticks to hold the bundle in oil heated to 375°F, until the batter cooks. Then release to allow the noodles to spread into a brush shape. Cook about 45 seconds longer and remove from the oil.

Noodle brushes

Noodle Baskets or Nests

You will need a Chinese "noodle nest" frying basket to make these with ease, but you can improvise with two wire-mesh strainers, one slighty smaller than the other. Dip them into cold oil before lining with noodles, to prevent the nests from sticking.

Fine or narrow flat egg noodles
Vegetable oil for deep-frying

Cook the noodles in boiling water until tender. Drain but do not rinse. Heat deep oil to 375°F. Oil two wire-mesh baskets and spread a thin layer of noodles evenly around the inside of the larger basket, allowing some of the noodles to loop over the edge, if you like.

Press the other oiled basket on top. Hold the two handles firmly together as you lower into the oil. Cook until the noodles are golden and crisp. Turn onto a rack over a double layer of paper towel to drain before using.

Noodle Cages

Decorative noodle "cages" can be fashioned in the same way as noodle nests or baskets, except only a few strands of noodles are evenly laid in the frying basket, so the result is an open-weave cage of crisp noodles which can be placed like a lacy dome over an appetizer.

index